D1526160

Ministry, Word, and Sacraments

Ministry, Word, and Sacraments

An Enchiridion
Martin Chemnitz

Edited, translated, and briefly annotated by
Luther Poellot

The German edition of 1593 and the Latin edition of 1603
were used in this work.

Note:

This work was written for use in periodic
(bis quotannis, twice a year) examination of pastors
by superintendents.

Copyright © 1981 Concordia Publishing House
3558 South Jefferson Avenue, St. Louis, Mo. 63118

Manufactured in the United States of America

Library of Congress Cataloging in Publication Data

Chemnitz, Martin, 1522-1586.
    Ministry, word, and sacraments.

    Translation of 1593 German ed. of Enchiridion D.
Martini Chemnitii and the 1603 Latin ed. of D. Martini Chemnitii
Enchiridion.
    Includes bibliographical references.
    1. Lutheran Church—Catechisms and creeds—English
2. Clergy—Office. I. Poellot, Luther. II. Title
BX8070.C413   230.41   80-15883
ISBN 0-570-03295-4

3 4 5 6 7 8 9 10 11 12 MAL 96 95 94 93 92 91 90 89 88 87

0 78777 03295 1

Contents

Abbreviations
of Books of the Bible

Old Testament	New Testament	Apocrypha
Gn	Mt	1 and 2 Esd
Ex	Mk	Tob
Lv	Lk	Jdth
Nm	Jn	Ap Est
Dt	Acts	Wis
Jos	Ro	Ecclus*
Ju	1 and 2 Co	Bar
Ru	Gl	L Jer
1 and 2 Sm	Eph	Ap Dn
1 and 2 K	Ph	Sus
1 and 2 Ch	Cl	Bel
Ez	1 and 2 Th	Man
Neh	1 and 2 Ti	1 and 2 Mac
Est	Tts	
Jb	Phmn	* or The Wisdom of
Ps	Heb	Jesus Son of Sirach
Pr	Ja	(sometimes simply
Ec	1 and 2 Ptr	called Sirach)
SS	1—3 Jn	
Is	Jude	*Full names:*
Jer	Rv	
Lm		Esdras, 1 and 2
Eze		Tobit
Dn		Judith
Hos		Apocryphal Esther
Jl		Wisdom
Am		Ecclesiasticus
Ob		Baruch
Jon		Letter of Jeremiah
Mi		Apocryphal Daniel
Nah		Susanna
Hab		Bel and the Dragon
Zph		Manasses
Hg		Maccabees, 1 and 2
Zch		
Ml		

Translator's Foreword

This English translation of Martin Chemnitz's *Enchiridion* is, with its prefaces, based on the following two texts: (1) *Enchiridion D. Martini Chemnitii. Darinnen die Häuptstück der Christlichen Lehr, durch Frag und Antwort, auss Gottes Wort eynfältig und gründlich erkläret werden. Sampt angehencktem Tractätlein D. Vrbani Regij. Wie man fürsichtiglich, und ohne Ergernuss von den fürnembsten Artickeln Christlicher Lehr reden soll. Allen jungen einfältigen Predigern und Studiosis Theologiae, wie denn auch allen frommen Christen in gemein, auffs Neuw zusammen geordnet: Durch Polycarpum Lyserum, der H. Schrifft D. und der Statt Braunschweig Superintendenten. Getruckt zu Franckfurt am Mayn, durch Johann Spiess. M.D.XCIII [1593].* (2) *D. Martini Chemnitij Enchiridion, de praecipvis Doctrinae Coelestis capitibus, per Quaestiones & Responsiones ex verbo Dei simpliciter ac solide declaratis. Accessione dictorvm Scripturae, quorum loca tantummodo ab Authore citantur, auctius nunc editum, studio & opere Pavli Chemnitii F. Iam denuo Accesserunt Formulae quaedam caute & citra scandalum loquendi de praecipuis Christianae doctrinae locis Vrbano Regio autore. Indice rerum & verborum vtrobique addito. Lvbecae [Lübeck]. Anno M. D. CIII [1603].*

For a list of other editions see Georg Williams, "The Works of Martin Chemnitz," *Concordia Theological Quarterly,* XLII (1978), 103—114. Editions appeared at various times from 1569 to 1886, with the greatest gap between 1608 and 1886. Anniversary buffs will note that an edition appeared in 1578.

The 1593 edition has 30 unpaginated pages of introductory material after the title page folio (a 17-page preface by Polycarp Leyser, a 10-page preface by Chemnitz, and a 3-page "Register"). The "Register" is a list, neither alphabetic nor in the sequence of a table of contents; it is a kind of subject-grouping of the doctrinal points in the whole volume. The following 534 pages are numbered consecutively through the volume, which has no index. The 294-page *Enchiridion* is followed by the 84-page *Wie man fürsichtiglich . . . .*, which is in turn followed by a 156-page work

9

entitled *Wolgegründter Bericht von den fürnembsten Artickeln Christlicher Lehre, so zu unsern Zeiten streitig worden seyn. Was eines jedern Artickels rechter Verstand sey, unnd wie man in Gottes Furcht, ohne Abbruch der Wahrheit, von einem jedern Artickel, auss der rechten Grundfest dess Göttlichen Worts, mit Bescheidenheit reden möge und solle.* There are some minor variations between the wording of the latter title on the title page for *Wie man fürsichtiglich* . . . and the wording at the head of its own section. Page 535 is the volume's colophon page.

In the 1603 edition, which has no table of contents and has 10 unpaginated pages of introductory material after the title page (a 3-page unsigned preface, and a 7-page preface by Chemnitz), the pages are numbered from page 1 of the *Enchiridion* to its end on page 546. Then follows an unpaginated 31-page index of subjects and words, a page listing errata, a colophon page, and three blank pages. Then follows *Formulae quaedam cavte et citra scandalum loquendi de praecipuis Christianae Doctrinae locis, pro iunioribus Verbi Ministris,* by Rhegius; on this see Leyser's preface. The *Formulae* covers 102 numbered pages plus a 12-page unpaginated index, a colophon page, and a blank page. Thereafter follows *Theologiae Iesuitarum praecipva capita* . . . , by Chemnitz, which includes 17 pages of introductory material after the title page (1-page table of contents, 5-page preface to the reader, 6-page dedicatory epistle signed by Chemnitz, 2-page Greek poem, and a 3-page Latin poem) and 244 pages of text in which there is no pagination but the folios are numbered from 1 to 122.

The pages of the 1593 edition are about 3.75 by 6 inches, and the volume is about 1.5 inches thick. The pages of the 1603 edition are about 2.75 by 5 inches, and the volume is about 2 inches thick.

This bibliographical material is herewith supplied, as drawn from the translator's personal copies, because it is not easily found elsewhere and in order to help show the origin of the *Enchiridion,* the history of its printings, and some of the concerns with which it was associated.

As for the rest, the questions in the *Enchiridion* are not numbered in the original texts; for the sake of reference they have been numbered in the present translation. In this translation, also, Bible passages are not quoted unless they are an integral part of the text or are necessary to its flow of thought; but verse numbers (which are not in the German text) have been included to aid the reader. Some corrections have been made in the Bible references. No one English Bible was used for Bible texts because (1) the Bible text generally accepted as original today is not necessarily the same in wording in every case as that used by Chemnitz and Zanger, who were to some extent also influenced by the Vulgate, and (2) the Bible references are often exactly that—references—rather than precise verbatim quotations, with the result that one and the same passage may be referred to in the German and the Latin texts at various places in various wordings. Since the present work is a translation, Chemnitz and Zanger speak for themselves, so far as possible, and are not bound to a modern Bible translator's wording.

In order to retain some of the flavor of the German and Latin originals, the sentence structure generally follows their pattern instead of being reduced to our more clipped style. And this translation was not originally made for publication. It had its origin in the translator's personal interest and delight in the work as a window to the 16th-century roots of Lutheranism. It does not answer all questions that might be raised by scholars, who, in the translator's hope, may be restrained in criticism of his work by the challenge to engage in further research and improvement. As for inconsistencies in form that may occur, let them be tested by Ralph Waldo Emerson's dictum, "A foolish consistency is the hobgoblin of little minds."

Finally, to borrow a thought from an unknown author: Dear reader, receive this our little work graciously and, if it please you, use it and enjoy it!

Luther Poellot
Tuesday, April 22, 1980

[Preface[1]]

To the Christian[2] and Candid[3] Reader Greeting[4]

This little book, dear[5] reader, was first written by the author in the vernacular tongue in the form of an examination for the use of less-well-trained[6] pastors very many years ago, toward the beginning of the reformation of the churches of the glorious duchy of Brunswick, [which reformation] was undertaken by the most illustrious prince His Lordship Julius, of most praiseworthy memory, as the author himself set forth at length the occasion, purpose, and intent of this writing in the preface of the German edition, which [preface] we have supplied in Latin translation. Moreover, for the sake of pious youth that studies Holy Writ it [the little book itself] has been issued also in Latin with the consent of the author, with Dom.[7] Johann Zanger,[8] formerly a coauditor of Dom.[9] Chemnitz, as translator. And so that *Enchiridion* has indeed been read eagerly and used profitably till now in both editions by many. Besides, whereas for the most part only the mere chapters of Scripture passages are referred to therein, learned men have held that profitable work would be done by learners if the very statements of Scripture were added to the passages cited. For even if the author for some certain reason did not want to add the whole statements of Scripture, content to note only their chapters, so that, namely, he would send the pastors whose examinations he at first wanted this little book to serve back to the very sources of

Scripture, where they themselves might become accustomed to search out those proof texts, weigh the connection of the context, and thus discover their true sense, import, and emphasis, yet novices, for whose use this *Enchiridion* is now especially designed, are not all of that discernment nor so trained in reading Holy Writ that they might everywhere correctly track down and look into those statements of the cited chapters that are properly pertinent to the question at issue, especially since the author, in citing and applying proof texts of Scripture, follows a certain line of thought of his own that perhaps will not thus be obvious to those less familiar with his writings. In order, then, that their studies might be aided, the whole statements of Scripture, with the places noted by the author, are repeated and added in this edition, with other writings of the same author considered on that subject, where he treats the same matters with express proof texts. Care was also taken that statements of Scripture, as also of the fathers, be set forth in different type, so that they might the more easily be distinguished from the rest of the text. You, Christian[10] and gentle[11] reader, receive this our little work graciously and, if it please you, use and enjoy it. Farewell.

Preface[1]

To the reverend in Christ, venerable, most illustrious, and very learned lord abbots[2] and heads of monasteries, as also the lord superintendents and pastors of the churches of the glorious duchy of Brunswick, my honorable lords and dearly beloved brothers in Christ:

The grace of God in Christ Jesus, our only Redeemer and Mediator.

Reverend in God,[3] venerable, pious,[4] and very learned men, honorable lords, and dearly beloved brothers in Christ:[5] The highest favor that can come from heaven to any province, city, or people is this, when God kindles and causes to arise the light of His saving Word, by whose splendor all darkness of errors, abuses, superstitions, and idolatrous worship are put to flight, and hearts are enlightened by the true and salutary knowledge of God. For Scripture calls it the accepted time, the day of salvation, a blessed people and a blessed land, Lk 10:23[6]; 2 Co 6:2; Ps 144:15; 147:13. And it praises this treasure as more excellent than any purest gold and most-precious stones, Ps 19:10; 119:72, 127.[7] For it is the only and ordinary means whereby the Holy Spirit calls, gathers, enlightens, and keeps a true Christian[8] church on earth, which [church] in this life rejoices and delights in a gracious and merciful God and in [the life] to come[9] in eternal blessedness. Since, then, the most merciful God[10] has richly bestowed that great favor according to His singular mercy on the churches of this glorious duchy, so that namely, with the tables of the money changers of the Roman Antichrist overturned and his traffickings, together with his rotten, evil, false, and venomous[11] wares driven out, the pure and salutary doctrine of the divine Word from Holy Scripture has been sown and planted in their place through a Christian[12]

15

reformation in monasteries, churches, and schools, we surely can never give the very great and good God[13] enough thanks for that boundless goodness and mercy. Yet it behooves us by all means[14] to acknowledge, take to heart, and ponder[15] it and—to prove and show[16] our thankful Christian heart and mind[17]—to use that gift of God in a Christian and blessed way to His honor[18] and the welfare and salvation[19] of our poor soul,[20] lest, with blessing spurned, the fearful curse await us of which it is written, Mt. 11:23[21]: And you Capernaum, which are exalted even to heaven, will be brought down to hell.[22] Likewise Lk 11:26: The last state becomes worse than the first.

But indeed, since that great and arduous work cannot, at the beginning of these budding,[23] tender churches, immediately be complete and perfect in every respect, God, who has begun the good work in us, is to be implored to continue completing it until the day of Jesus Christ, Ph 1:6, and preserve and confirm what He has graciously begun to work, Ps 68:28.

And since God[24] instituted the ministry for this reason and uses it to this end, that the body of Christ, that is, His church,[25] might be built, and ever grow, unto the edifying of itself, Eph 4:16, they that are in the ministry must, with all concern, diligence, and faithfulness, be God's colaborers, plant, and water, 1 Co 3:6-9,[26] that the Word of God might dwell among us richly in all wisdom, Cl 3:16, and all manner of tares[27] of false, erroneous doctrine be rooted up and kept away from these churches by the grace of God,[28] Mt 15:1-13; Acts 20:28-31.[29] For that reason and in view of this it is decreed in the Christian church order of our illustrious prince and ruler, Lord Julius, duke of Brunswick and Lüneburg, that the examinations be held not only when someone is to be accepted and received into the church ministry, but that the superintendents twice a year [30] examine the pastors assigned to their supervision, so that it might at one and the same time be an indoctrination and instruction regarding the basis and true meaning of the pure doctrine, and how less-learned pastors[31] might arrange their studies, guard against false doctrine, and set the doctrine before their hearers in plain and simple terms, so that through such examinations the whole church, both preachers and hearers, might be edified under divine blessing with great profit and benefit. But in order that equality might be preserved in the examinations and the less-learned be able the better to prepare themselves for them, it was resolved in the church consistory, with the gracious previous knowledge and consent of our[32] gracious prince and lord, etc., that the form of examination—like that in the consistory—used with those who are to be ordained and received into the church ministry be published in written form, so that the superintendents might be able to follow it in the annual visitations. And that was not done with this intent, herewith to reject other useful little books of this kind (for in this little booklet reference is made in many places to the *Examen* of Dom. Philipp[33] and to other writings), but that for the sake of these new, budding churches one might have a simple form for bringing pastors to the true fundamentals of pure doctrine. Therefore the chapters of passages of Scripture are everywhere noted, so that the pastors themselves should learn to search in the Bible and be able to advance sure testimony of the Scripture on each point. And this form of examination is drawn up in the German language, not with the intent that the pastors should be educated only by the medium of German[34] and take this little book as a *Dormi secure*[35] (for the examinations are held, and should also be chiefly held, in the Latin language), but [1] because one often finds that many recite the customary definitions like a parrot[36] and either do not understand their true meaning or are unable to show any basis for them in God's Word, and [2] because it is one thing to discuss something in the schools in Latin but quite another to set the same before the common man in such a plain way[37] that he can thoroughly understand, grasp, and receive it. Finally [3], also, it [this little book] is written in German so that the laity might read and know what is discussed in examinations and what is the model in the chief heads of salutary doctrine, according to which also the hearers might judge whether their pastors follow the true voice of Christ, the only Chief Shepherd, or if they speak with the voice of a stranger,[38] Jn 10:3-5.

Now, when this little book was to be published, I then[39] dedicated and addressed it first to you, reverend heads of the monasteries of this duchy, because the reformation of the monasteries was directed to this end, that the prelates should gradually be drawn in and used in the consistory, for visitations, for examinations, and for synods, etc. and because the examinations of pastors in the first visitation were for the most part held in the monasteries—so that this little book might publicly testify what kind of doctrine it is regarding which pastors were examined toward the beginning of the reformation, which [doctrine] also Your Reverences embraced and still profess. Moreover, at the same time I also addressed you, the superintendents, general and special, and all pastors of the churches of this duchy, to testify publicly, confirm thoroughly, and firmly preserve Christian,[40] salutary unity in pure doctrine, against all[41] pernicious corruptions, among the ministers of the churches in the duchy and in the city of Brunswick, as this very model of pure, incorrupt doctrine resounded by divine grace in all these neighboring and other nearby churches of Saxony, in thesis and antithesis, till now and still resounds, as the chief points are explained in a simple manner in this manual. And since God[42] has given His special grace and blessing, so that the Christian declaration of the disputed points of religion—which [declaration] was incorporated in the church order of the duchy of Brunswick, from which also this manual was for the most part drawn—is approved and praised as correct by many leading churches, not only nearby but also far away, I could not object when the printer wanted to issue this little book anew, and I have also improved it in some places. And I hereby want the first, previous dedication of this little book to Your Reverence and Honor to be repeated and confirmed.

May the faithful and most merciful[43] God rule, teach, bless,[44] and keep us in pure doctrine and unity of the Spirit, so that we may one and all, by the grace and help of the Holy Spirit, according to the teaching of Paul, hold steadfastly to the Word, which is salutary and sure, refute those who contradict, Tts 1:9, and endeavor to keep—besides pure doctrine—Christian, brotherly unity and the bond of peace, Eph 4:3. Let us guard against unnecessary, vexatious division and schism, Ro 16:17. Let us not give way or place, even in the least, to the wolf and to tares of false doctrine, Jo 10:12, but, as Luther says, do both faithfully and diligently: feed the sheep and drive away the wolf. Amen. Written at Brunswick, August 6, A. D. 1574.

Martin Chemnitz
Lord Superintendent

Preface[1]

To the venerable in God, abbots and heads of monasteries, also the the venerable, worthy, high, and very learned general and special superintendents, with all pastors and ministers of the churches of Christ in both praiseworthy duchies of Brunswick and Lüneburg, his very gracious lords and dear fellow brothers in Christ:

Dom. Polycarp Leyser wishes grace and blessing through Christ Jesus, besides first offering his willing service and prayer:

Venerable in God, worthy, devout, high and very learned, dear gracious lords and brothers in Christ: After the bookstores sold out these two little books, namely the *Enchiridion* of Martin Chemnitz and the little book *De formulis caute loquendi* of Urbanus Rhegius, two distinguished theologians now resting in heavenly peace, both of greatest importance for all students of theology, young beginning preachers, and other pious Christians—so far as they have thorough instruction in the chief parts of Christian doctrine and fit themselves properly into the religious controversy raging in our time and want to speak or teach regarding them in a reasonable, Christian, and restrained way and on a good and lasting basis—on the urging and request of several kindhearted people and with the consent of the heirs I have had them printed together in one little manual, wishing to share them again under one title with one and all in the hope that thereby many pious hearts may be served and that no one might take it amiss, because Dom. Chemnitz is not only the sole author of the *Enchiridion* but also—on the gracious commission of the late serene and noble prince and lord, Lord William the Younger, duke of Brunswick and Lüneburg, etc., of most praiseworthy, Christ-tempered[2] memory—enlarged and improved the other little book with explanation of the newly arisen controversy to such an extent that it might indeed well be regarded as new and almost his own work.

But since the first work, namely the *Enchiridion*, was previously and indeed soon upon its appearance dedicated and inscribed to Your Venerable Esteem and Grace, the lord abbots, superintendents, and pastors of the praiseworthy duchy of Brunswick, Wolfenbüttel part, I also let it stand as proper and did not change that dedication in the least. For it was written and published by the author 20 and some years ago mainly for this purpose, that by it the newly planted and at that time reformed churches of this duchy and the preachers in it might be served.

But the other work, namely *De formulis caute loquendi*, since it originally came from Celle and was improved and produced by gracious arrangement of highly esteemed princes and lords—the aforementioned[3] lord abbots, superintendents, and pastors will also kindly note that in this edition, since these little books are printed together, I at the same time address and salute the Lord superintendents, pastors, and preachers of the duchy of Brunswick and Lüneburg, Celle part.

But beyond that and mindful that this little book, *De formulis caute loquendi*, is incorporated in the collection of doctrinal statements in both parts of the praiseworthy duchy and therefore cannot properly and rightly be withdrawn from either part, I have besides also another important reason why I do not want to fail on this occasion to address the theologians of both duchies in public print, praying subserviently and earnestly that it be favorably heard and altogether well received.

It is more than five years now, my gracious lords, since I was called to your ministration by an honorable and very wise council of this distinguished and far-famed city of Brunswick. At that time I resolved immediately upon acceptance and approval of the call that, as I had previously lived in good and warm friendship and unity with all preachers in the region of Meissen (not to boast), I would also likewise here in Lower Saxony, and particularly in the praiseworthy duchies of Brunswick and Lüneburg, live in peaceful unity and good relationship with their theologians, into whose very near neighborhoods I would now come.

And in His faithfulness God, to whom I henceforth humbly give due praise and thanks, has granted me grace that even so the highly esteemed clergy of these Lower Saxony churches received me with all goodwill, acknowledged me as a brother in Christ and colaborer in the vineyard of the Lord, and by letter and in other ways have maintained close-knit unity, except what happened with some few, whom Your Venerable Esteem and Grace knows, and who, because of the unpleasant controversy about the ubiquity of the body of Christ—which controversy they began against me against my will—said what they thought of me and gave me a hard time also in other ways, and have aroused suspicion not only regarding me but also these famous churches, well-regarded far and wide, of the city of Brunswick, as though they [the churches] had departed from their old steadfast confession of the pure doctrine regarding the article on the person and majesty of the Lord Christ.

This charge hurt many Christian hearts very much. But especially did it of course give me very much pain to see that thereby the bond of Christian unity, which [unity] was attained a few years earlier among the churches of the Augsburg Confession, would be greatly weakened, the weak in faith led astray, good consciences disturbed, and occasion for rejoicing given to the common enemies of our confession. But this pained me most of all, that I had to experience this, that although not only some distinguished theologians but also the praiseworthy reigning prince took pains to become involved in the matters and settle the controversy out of Christian zeal and concern for the peace of the churches, yet a foreign view, completely contrary to my faith, was ascribed to me and condemned as my own.

For I was charged with daring to sneak general ubiquity of the body of Christ into the churches of this land, that is, that I hold this teaching and try to persuade others of it, as though the body of Christ were present not only in the consecrated bread of the Holy Supper but also in all wood, stone, leaves, grass, and all other creatures, whatever they might be called, also in a cow (as yon[4] doctor said, but without basis). All this has till now been called the general ubiquity of the body of Christ. Not only did I never share this view and gladly let the matter rest with the advice of Luther, who is cited and approved on page 399 of this little book,[5] but have in fact always had an abhorrence of such talk and propositions, which serve neither for the honor of Christ nor for the edification of the Christian churches, nor for common piety or comfort.

Therefore, if there is someone who, when he contends and fights against the ubiquity, understands these and similar propositions in which one refers to the body of Christ to wood, stone, leaves, and grass, etc. or seeks it therein, and cannot bear or suffer them, let him herewith know that he will not only not have me as an adversary, but I will much rather step to his side and lend counsel and aid, so that such unnecessary, idle, and prolix disputations be cut off once and for all.

Side by side with this, however, I confess freely and willingly that if the question were asked regarding this proposition: Is the person of Christ, whole and undivided, in and with both natures, divine and human, present in ruling all creatures, or is this done in such a way that the divine nature is present but the human absent?—there I unabashedly and openly confess that I approve and, according to my ability, defend the doctrine and view that teaches that the whole Christ now, after He has entered His glory, is present not only as God but also as man, first indeed for His Christian churches with all graces, but then for all creatures with His almighty power and powerful rule, and that all this takes place not only according to His divine nature but also with, in, and according to

21

His adopted human nature (which two natures united together make one whole Christ), but with this difference, that the divine nature is present by virtue of its natural quality, but the human not by natural power, nor as it would be considered in and for itself, nor as if it had received from the divine nature such an essential quality or power of its own or one that belonged to its human essence—but as it is, considered in the person of the Son of God, one person with the Son of God.

Now, if someone, because of this doctrine and view, is not at one with me but is my enemy and hates me, even stirs up a controversy against me, I must let it happen and commit it to God and by His aid see how I might defend myself against attack and champion this infallible truth. For this doctrine is set forth from God's Word so powerfully against the Zwinglians by our German prophet and man of God, Martin Luther,[6] of holy and Christ-tempered[7] memory, and later explained so faithfully by our dear preceptor and faithful superintendent, Dom. Martin Chemnitz, of blessed memory, in his fine and worthwhile book, *De persona Christi,* is also approved clearly enough in this little book, *De formulis caute loquendi,* page 400 ff.,[8] under the heading, Of the Ascension of Christ and His Sitting at the Right of God the Father, and then finally so confirmed and preserved in the Christian Book of Concord and in the Apology that followed it, published in the name and with the consent of high potentates and many churches, that I could not, for the sake and service of anyone, let it drop and so surrender the truth.

Be that as it may, it is not now my intent that I want to engage in this controversy in this writing, or deliberately stir up again all that has to some extent been quieted, and so cause a new dispute and quarrel. But my intent is directed toward something else, namely that after the almighty God, in His secret counsel and hidden will, has so disposed, that I have now again been called to Wittenberg, to my former office and post, by the Most Serene Noble Prince and Lord, Lord Frederick William, duke of Saxony, and the administrator of Electoral Saxony, etc., my most gracious lord, as also by the praiseworthy university and the honorable council at Wittenberg, to which call, extended elsewhere, an honorable, very wise council here has granted me gracious leave, and I would therefore again leave this land—that I much desire, so far as might be possible, also after my departure, to keep close-knit unity in matters of religion and faith also with the theologians and pastors[9] also of these two praiseworthy duchies, as with others of Lower Saxony.

For the church of Christ is always built with less trouble and more profit where the preachers, as the spiritual builders, keep harmony, peace, and unity with each other, than where each on his own again tears down through quarrel and dispute what another has built.

And though indeed I feel sure that there is nothing but all good friendship between me and most preachers of both duchies, above all those whom I know, even though I would not have openly sought it hereby, yet, to make assurance double sure, I did not want to let pass this welcome opportunity to address Your Reverence, Honor, and Grace in these matters, in comfortable assurance that they would not be displeasing.[10] For I really want it done to this end, that this my preface be a public testimony that I am minded to maintain ongoing and brotherly unity with each and all theologians, preachers, and ministers of the churches of Christ in both praiseworthy duchies, Brunswick and Lüneburg, in the doctrine whose sum and foundation is contained in these two little books that are common to both duchies, with regard to thesis and antithesis, and remain, live, and die in it. But he that is not pleased and satisfied with this doctrine or in unnecessary zeal for dispute dares to undermine and overthrow the foundations of this salutary doctrine should not be angry if I do not care to have any fellowship with him or, according to the teaching of John, also do not wish to greet him. For no unity is lasting or salutary but that which is based on Christ and on the truth.

And since the first part of this little book[11] contains very good and Christian instructions how to examine the young preachers before ordination, when they want to enter their office, it would also be much better simply to follow such a Christian and approved form and exhort beginning preachers to study this little book diligently, than to use the whole time of the examination for irrelevant questions and idle quarrel about ubiquity or to hang gratuitous tags and nicknames in adverse reflection on one's neighbors, as has heretofore been done much and often, but doubtless those who have proper supervision of this matter would now be well advised to make an end of it. In connection with it I have been reliably informed, however, not only that the dreadful clamor about ubiquity has measurably subsided but also that a beginning is being made to teach and to express oneself more restrainedly regarding the whole main issue. From this I draw hope that perhaps God might grant success and blessing for a complete settlement also of this disputed article of religion, so that those who till now felt such great aversion against our teaching and position, and yet could never make a charge of error in our teaching hold and therefore now draw closer to us again, might finally become altogether one with us again.

To that end may God the Father, who is a God of peace and of the truth, graciously grant the grace and power of His Holy Spirit for the sake of His dear Son Jesus Christ. To Him and His gracious defense and shield I herewith faithfully commend Your Reverence, Honor, and Grace. Written at Brunswick on the day after that of Polycarp, A. D. 1593.

Your Reverence's, Honor's, and Grace's ready servant
Polycarp Leyser D.

The *Enchiridion*
of
Martin Chemnitz

Introduction

1   *What is the nature of the ministry of the church?*

It is not civil government, by which political affairs, or the matters of this world, are administered. Lk 22:25-26; 2 Ti 2:4. Nor is it spiritual power lording it arbitrarily and, as it were, by naked power over the church of God in matters of faith. 2 Co 1:24; 1 Ptr 5:3. Nor is it a business or a tricky way for indulging greed. 1 Ti 3:2-3, 8; 6:5; 1 Ptr 5:2. But it is a spiritual, or ecclesiastic, office, instituted and ordained by God Himself for discharging and performing necessary functions of the church, so that pastors, or preachers, are and ought to be ministers of God and of the church in the kingdom of Christ, and stewards of the mysteries of God. 1 Co 4:1; Cl 1:25; 2 Co 4:5.

2   *What, then, is the office of ministers of the church?*

This office, or ministry, has been committed and entrusted to them by God Himself through a legitimate call

I. To feed the church of God with the true, pure, and salutary doctrine of the divine Word. Acts 20:28; Eph 4:11; 1 Ptr 5:2.

II. To administer and dispense the sacraments of Christ according to His institution. Mt 28:19; 1 Co 11:23.

III. To administer rightly the use of the keys of the church, or of the kingdom of heaven, by either remitting or retaining sins (Mt 16:19; Jn 20:23), and to fulfill all these things and the whole ministry (as Paul says, 2 Ti 4:5) on the basis of the prescribed command, which the chief Shepherd Himself has given His ministers in His Word for instruction. Mt 28:20.

3   *Is it right to ordain and admit to the ministry of the church those who have been called, without prior appropriate and solemn examination, as is generally done among papal suffragans[1]?*

By no means. For in His Word God has prescribed a certain form regarding the call, doctrine, and conduct, or life, of those to whom the functions of the church are to be entrusted. One should therefore first carefully test and examine them as to whether they are legitimately called, whether they rightly hold the fundamentals of salutary doctrine and reject fanatic opinions, whether they are endowed with the gifts necessary to teach others sound doctrine, and whether they can prove their lives to be honorable, so that they can be examples to the flock; for this concern we have the very solemn precept of Paul. 1 Ti 5:22; 2 Ti 2:2. The older councils therefore decreed many things regarding examination of those who are to be ordained; these things are found in Gratian, Distinct. 23, 24, and 81. And canon 4 of the 4th Council of Carthage, at which Augustine was present, decreed thus: Let one who is to be ordained be ordained when he has, in an examination, been found to be rightly instructed. And the canon of Nicaea, Distinct. 81,[2] says: If any are promoted [to be] presbyters without examination, church order does not recognize them, because they are ordained contrary to the rule.

4   *What, then, are the chief parts regarding which either one who is to be ordained, or one who already is pastor of a church, is to be examined?*

There are four[3] chief parts:

1. The call.
2. The doctrine of the Word and of the Sacraments.
3. Ceremonies to be observed in church assemblies and in the administration of the sacraments.
4. The life and conduct of ministers of the church.

Part 1

The legitimate and ordinary call of ministers of the Word and of the Sacraments

5   *May one seek or undertake the ministry of the church who has neither learned the fundamental Christian doctrine, nor understands [it], nor has the gift to teach others?*

By no means. For Paul commands Timothy and Titus to entrust the ministry to faithful and able men. 2 Ti 2:2; 3:2; Tts 1:9.

6   *Should, then, one who is somewhat endowed with those gifts, on his own initiative and personal judgment, without a special and legitimate call, undertake and claim for himself the office of teaching in the church?*

By no means. Ro 10:15; Jer 23:21; Heb 5:4.

7   *Are they to be heard, or can they be profitably heard by the church, who have no proof of a legitimate call?*

No. Ro 10:14-15; Jer 27:14-15. And for this reason the prophets and apostles so earnestly emphasize the prerogatives of their call at the beginning of their writings. And experience shows that they who thrust themselves into ecclesiastical functions without a legitimate and regular call experience little blessing of God and contribute little to the upbuilding of the church.

8   *But Paul says, 1 Ti 3:1: "He that desires the office of bishop desires a good work." Is it therefore necessary for one to wait until he is called?*

To desire the office of bishop is not to thrust oneself into ecclesiastical functions without a legitimate call; but if one has learned and understands the fundamentals of Christian doctrine and is somewhat endowed with the gift of teaching—when he offers his service to God and the church, he thereby seeks nothing else than that God would declare through a legitimate, or regular, call whether He wants to use his service in His church. And he ought to be so minded, that, if a call does not follow his request, he does not cunningly work his way in. 2 Sm 15:26.

9   *But all believers are called priests, Rv 1:6; 5:10; 1 Ptr 2:9. Have all, therefore, a general call to the ministry?*

All we who believe are indeed spiritual priests, but we are not all teachers. 1 Co 12:29-30; Eph 4:11-12. And Peter explains himself: All Christians are priests—not that all should function without difference in the ministry of the Word and of the Sacraments, without a special call, but that they should offer spiritual sacrifices. Ro 12:1; Heb 13:15-16.

10   *Yet all Christians have a general call to proclaim the virtues of God, 1 Ptr 2:9, and especially family heads, to instruct their households, Dt 6:7; 1 Co 14:35.*

It is true that all Christians have a general call to proclaim the Gospel of God, Ro 10:9, to speak the Word of God among themselves, Eph 5:19; to admonish each other from the Word of God, Cl 3:16; to reprove, Eph 5:11 [and] Mt 19:15; [and] to comfort, 1 Th 4:18. And family heads are enjoined [to do] this with the special command that they give their households the instruction of the Lord. Eph 6:4. But the public ministry of the Word and of the Sacraments in the church is not entrusted to all Christians in general, as we have already shown, 1 Co 12:28; Eph 4:12. For a special or particular call is required for this, Ro 10:15.

11   *For what reasons is it so very important that a minister of the church have a legitimate call?*

One must not think that this is done by human arrangement or only for the sake of order; but there are many weighty reasons, consideration of which teaches many things and is very necessary for every minister of the church.

I. Because God Himself deals with us in the church through the ministry as through the ordinary means and instrument. For it is He Himself that speaks, exhorts, absolves, baptizes, etc. in the ministry and through the ministry. Lk 1:70; Heb 1:1; Jn 1:23 (God crying through the Baptist); 2 Co 2:10, 17; 5:20; 13:3. It is therefore absolutely necessary that the minister as well as the church have sure proofs that God wants to use this very person for this His ordinary means and instrument, namely the ministry.

Now, a legitimate or regular call provides these proofs; for in this way every minister of the Word can apply to himself the statements of Scripture [in] 2 Co 5:19; Is 59:21; Mt 10:20; Lk 10:16; 1 Th 4:8.

II. Very many and necessary gifts are required for the ministry. 2 Co 2:16. But one who has been brought to the ministry by a legitimate call can apply the divine promises to himself, ask God for faithfulness in them, and expect both, the gifts that are necessary for him rightly to administer the ministry (1 Ti 4:14; 2 Ti 1:6; 2 Co 3:5-6) and governance and protection in the office entrusted to him (Is 49:2; 51:16).

III. The chief thing of the ministry is that God wants to be present in it with His Spirit, grace, and gifts and to work effectively through it. But

Paul says, Ro 10:15: "How shall they who are not sent preach" (namely in such a way that faith is engendered by hearing)? But God wants to give increase to the planting and watering of those who have been legitimately called to the ministry and set forth doctrine without guile and faithfully administer whatever belongs to the ministry (1 Co 3:6; 15:58), that both they themselves and others might be saved. 1 Ti 4:16.

IV. The assurance of a divine call stirs up ministers of the Word, so that each one, in his station, in the fear of God, performs his functions with greater diligence, faith, and eagerness, without weariness. And he does not let himself be drawn or frightened away from his office by fear of any peril or of persecution, since he is sure that he is called by God and that that office has been divinely entrusted to him.

V. Finally, on this basis the hearers are stirred up to true reverence and obedience toward the ministry, namely since they are taught from the Word of God that God, present through this means, wants to deal with us in the church and work effectively among us.

12 *Who, then, properly has the right or power to send and call ministers of the Word and of the Sacraments?*

At all times there have been great, often also bloody, controversies regarding the right to call; but, speaking properly and on the basis of Scripture, the right to call and to send laborers into the harvest belongs to Him who is the Lord of the harvest, and it is good to note in Scripture that the right and administration of this call are ascribed expressly to the individual persons of the Trinity. For the Son says of the Father, Mt 9:38: "Pray ye the Lord of the harvest to send laborers into His harvest"; Paul testifies of the Son of God, Eph 4:8, 11-12: "He ascended on high [and] gave gifts to people. . . . And He gave some [as] apostles, some [as] prophets, some [as] evangelists, and some [as] pastors and teachers . . . for the upbuilding of the body of Christ"; the same is also attributed to the Holy Spirit [in] Acts 13:2, 4; 20:28. Therefore also God does not recognize as true pastors those who have not been sent by Him, even if they have been called and appointed by kings or [by] a political magistrate. Jer 23:21; 27:14-15.

13 *But how and in what way does God call and send ministers to the church?*

There is no legitimate or ordinary call to the ministry except from God, and it is twofold: either without means or through means.

14 *What is a call without means, and how does it take place?*

When someone is called and sent to the ministry neither by men nor through men as through regular means, but without means, by God Himself, and through God Himself, as God in this way called the patriarchs, prophets, and apostles, without any intervening human means. And they who have thus been called have the testimony of the Spirit and of miracles that they do not err in doctrine. And the rest of the ministers of the church take their doctrine from them, and they must prove it thereby. And besides, the ministry of those who have been called without means is not bound and anchored to a certain church at only one place, but they have the command to teach all people everywhere.

15 *Is one, therefore, immediately to believe all fanatics when they claim that God has appeared to them, that the Lord has spoken to them, that the Father has given them this commission, and that they are thus stirred up and moved by the Spirit?*

By no means. For God has forbidden this with an express warning. Jer 14:14. But God endows those whom He calls without means either with the gift of miracles or with other testimonies of the Spirit with which to prove and confirm their call. Thus Moses established his call before Pharaoh with the gift of miracles, Ex 4:1 ff. Therefore Paul also calls signs, wonders, and mighty deeds proofs of the apostolate, 2 Co 12:12. Christ speaks of these, Jn 5:36; Mt 10:8. But one should not believe false doctrine that leads away from God and conflicts with the Word, even if miracles follow it. Dt 12:1 ff; Mt 7:22-23; 24:23-24; 2 Th 2:9.

16 *Should one also in these times expect from God a call like that without means?*

We neither want nor ought to prescribe anything to the free will of God and His infinite power. But since in the New Testament we neither have any promise that after the apostles God wants to send laborers into His harvest through an immediate [i.e., without means] call, nor is there a command that we should wait until ministers are appointed by an immediate call, we therefore observe, and should observe, the form that the apostles have prescribed for us by the Holy Spirit, namely that, and how, God at this time wants to call and send ministers to His church through a mediate [i.e., through means] call or regular means.

17 *What, then, is a mediate call?*

When any minister is called and appointed to the ministry of the church, indeed by God and divinely, but not without means, as the prophets and apostles [were], but through regular means, in a legitimate way. For a mediate call is as much from God as an immediate one, but they differ in the manner of the call. For God called the prophets and apostles immediately, through Himself. But God called and sent Titus, Timothy, Sosthenes, Silvanus, and others likewise, but not immediately, rather through means instituted and ordained by Himself for this purpose.

18 *Is a mediate call based on the Word of God?*

It certainly is. For the apostles appointed elders in every church by an election of the church, Acts 14:23. Thus the ministry of the church was entrusted to Timothy by the laying on of hands of the presbytery, 1 Ti 4:14. But lest this call appear to rest only on examples, without divine command, Paul commands Timothy and Titus to appoint ministers in every city and at the same time prescribes a form for them, how they should do that. Tts 1:5; 2 Ti 2:2; 1 Ti 3:2 ff.

19 *Show with statements and examples of Scripture that they who are legitimately called through regular means are called and sent by God Himself.*

Timothy, bishop of the church at Ephesus, was not called immediately, but through Paul and the presbytery. 1 Ti 4:14; 2 Ti 1:6. And he had a mandate similarly also to appoint other ministers of the church. 2 Ti 2:2. And yet Paul says to the elders of the church at Ephesus, Acts 20:28: "The Holy Spirit has made you overseers, to rule the church of God." And in the 2d Epistle to the Corinthians [5:19-20], which Timothy also signed, Paul says in his own name and that of Timothy: "God has given us the ministry of reconciliation and has entrusted to us the Word of reconciliation. We therefore function as ambassadors in the name of Christ, God exhorting through us." Paul likewise declares that God gives and places in the church not only apostles, who are called immediately, but also teachers and pastors, who are called mediately. Eph. 4:11; 1 Co 12:28.

20 *May he, then, who has been properly chosen for the ministry by a mediate call, refer and apply also to himself, each according to his own measure, equally as well as also the prophets and apostles, the promises of grace, help, power, and divine efficacy in the ministry?*

The prophets and apostles, who were sent by an immediate call, indeed have many and great prerogatives, in accordance with a larger measure of divine gifts. But the promises of grace, help, power, and divine efficacy in the ministry also apply nonetheless, according to each one's measure, to those who have been mediately called in a legitimate way. Paul declares this regarding Timothy. 2 Ti 1:6. And lest anyone think that this applies only to those who have indeed been called mediately, but by the apostles themselves, he says, 1 Ti 4:14: "Do not neglect the grace which has been given you by prophecy, with the laying on of hands of the presbytery." And 1 Ti 4:16 he writes regarding the efficacy of the ministry itself. And when the Corinthians measure the efficacy of the ministry in their church on the basis of the persons, called either immediately or mediately, likewise on the basis of diversity of gifts in ministers, Paul cries out, 1 Co 3:5 ff.: "Who is Apollos? etc." and for this reason Paul, who otherwise strongly emphasizes his apostolic call, nevertheless in the subscription of several epistles modestly adds also others mediately called. Thus Timothy signed 2 Co together with Paul, likewise Ph and Cl; Sosthenes signed 1 Co; Paul, Timothy, and Silvanus together signed 1 and 2 Th.

21 *What, then, are the regular means that God wants to use for a mediate call?*

For a mediate call God ordinarily does not use the ministry of angels, but the ministry of His church, which is a royal priesthood. 1 Ptr 2:9. For to it as to His spouse has Christ entrusted the keys of the kingdom. Mt 18:18. Likewise He entrusted the Word and the Sacraments. Ro 3:2; 9:4. And briefly, all things are of the church, both the ministry and the ministers. Eph 4:12; Co 3:21-22.

22[1] *Does the Roman pontiff do right in that he excludes pious rulers and the rest of the lay church from the election and call of bishops or ministers of the church?*

It is clearly and surely evident from both the commands and the examples of Scripture, that when the ministry is to be entrusted to someone through a mediate call, those who are already in the ministry and profess sound doctrine are to be used. Tts 1:5; 1 Ti 4:14; 2 Ti 2:2; Acts 14:23. But since ministers are not the whole church, but only part of it (Eph 4:11-12), and they are not lords of the church, but ministers and overseers (2 Co 1:24; 4:5; Eze 33:7), therefore they neither can nor should seize to themselves alone the mediate call, with the other members of the church excluded; for not even the apostles did this, but drew the rest of the church in with themselves. Acts 1:15-16; 6:2-3; 14:23. And with the name elders are meant not only ministers of the Word, but included in the presbytery are also those who were appointed by the whole church to administer the work of the church, as Tertullian and Ambrose testify.

23 *But with what right does political authority take for itself the power to call and appoint ministers of the church?*

The ecclesiastical ministry belongs to the kingdom of Christ. And since Christ wants His kingdom and the kingdom of the world with its functions to be separate, therefore the appointment of the ministry does not properly belong to the political rights of a magistrate like the rest of the things that are called regalia. But since a political magistrate, if he is a Christian and pious, is a member of the church (Ps 47:9; 102:23) and thus has a mandate not only to love the teaching of the divine Word and practice piety himself (Ps 2:10-11) but with his office also to be a nursing father of the church (Is 49:23), and in order that the gates of the world lift up their heads, that the King of glory might enter through them (Ps 24:7), this is therefore the concern also of a pious magistrate, that the ministries of the church be rightly ordered and administered.

24 *Is a Christian magistrate, therefore, permitted to call and appoint ministers in the church without the will and consent of the ministry and the rest of the church?*

As the Roman pontiff, with them who are his, has committed a great sacrilege in this, that he has taken the election and call of ministers away from the church and transferred [it] to himself alone, so a political magistrate also becomes guilty of the same offense when he takes for himself alone the power to appoint the ministries in the church, with the ministry and the rest of the church excluded. For a pious magistrate is not the whole church, but only part of it. Ps 47:9. Nor is he the lord of the church, but nursing father (Is 49:23), in fact, its servant (Is 60:10).

25   *But do Anabaptists do right, who entrust the whole right of calling to the common multitude (which they take the word ekklesia to mean), with the ministry and pious magistrate excluded?*

By no means. For the church in each place is called, and is, the whole body embracing under Christ, the Head, all the members of that place. Eph 4:15-16; 1 Co 12:12-14, 27. Therefore as the call belongs not only to the ministry nor only to the magistrate, so also is it not to be made subject to the mere will [and] whim of the common multitude, for no part, with either one or both [of the others] excluded, is the church. But the call should be and remain in the power of the whole church, but with due order observed.

26   *Ought then the whole multitude (especially where it is very large) indiscriminately and without order handle the matter of election and call?*

God is not a God of confusion; He rather wants all things to be done and administered decently and in order in the church. 1 Co 14:40. Therefore to avoid confusion, at the time of the apostles and also after their time in the ancient and pure church, the matter of the election and call of ministers of the Word was always handled according to a certain order by the chief members of the church in the name and with the consent of the whole church. Thus the apostles first set forth a directive as to what kind of persons are to be chosen for the ministries of the church. Acts 1:15 ff.; 6:2 ff. Then the church, according to that rule of the directive, chose and set forth some. But since the call belongs not only to the multitude or common people in the church, therefore they submitted those who were chosen and nominated to the judgment of the apostles, whether they be fit for that ministry according to the rule of the divine Word. And so the election of the multitude was confirmed by the approval of the apostles.

And thus finally the ministries are committed to those nominated, elected, and called, with the solemn prayer of the whole church and public testimony, namely laying on of hands. Acts 6:5-6. But since the multitude of the church is not always such that it can search out and propose for election those that are fit, the apostles themselves often nominated suitable persons and proposed them to the churches. Tts 1:5; 1 Ti 1:3, 2 Ti 2:2.

Thus Paul sent Titus, Timothy, [and] Silvanus to churches. But the apostles did not thrust those persons on the churches without either invitation or consent, but nominated or presented them to the churches, which then approved and confirmed that nomination or election with their own free election, as Luke describes this custom with the word *cheirotonia*, Acts 14:23.

Finally, after the church had grown into a large multitude, a presbytery was arranged and set up already at the very time of the apostles to handle this matter. 1 Ti 4:14. In this [presbytery], according to the accounts of Tertullian and Ambrose, some were chosen and appointed, from all the orders or members of the church, to take care of and administer these and similar church matters in the name and with the consent of the whole church. And thus the call remained that of the whole complete church, yet with proper and decent order observed. The church immediately following diligently followed these apostolic footsteps. And since the government also began to embrace the doctrine of the Gospel, the whole matter of the election and call of ministers was ordinarily best distributed among the three chief orders of the church, namely clergy, the pious ruler, and the faithful people. Many notable old canons are quoted regarding this rite, Dist. 23, 24, 62, 65, and 67. And the old church histories testify that at times the bishops and clergy proposed persons to be called, at times a pious ruler nominated [them], at times the people requested [them], but they then presented those proposed, nominated, and requested persons to the other orders or members of the church, that the election might be approved and confirmed by their judgment and consent, Cyprian, Book 1, Ep. 4; Augustine, Ep. 100. From this there still remain the words nomination, request, presentation, consensus, confirmation, and conferring; from these words, rightly considered, it can be understood how and with what order the call of ministers of the church both was once regulated and ought to be properly administered in our time.

27²   *But whence does the right of patronage originate, and how far does it extend?*

That right has its origin in this, that some pious people gave certain returns and assessments of their goods to parishes to take care of church functions, and they reserved for themselves this right, that with their consent the profit of those returns be given to suitable persons. But that right did not extend so far that it was left free to the patron to put at the head of the ministries of the parishes whomever they wished, without the judgment and consent of the church of that place. But because the parochial returns flow from the patrons, it [the church] therefore either presents and sets before the patron of the church some suitable person and requests that the profit of those returns be conferred on him, or the patron himself nominates and presents to the church some person equipped with necessary gifts, but always with both the judgment of the ministry and the consent of the rest of the church preserved and free. And in this way the call remains nonetheless that of the church, and that old canon is observed: Let no one be given to the unwilling.

28   *Does the church have free power to call to the ministry whomever it wishes?*

The Lord of the harvest has prescribed a certain form and rule through His apostles, which is, as it were, a kind of heavenly instruction as to what kind of people they should be, both in doctrine as well as in conduct, or life, who are to be chosen and called for the church ministries. 1 Ti 3:2 ff; Tts 1:6 ff. And the church should recognize in the fear of God that this norm or instruction is to be followed if it wants a call both to be called [divine] and to be divine.

29   *If a legitimate call consists in the things that have been said so far, what, then, does the public rite of ordination confer?*

This rite is to be observed for very weighty reasons.

The first reason is that, because of those who run and have not been sent, a call ought to have the public testimony of the church. But that ceremony or rite of ordination is nothing else than the kind of public testimony by which the call of that person who is ordained is declared before God and in His name to be regular, pious, legitimate, and divine.

Second: By that rite, as by a public designation or declaration, the ministry is committed in the name of God and of the church to him who has been called.

Third: By this very thing also, as by a solemn vow, he who has been called becomes obligated to the church in the sight of God to render the faithfulness in the ministry that the Lord requires in His stewards, regarding which He will also judge them. 1 Co 4:2.

Fourth: The church is reminded that it is to recognize that this pastor has divine authority to teach, and to hear him in the name and place of God.

Fifth, and this is most important: That rite is to be observed for this reason, that the whole church might, by common and earnest prayers, commit to God the ministry of him who is called, that He, by His Holy Spirit, divine grace, and blessing, might be with his ministry.

30   *Whence is the rite of laying on of hands taken, and what does it mean?*

The rite of laying on of hands was common in the Old Testament when something was to be put solemnly in the sight of God, as it were, and committed to Him in a special way. Gn 48:14, 20; Lv 1:2, 4; Mk 10:16. And since public functions were at times entrusted to certain persons by laying on of hands (Nm 27:18-20; Dt 3:28; 34:9), therefore the apostles, in the ordination of ministers, out of Christian liberty retained and used that common rite as a thing indifferent [and] helpful in teaching many things. Acts 6:5-6; 13:3; 1 Ti 4:14; 5:22; 2 Ti 1:6. And thus also the ancient church observed the act of ordination without anointing and without other superstitions, simply with laying on of hands (Dist. 23 of the Council of Carthage). Therefore we also in our churches observe the same rite. For through laying on of hands the person called is set before God, as it were, so that there might be a public and outward testimony that the call is not only a human matter, but that God Himself calls, sends, and appoints that person for the ministry, though by regular and legitimate means. Moreover, by this solemn act he that is to be ordained is obligated and, as it were, consecrated to Christ for the ministry. Besides, by that rite, as in the sight of God, the church is entrusted to the minister and, on the other hand, the minister to the church, through whose ministry, namely, God wants to teach, exhort, administer the Sacraments, and work effectively in us. But the laying on of hands in ordination is observed chiefly because of the common prayers of the church, that they may be made with greater diligence and warmer desire. For it is, as it were, a public reminder of the difficulty of the ministry, which cannot be made able except by God. 2 Co 3:5-6. Therefore that minister is presented to the Lord of the harvest through laying on of hands, and the church, reminded of the institution of the ministry and of the divine promises attached to it, reminds God of His promises and asks that by their power He would graciously be with the present minister with His Spirit, grace, blessing, efficacy, working, governance, and direction. And Paul and Moses testify that these prayers of the church are not in vain. 1 Ti 4:14; 2 Ti 1:6; Dt 34:9. And thus the act of ordination publicly shows forth the whole doctrine of the call of ministers and sets it, as it were, before [one's] eyes.

31 *But what if some minister is to be dismissed or removed from office?*

Just as God properly claims for Himself the right to call, also mediately, and it is accordingly necessary for it to be done according to divine instruction, so also has God properly reserved to Himself alone this power of removing someone from the ministry. 1 Sm 2:30, 32; Hos 4:6.

But since that dismissal takes place mediately, it is therefore necessary that it not take place except by instruction and divine direction. Therefore as long as God lets in the ministry His minister who teaches rightly and lives blamelessly, the church does not have the power, without divine command to remove an unwanted man, namely [if he is] a servant of God. But when he does not build up the church by either doctrine or life, but rather destroys [it], God Himself removes him, 1 Sm 2:30; Hos 4:6. And then the church not only properly can but by all means should remove such a one from the ministry. For just as God calls ministers of the church, so He also removes them through legitimate means. But as the procedure of a call is to follow the instruction of the Lord of the harvest, so also if one is to be removed from the ministry, the church must show that that also is done by the command and will of the Lord. And just as the call, so also the removal or deposition belongs not only to some one order of the church, but to the whole church, with that order preserved of which we spoke a little while ago. Thus also the ancient church[3] handled cases of deposition in the councils with diligent inquiry and careful judgment (ch. 15, q. 7); on this basis one can also answer the other question about moving a minister from one church to another, about which there are helpful canons (ch. 7, q. 1).

The office of a minister of the church

32   *Should one who has been legitimately called be concerned only about ecclesiastical returns?*

Christ declares that laborers have wages coming. Mt 10:10; Lk 10:7. And Paul says, 1 Co 9:14: "God has so ordained, that they who preach the Gospel should live of the Gospel." But this should not be the chief concern in the ministry. Eze 34:2-3. Therefore Scripture calls pastors and teachers ministers, stewards, and laborers of God. 1 Co 3:5; 4:1; Mt 10:10; 2 Ti 2:15. But [Scripture calls] their ministry service, labor, and work. 1 Ti 5:17; 3:1.

33   *What, then, is the office or work of the ministry of the church?*

Sirach says, 38:25-26: "The wisdom of a scribe (namely for the kingdom of heaven) requires opportunity for leisure; and it is necessary for him to be free of other matters, who wants either to obtain that wisdom for himself or impart it to others. For how can he deal with wisdom, who must hold the plow and drive oxen, etc.?" The office of a minister of the church therefore is, that he diligently study the holy Scriptures and give himself to reading them (1 Ti 4:13), moreover, that he labor in the Word and doctrine (1 Ti 5:17), that he feed the flock of Christ and the church of God (1 Ptr 5:2; Acts 20:28); that is, he is to serve the church with the preaching of the Word and administration of the Sacraments and the use of the keys. As Origen aptly writes on Lv 8: "These two are works of a priest: First, that he learn of God, by reading the Holy Scriptures and frequent meditation, and that he teach the people, but that he teach the things that he himself has learned from God. There is also another work, which Moses does: he does not go to war, but prays for the people, etc."

Part 2

The Word and the Sacraments

The Word of God

34   *Which doctrine, then, or which word, ought a minister set before the church of God?*

Neither his dreams, nor the visions of his heart, or whatever seemed good or right to him (Jer 23:16, 25); also not human traditions or ordinances (Is 29:13; Mt 15:9). But let him who teaches in the church teach the Word of God (1 Ptr 4:11), so that the heart of the ministry is and remains this, Is 59:21: "I have put My words in your mouth," and as Augustine aptly says: "Let us not hear in the church: I say this, you say this, he says that; but: Thus says the Lord."

35   *What is the Word of God?*

It is the wisdom of God hidden in a mystery (1 Co 2:6-7), by which [wisdom] God has made known and revealed to mankind, by a certain Word which has been given, His essence and will (at least so far as it necessary for us in this life), so that we thereby recognize sin and the miseries into which we fall through sin, and know how and through whom we are freed from these evils, so that we as a result rightly recognize and worship God and learn well to arrange and conform our life according to the norm and rule of His commandments, and finally that we be taught what will be and what is to be expected for us after this life.

36   *Can a man by his own knowledge or by the perception of his own reason obtain that knowledge for himself?*

So great a darkness of the human mind followed upon the fall of [our] first parents that by itself or of itself it does not know or understand anything certain or sound of these matters. 1 Co 1:21; 2:14. For in spiritual things the human mind is not only blind, but Scripture declares that it is darkness itself. Jn 1:5; Eph 5:8. Man indeed has some obscure knowledge, as by a dream, that there is a God, who must also be worshiped. But who and what kind of God this is, and how He wants to be worshiped, he knows not at all; indeed, indulging his own thoughts and wisdom, he engages in pure idolatry. Ro 1:21-23. Thus human nature still indeed has a little part of the divine law written in the heart, regarding some outward and civil functions. But of the true knowledge of sin, and of the true worship of God, human reason, without the light of the Word of God, knows or understands nothing whatever. Rather, the whole doctrine of the Gospel is a mystery, unknown and hidden to human reason and wisdom. 1 Co 1:18, 21. But God, coming forth out of His secret dwelling place, moved by great mercy toward lost mankind, by a sure and special Word, given partly immediately, partly mediately, has made known and revealed that mystery to His church, which [mystery] He also confirmed with notable testimonies and miracles, lest one could doubt its truth. Mk 16:20; Heb 2:3-4.

37   *Can anyone, as some think, be saved in his religion and faith, without the Word of God, but having formed a good intention?*

By no means. For God says only of His Word that it is the Word of life (Jn 6:63, 68; Ph 2:15-16 ["the Word of life": the Word of salvation]; Acts 13:26); it saves our souls (Ja 1:21; Ro 1:16; Lk 11:28).

But Scripture declares of all other sects, conceived beyond, outside of, or contrary to the Word of God, that they are without Christ, outside the promises of the covenant, having no hope, and without God in the world, Eph 2:12. Jn 5:23; 3:36; 1 Co 3:11. And flesh and blood does not reveal this Christ, but the Father in the Word and through the Word. Mt 16:17; Gl 1:12, 15-16.

Holy Scripture

38   *Where is that Word of God to be looked for, and whence is [it] to be sought? Are new and special inspirations and revelations to be expected?*

At one time God revealed His Word by various ways and means. For sometimes, appearing Himself to the holy fathers, He spoke in their presence, sometimes through prophets inspired and moved by His Spirit; finally He spoke to mankind through His Son and the apostles. Heb 1:1-2; 2:3; 2 Ptr 1:21; 2 Ti 3:16; Lk 1:70. But He gave us neither command nor promise to expect that kind of inspirations or revelations. Yet for the sake of posterity He saw to it that this Word of His, first revealed by preaching and confirmed by subsequent miracles, was later put into writing by faithful witnesses. And to that very same Word, comprehended in the prophetic and apostolic writings, He bound His church, so that whenever we want to know or show that a teaching is God's Word, this should be our axiom: Thus it is written; thus Scripture speaks and testifies.

39   *Are all things that are sufficient for people as the Word of God for faith and conduct of life contained in the sacred writings?*

Jn 15:15; Acts 20:27. The Holy Spirit therefore will not, through prelates of the church or [through] councils teach other, new, and different things than those that have been revealed through Christ and proclaimed through the apostles. For it is a function of the Holy Spirit to suggest and, as it were, recall to mind, the things that Christ said and taught. Jn 14:26. And though not all miracles, just as not all discourses of the prophets, Christ, and the apostles are individually set forth, yet the Holy Spirit included in Scripture the sum of the whole heavenly doctrine, as much as is necessary for the church and suffices for the faith by which believers obtain life eternal. Jn 20:31. And Paul ascribes two things to Holy Scripture. First, that it can make the man of God, that is, a teacher of the church (for they are called people or men of God) perfect, sufficiently equipped for every good work (which is namely necessarily required to perform the ministry of the church). 2 Ti 3:16-17. Second, that a believer might be made wise unto salvation through faith. 2 Ti 3:15. Since, then, we have in Scripture the things that are necessary for salvation and life eternal, therefore in matters of faith it alone is properly sufficient for us.

40   *Why do the ancients call Holy Scripture canonical?*

Because there is and ought to be in the church a definite canon and a single norm or rule according to which all religion and doctrine ought to be examined, tested, and judged. Therefore, that which does not have foundation in Holy Scripture and cannot be proved by it and is not in harmony with it, but contrary to it, this we neither can nor ought to set forth and receive as the Word of God. But the doctrine that is founded in Holy Scripture, this alone we acknowledge, approve, and receive as true and salutary, and with this judgment and distinction we read the writings of the fathers. And within those limits we also embrace the doctrine rehearsed in the Augsburg Confession.

The true ancient catholic religion or faith

41   *Is any new doctrine to be set forth or new faith to be received in the church of God?*

By no means. For as there is only one God, so also is there no faith but one. Eph 4:5. And this is that one true and very ancient faith (2 Co 4:13) which is founded not in new but most ancient doctrine and is in the true ancient and catholic church. For these things are and have been joined and mutually connected: God, the Word, faith, the church, salvation, and life eternal.

42   *If religion and faith are to be judged on the basis of antiquity, why, then, do we depart from the papistic religion, faith, and church, which can defend themselves by the pretext of many years?*

The Pharisees charge Christ with new doctrine (Mk 1:27) since it namely did not agree with the traditions of the ancients now accepted and common for many years. Mt 5:21 ff; 15:2. And the Gentiles censure and accuse Paul's doctrine as new because they believed their idolatry, now current for many years, to be the ancient and true religion. Acts 17:18, 19-20. Moreover, when one inquires and disputes about the ancient faith, proofs of only some hundreds of years are not enough, but one must go so far back until it is shown and proved that the doctrine and faith in question is the very same as that which Christ and the apostles taught, the prophets prophesied, and the patriarchs testified, which was, in fact, ordained before the foundation of the world. Eph 1:4; 1 Co 2:7. But that true and most ancient faith and religion is found surely and firmly taught and recorded nowhere else than in the Biblical Scriptures. Since, then, the Roman pope has departed from this most ancient faith and has thrust on the church of God an altogether strange and new doctrine contrary to Holy Scripture, we are obliged by divine command to go out of that congregation of evildoers (Jn 10:5; Gl 1:9; Heb 13:9; Ps 26:5) and to return to the true ancient and catholic religion and faith contained in the Holy Scriptures. 2 Ptr 1:19; 2 Ti 3:14.

43   *But the question is not about Scripture (for Biblical Scriptures are received by both sides), but the point in controversy is this: What is the true, ancient, and catholic sense of the Holy Scriptures? This [is] the whole controversy: How can a common person and layman decide?*

It is easy to settle this controversy. For since Holy Scripture is a light shining in darkness and enlightening the eyes (Ps 19:8; 2 Ptr 1:19), it sets forth and interprets itself in clear words. For one and the same doctrine is repeated in Scripture in many places and is gradually explained more clearly for this reason, that one might more surely and certainly seek the true sense by comparing passages. Besides, God Himself has drawn together into a brief summary from the entire Holy Scripture summary heads of the heavenly doctrine, as much as necessary for everyone unto salvation. The Greeks aptly gave this summary the name *katechesis*. But the old Germans had an even better term for it: Laymen's Bible.[1] If, then, a layman understand Scripture according to those chief parts of catechesis, the true meaning and interpretation will in no wise escape him.

44   *Are people to be exhorted to read, hear, and meditate on that Word, both written and oral (as it is commonly called)?*

By all means. For Scripture can make us wise unto salvation, and it is profitable for doctrine, patience, comfort, admonition, reproof, correction, and instruction in righteousness, that a man might be equipped and prepared for every good work. Ro 15:4; 1 Co 10:11; 2 Ti 3:15-17. And that Word, preached and heard, is the power of God unto salvation to everyone who believes, Ro 1:16. It is likewise the immortal seed by which people are reborn. 1 Ptr 1:23. On hearing this Word of God people were pricked in the heart. Acts 2:37. And Paul declared that faith is [comes] by hearing the Word of God. Ro 10:17 And Ps 1, 19, 77, and 119 speak very aptly of meditation on the divine Word.

45 *But it is certain that God Himself works all these things. Is it, then, magic to ascribe to either the syllables and letters of Scripture or to the frail voice of a preacher such power and efficacy?*

It is doubtless true that this power and efficacy does not lie in syllables as characters. Nor do we mean this, that the voice of the preacher, which passes away, is so efficacious of itself. For to illumine and convert hearts and initiate and effect repentance, faith, and new obedience are solely works of God Himself, who works these things in men by His almighty power. And without that power of the Spirit Scripture is only a dead letter. 2 Co 3:6. As for the rest, God does not want to use such power without means, but has for that end appointed the ministry of the Word and of the Sacraments, through which, as regular means and instruments, He works, gives increase, and preserves. For therefore is the ministry of the New Testament called the ministry of the life-giving Spirit; through this ministry, namely, the Spirit, who makes alive, writes the Word into hearts, so that we are thus transformed into the image of the Lord. 2 Co 3:6, 8, 18. And Paul declares that God is powerful or efficacious through the weapons of our warfare, which are [those of] the ministry itself. 2 Co 10:4-5; Gl 2:8; 1 Co 3:6, 9. Thus God illumines hearts through the Word. Ps 19:8. He opens the heart of Lydia, but through the Word, heard from Paul. Acts 16:14. He converts, but through the Word. Acts 26:17-18. He works and gives repentance, but through the hearing of the Word. Acts 2:37-38. He stirs up faith by hearing, namely of the Word preached. Ro 10:14, 17. He is a God of all comfort, but through patience and comfort of Scripture. Ro 15:4. He works obedience, but through the apostolic ministry. Ro 1:5; 15:18. Therefore people are to be diligently admonished often and attentively to read, hear, and meditate on that written and preached Word, if they want God to work, increase, confirm, and preserve in them these great and salutary gifts.

46[2] *How are the Biblical books divided?*

In two ways:

I. Into the books of the Old and New Testament.

II. Into the canonical and apocryphal[3] books of each Testament.

47 *Which are the canonical books of the Old Testament?*

The five books of Moses:
- Genesis
- Exodus
- Leviticus
- Numbers
- Deuteronomy

Joshua
Judges
Ruth
1 and 2 Samuel
1 and 2 Kings
1 and 2 Chronicles
Ezra
Nehemiah
Esther
Job
Psalms
Proverbs of Solomon
Ecclesiastes
Song of Songs

Major Prophets — four:
- Isaiah
- Jeremiah [including Lamentations]
- Ezekiel
- Daniel

Minor Prophets — twelve:
- Hosea
- Joel
- Amos
- Obadiah
- Jonah
- Micah
- Nahum
- Habakkuk
- Zephaniah
- Haggai
- Zechariah
- Malachi

48   *Which are the apocryphal books of the Old Testament?*

Judith
Wisdom
Tobias
Sirach
Baruch
1 and 2 Maccabees
Esther—of Haman and Mordecai

Fragments of the history of } { Daniel / Susanna / Bel of Babylon / The Dragon of Babylon

Fragments of the prayer of } { Azariah / The Three Children / Manasseh

49   *Which are the canonical books of the New Testament?*

Evangelists { Matthew / Mark / Luke / John

Acts of the Apostles

Epistle {
  of Paul to { Romans / Corinthians 1 and 2 / Galatians / Philippians / Ephesians / Colossians / Thessalonians 1 and 2 / Timothy 1 and 2 / Titus / Philemon
  1 of Peter
  1 of John
}

50   *Which are regarded apocryphal[4] books in the New Testament?*

Epistle { 2 of Peter / 2 and 3 of John / to the Hebrews / of James / of Jude

Revelation of John.[5]

And since of old the order of the canonical hours and of the breviary was especially arranged for this purpose, that the ministers of the church might become accustomed to daily reading [of] and meditation on Holy Scripture, the superintendents enjoin the pastors to read something daily in the Old and New Testament. And in the following examination they will explore how many chapters they have read, what is the content of each chapter, how they understand the text, to which commonplaces it is to be referred, [and] how it is to be used in application. Thus the diligence and progress of each will be most correctly discovered.

51 *What does God require of ministers of the church, and how does He want them to dispense His mysteries?*

Paul covers this very briefly 1 Co 4:2, 4. Let the dispensers of the mysteries of God therefore set before themselves the future judgment of God, in which they will be rewarded [according to] the measure of faithfulness before the judgment seat of Christ.

52 *What things are required to render that faithfulness?*

Very many. For since he who wants to teach in the church ought to be certain that he speaks the oracles of God, 1 Ptr 4:11, or what is right before God, Jer 17:16, and to preserve knowledge or doctrine, Ml 2:7:

First, then, it is necessary that he rightly hold fast and understand the principles of sound doctrine and that he be equipped with an average gift to set forth the sum of heavenly doctrine clearly and humbly. 1 Ti 3:2; 2 Ti 2:2; 3:17. For how shall he render due faithfulness in office, who himself either does not understand the doctrine or does not know how rightly to teach and explain the meaning to others?

Second. Let him speak the Word of God not only in general, but let him with special love and diligence so form and apply his sermons to himself and the hearers that the whole church is edified thereby. 1 Co 14:12, 26; Eph 4:11-12. This is what happens when both in sermons and in his whole ministry he sets before himself the chief parts that the Holy Spirit Himself has prescribed, so that he namely refers and directs all things either to doctrine, or to comfort, or to patience, or to directive, or to reproof, or to correction, or to repentance, or to faith, or to righteousness, or new obedience in good works commanded by God. Ro 15:4; 1 Co 10:11; 2 Ti 3:16; Tts 1:7, 9; Acts 20:21; 26:20. And in Eze 34:15-17 the office of a good and faithful pastor is well described, namely that he feed the sheep, seek the lost, lead back the erring, care for the wounded and the weak, encourage the strong, distinguish sheep from goats, etc.

Third. A minister of the Word ought not only teach things true and in harmony with the divine Word. But he ought also render his faithfulness to God and the church entrusted to him in this, that he at the same time rightly feed the sheep and hold off the wolf from the sheepfolds, or as Luther says, he should do both, nourish and defend. He ought therefore neither defend nor cover up or paper over false doctrine, but oppose it openly and plainly and warn his flock to beware of it. Eze 13:10; Jn 10:5; Mt 7:15; Tts 1:9-11, 13; Acts 20:29, 31. But he is not to stir up all kinds of unnecessary disputes and strifes about words instead of a discourse, and arouse his hearers with untimely clamoring, but only fight against adversaries in necessary conflicts, without which purity of doctrine cannot be retained. And in these very things let him always have regard to his hearers, as to what is useful and necessary for their edification, so that they might continue in sound doctrine and be able to protect themselves against the ferment of false doctrine.

Fourth. Let a faithful minister of the Word consider that he has been set by God as a watchman and lookout of the church, so that, when he notices that some of his sheep have gone aside from the way of the righteous and have turned aside into the way of sinners, he be neither a sleeping and blind watchman nor a dumb dog. Is 56:10. Nor ought he provide soft pillows for the impious. Eze 13:18. But let him cry out against sins with a loud voice. Is 58:1. And let him be instant in prayer and exhortations, threats and rebukes in all patience and teaching, both in season and in a spirit of gentleness and also out of season with severe rebukes. Eze 3:17; 33:7; 2 Ti 4:2; Tts 2:15; 1 Co 4:21. For through these means God recalls the erring and raises the fallen. Otherwise, if a pastor neglect this, God will require the blood of lost sheep at his hand. Eze 3:18.

Fifth. He ought not give anyone offense by an evil life, but is to be a type and example for the flock of the Lord with a pious and honorable way of life. 1 Ti 4:12; 2 Th 3:9; Tts 2:7; 1 Ptr 5:3; Ph 3:17. For as Augustine says, A wicked pastor only destroys as much by life as he builds up by teaching, if indeed he builds anything who lives wickedly, for his teaching is cold who is not affected by the doctrine that he teaches in place of God and does not live it. Nazianzen[6] was accustomed to say: He that teaches well, but lives ill, takes away with one hand what he gives with the other.

Sixth. Since no one is of himself fit and sufficient for so great and arduous an office (2 Co 2:16; 3:5), and no one can successfully sow in the church unless divine blessing be added (1 Co 3:6), therefore let the minister of the Word earnestly and ardently pray, and in united prayers with the church diligently commit both himself and his ministry as well as the whole church to God, following the example of Paul in nearly all his epistles. Cf. 1 Sm 12:23. And let the ministers of the church often and diligently consider all these things that belong to the faithfulness of a true pastor, that, with the Holy Spirit of God governing and assisting them, they might try in the ministry to render that faithfulness to God and know, that if they do this, their labor will not be in vain in the Lord (1 Co 15:58), but that they will by the grace of God save both themselves and their hearers (1 Ti 4:16), or at least their souls go free (Eze 3:19). But if they be found lazy, negligent, and unfaithful, let them know that they must render account before Christ, the chief of shepherds, on the day of judgment.

The chief parts of heavenly doctrine and of the whole ecclesiastical ministry

53   *Which are the chief parts into which the whole doctrine of the divine Word or Sacred Scriptures can be divided and summarized?*

Christ summarized all heavenly doctrine. Lk 24:46-47; Mk 1:15; 16:15; Mt 28:19-20. John the Baptist set forth that sum total in these chief parts: repent, believe in Christ, and bear fruit worthy of repentance. Mt 3:2, 8; Acts 19:4. And Paul declares that this is the sum of his whole doctrine; repentance, faith in Christ, and true obedience toward God. Acts 20:21; 26:20

One may also rightly answer thus: The sum of all Scripture consists in the knowledge of God and of His essence and will. Eph 1:17; Cl 1:9. But this is the will of God, that we turn from sins (Eze 18:23), that we believe in Christ (Jn 6:40), and that we lead a holy life (1 Th 4:3).

The sum of Christian doctrine, finally is also contained in very simple form in the chief parts of the Catechism and consists in the doctrine of the Law, or Decalog, and the doctrine of the Gospel.

God

54   *Is there a God? And whence can it be known what God is?*
55   *Is God one?*
56   *Or are there more Gods?*
57   *Which testimonies of the Old and New Testament prove that there is only one God?*
58   *Who and what is God?*
59   *Is there only one Person in the divine essence?*
60   *Which testimonies prove that there are three Persons of the Godhead?*
61   *Who is God the Father?*
62   *Who is God the Son?*
63   *Who is God the Holy Spirit?*
64   *How are the Persons of the Godhead distinguished from each other?*
65   *What is the special nature of each Person?*
66   *What is the function of each Person?*
67   *What benefits has each Person conferred on us, and does He still confer?*

Answers and statements on these questions are to be sought from the teaching of the Catechism [and] from the Commonplaces and *Examen* of D.[7] Phil. Melanchthon.

The word repentance and whence the doctrine of repentance is to be sought and taught

68 *In what sense does Scripture use the word repentance?*

Here and there it means the whole conversion of man, e.g., Lk 13:3, 5; 15:7, 10; Acts 11:18. In this sense it is taken also in Mk 6:12; Lk 16:30; Jer 18:8; Eze 18:30. But here and there it is put only for one, or the first, part of conversion, namely contrition, which is: to be greatly terrified by the knowledge of the wrath of God against sins, and to be sorry that we have offended God, plus a serious turning away from sin. This meaning applies where together in the same statement, or in the context of the presentation, repentance and faith, or remission of sins is distinctly mentioned, e.g., Mk 1:15; Lk 24:46-47; Acts 5:31; 20:21; 26:20. Thus, in common language, to preach repentance is the same as to rebuke sins, with threats added of the wrath of God, death, and damnation. But vain *logomachias* [strifes about words] about the word are not to be stirred up, but it should be clearly stated in what sense the word repentance is to be taken in each presentation.

But what repentance is when it is understood of the whole conversion of man, likewise which and how many are the true parts of repentance and how the papists teach and speak falsely about the parts of repentance is to be sought in the *Examen* of Philipp [Melanchthon].

69 *Whence, then, is the doctrine of repentance to be taken?*

When the word repentance is used for all of conversion, it is clear that its doctrine is to be sought not only in the Law, even as not only in the Gospel, but in both Law and Gospel. But when it is understood of only one part of conversion, namely contrition, it is clear that such repentance is to be sought and taught from the Law, as Scripture testifies Ro 3:20; 4:15; 7:7; 2 Co 3:6-8.

The divine law in general

70 *What is that which is in general called the divine law?*

It is the doctrine, given by God, that commands and points out how we ought to be, and what we ought to do [and] not to do.

71 *Are Christians to be compelled, according to the laws of the Old Testament, to be circumcised, bring sacrifices, observe the Sabbath [and] abstain from eating swine's flesh?*

By no means. For these laws have been abrogated and Christians are no longer bound to their observance.

72 *But these laws have been given by God no less than the law of the Decalog. Is it therefore rash boldness on the part of Christians, who, as though they had a choice, either reject or retain some of the divine laws, as they see fit?*

The Christian church by no means takes this liberty for itself by its own will. But God Himself has so made some laws, that not all men everywhere on earth are bound to their observance, but only in particular the people of Israel, so that namely that people itself might be distinguished from all other peoples by certain rites and special ceremonies, namely that out of it and in it the promised Messiah would be born. Therefore He also did not want those laws to be perpetual, but to continue only for the time predetermined by God, namely up to Christ. But God so promulgated the laws of the Decalog, that they bind all people of all times and places.

73   *Show this with firm proofs of Scripture.*

When Moses speaks of ceremonial and public laws, he usually uses this phrase: You shall keep these things in your generations. And where Paul treats of the same things, he says only that the Jews are under the Law, in the Law, and of the Law. Ro 3:19; 4:16; 1 Co 9:20. The Law was our pedagog up to Christ, Gl 3:23-24. [It was] imposed up to the time of correction, Heb 9:10. And it belongs to the Old Testament, which was outdated and abrogated at the time of the New Testament, Jer 31:31-32; Heb. 8:13. And there are two kinds of that law, namely ceremonial and political. Moral laws, as they existed before Moses, put into the minds of men in creation itself, and later often repeated by God Himself and by the patriarchs before Moses, were so retained by Christ and the apostles in the New Testament. Mt 5:17 ff.; Ro 3:31; 7:7, 12; 13:8-9. In fact, God Himself has clearly pointed out this difference between His laws. For He wrote the precepts of the Decalog with His fingers and gave command that they be put into the ark of the covenant. 1 Ki 8:9. But Moses wrote the rest of the laws, and they were kept in the temple. 2 Ki 22:8. On the basis of these principles one must search out the division of divine laws into their kinds, why they are commonly counted as threefold, namely moral, ceremonial, and political.

74   *When, therefore, Scripture says that we are not under the Law (Ro 6:15) but freed from the Law (Ro 7:6) and free from the condemnation of the Law (Gl 3:13), are these statements of Scripture to be understood only of the ceremonial and political laws of Moses?*

With regard to the curse and condemnation of the Law because of sins, likewise justification by the works of the Law, believers have been freed through Christ from the whole Law and all of its parts, so that, when we must deal with God, we be not condemned but He forgive us [our] sins, receive us into grace, adopt us as His sons, and receive us to life eternal—for this neither the whole Law nor any part or form of it is necessary, nor is it necessary that we seek or pursue these very great benefits by obedience with regard to any part of the Law. But they all come to us free, or by grace for the sake of Christ through faith. And though the Law always accuse and condemn us because of sins, yet, believing, we are delivered from this threatening accusation and condemnation. Ro 8:1, 33-34; 10:4; Gl 3:13; 4:4. But with regard to transgression or obedience, there is a great difference between the parts or kinds of divine law. For the ceremonial and political laws of Moses have so been abrogated that we are not obligated to obey them. For it is not sin now when we fail to keep those laws either by omission or by transgression; in fact, he that wants to observe them out of a feeling of necessity has lost Christ. Gl 2:21; 4:10-11; 5:2, 4. But all men are bound to obey the commandments of the Decalog and their transgression is in all men at all times accused and condemned, unless there is remission. And Christ bestows His Holy Spirit on the believers, so that in them an obedience according to the commandments of the Decalog is begun; Paul bears witness to this everywhere in his writings.

75 *Prove with passages of Scripture that the Mosaic ceremonies have been abrogated and abolished in this way.*

Gl 3:25, 28; 4:10-11. And the whole Epistle to the Hebrews deals for the most part with that one theme.

76 *Ought there then be no ceremonies whatever in the church of the New Testament?*

The chief true rites of the apostolic church are these: Baptism, Mt 28:19; Lord's Supper, 1 Co 11:23; holy assemblies to hear the Word of God, for common prayers, and collection of alms, Acts 2:42, 46; and the use of the keys of the kingdom of heaven, 1 Co 5:3 ff.; 2 Co 2:6 ff. But besides those rites the church has appointed and ordained also some other ceremonies in adiaphora, or things indifferent, namely things in harmony with the Word of God and useful to the church for this, that in the proclamation of the divine Word, in the administration of the Sacraments, in saying prayers, in gathering alms, and in the use of the keys all things be done in order, decently, and for the upbuilding of the church. And since Paul allows the churches this liberty (1 Co 14:26, 40), it will therefore be permissible to use this kind of ceremonies unto edification for that purpose and without loss of Christian liberty.

77 *Are all papistic ceremonies without distinction to be either rejected or accepted and observed?*

There are some ceremonies in the papal realm that are diametrically opposed to the Word of God and connected with manifest superstition or idolatry; such are the sacrifice of the mass, invocation of saints, etc. Those things are necessarily to be omitted and rejected. Some things originated in the ancient or primitive church; in so far as they are adiaphora and useful for edification they can be freely retained and used. But some have little use and do very little for either order, or decorum, or edification. In these things one must have regard for the weak instead of Christian liberty; for their sake they can be observed at the right time, according to the teaching and example of Paul, Ro 14; 1 Co 9. But there are in the papacy also many childish, useless, and truly histrionic ceremonies that are properly rejected and abolished, since they are not in harmony with ecclesiastical solemnity (1 Co 14:40).

78 *What if those indifferent ceremonies are imposed and required on basis of either necessity, or worship, or righteousness?*

In that case this is always to be observed, that Christian liberty remain intact, according to the teaching of Paul (Gl 5:1; Cl 2:16, 20, 22) and Christ (Mt 15:9, 14). When, therefore, the enemies of sound doctrine impose and demand such things as in their nature are adiaphora, either on basis of necessity or with this intent and purpose, that in this way the pure doctrine be gradually destroyed and uprooted, but the false gradually introduced and established, then one must follow the example of Paul, who said, 1 Co 7:19: "Circumcision is nothing," that is, it is a thing indifferent. And Ro 14:1-2, 6 he yields to the weak with regard to food and [observance of special] days. But after false brethren had unobtrusively entered in to spy on Christian liberty, [to see] how they might bring Christians into bondage and with such observations subtly introduce and establish their corrupt opinions, then he really declares most earnestly, Gl 2:5: "To them we gave place by subjection not even for the time being, that the truth of the Gospel might remain among you." Rather, he declares that those who in this case yielded to the adversaries did not approach the truth of the Gospel with the right foot. Gl 2:12-14; 4:10-11.

79 *Are the forensic or judicial and political laws of Moses likewise abrogated?*

God has shown that the political laws of Moses have been abrogated by the very fact of the complete overthrow and destruction of the whole Jewish state. For where there is neither authority nor state, there can be no use of public laws. The apostles also testified the same. For they did not impose the public laws of the Mosaic state on those converted from the Gentiles but permitted them freely to retain and use their accustomed judicial laws; rather, the apostles themselves submitted themselves to the public laws of the Gentiles and wanted Christians to be subject to those same laws. Acts 16:37; 22:25; 25:10-11; Ro 13:1-2; 1 Ptr 2:13.

80 *Do they, then, want this, that among Christians there ought to be no authority, no political government, no courts?*

Mt 20:25-26; 1 Co 2:15. Christ there speaks not of the office of a political magistrate, but of the ministry of the apostles, and that, he declares, ought not to be such a lordship or supereminence as there is in the states of this world. And Paul, in the passage cited, does not discuss this, whether and how the courts of the world are to be constituted and administered. But he treats of this, that natural *(psychikon)* and purely animal man of himself, by his own reason and understanding, can neither understand nor discern the spiritual things that concern God Himself and our salvation; but the spiritual *(pneumatikon)* man, who has been enlightened by the Spirit of God from the divine Word and according to that Word, both can and ought to discern all things. But the Gospel in the New Testament does not abolish political authority with the whole civil administration once instituted by God (Gn 9:6; Ps 82:6; Pr 8:15-16; Dan 2:21), but approves and establishes [them] as a divine ordinance, to which also Christians ought to be subject for the sake of the Lord and conscience. Ro 13:5; 1 Ptr 2:13. In fact, Christians can perform and administer the political functions of government in good conscience. Ps 2:10. So also testify the examples of Joseph of Arimathea (Mk 15:43), Cornelius (Acts 10:1), Sergius (Acts 13:7), etc.

81   *But since no state can exist without the order of courts and certain laws, and God Himself, in the Old Testament, has by the promulgation of certain public laws prescribed and established a form of court, would it not be better and safer for Christian authority to judge and pronounce sentences on basis of public Mosaic laws, rather than on basis of civil laws or [those] of heathen?*

God did not give and promulgate the judicial laws of Moses with this intent, that all nations be bound to them, nor did He want them to be a perpetual and universal norm, according to which states are necessarily always and everywhere to be set up, the order of courts to be formed, and sentences to be pronounced; but He prescribed those public laws only for His people Israel, according to the nature and condition of that place, time, and people, so that, aside from ceremonies, that people, from which the Messiah, the Savior of the world, was to be born, might be distinct from all other peoples also by a special form of the state. But by this very thing God did not reject and abolish the states of other peoples, courts, and laws in harmony with the Decalog; but in the New Testament the apostles themselves, in Christian liberty, not only submitted themselves to the laws of other states, but also enjoined other Christians to subject themselves for the sake of the ordinance of God and for the sake of conscience. Ro 13:2; 1 Ptr 2:13.

The Decalog

82   *When the doctrine of the Law is set before the church in the New Testament, what is meant by "Law"?*

The Decalog. For when Christ and Paul mention the Law in this sense, they simply mean the precepts of the Decalog. Mt 5:17 ff; 19:17 ff; Lk 10:26-27; Ro 7:7; 13:8-9.

83   *What is the teaching of the Decalog, or what is the Decalog?*

Here should be restated the definition of the moral law from the [Common] places and *Examen* of Philipp [Melanchthon].

84   *Is the Decalog to be taught in the church of the New Testament?*

Yes. For Christ and Paul by their examples have clearly given us this directive. Mt 5:17 ff; Ro 7:7 ff; 13:8-10.

85   *But Christ (Mk 16:15) commands to preach not the Law, but the Gospel.*

In that passage "Gospel" is generally taken for the whole doctrine of the divine Word, whose chief parts Christ and Paul list: repentance and remission of sins, or repentance toward God and faith in Christ. Lk 24:46-47; Acts 20:21. But since repentance, that is, acknowledgement of sins and of divine wrath, is properly not the teaching of the Gospel, but of the Law (Ro 3:20; 4:15), therefore Christ does not want only the Gospel but also the Law to be preached, for He also does not want only faith or remission of sins, but also repentance to be preached.

86   *Since the sum and purpose of the preaching of the Gospel is that God wants to remit sins and receive sinners into grace because of Christ, why, then, is it necessary first to rebuke sins on basis of the Law and reveal the wrath of God? Why do we not immediately begin with preaching the Gospel?*

Mt 9:12. The Gospel is to be preached to the poor, namely those whose hearts have first been terrified and broken by the preaching of the Law. Lk 4:18; Is 61:1; 66:2. For a pharisaic heart, swelled with pride in works of its own righteousness, thinks that it has need of neither the preaching of grace nor of Christ. And a secure or Epicurean heart is not concerned about those things and neither desires nor seeks [them]. Therefore the way is to be prepared for Christ the Lord through the Law in such a way, that it is pointed out to the Pharisees from the Law that they are under sin and the wrath of God and cannot stand before the judgment seat of God by their own righteousness, nor earn eternal salvation by works; and it should be made clear to the secure and Epicureans how dreadful and abominable their sins are before God, because of which they are held under the wrath of God in eternal damnation, so that in this way both Pharisees and Epicureans might begin to hunger and thirst after the righteousness that the Gospel reveals and freely sets forth in Christ.

87   *But in describing the passion of Christ the Gospel sets forth much clearer than the Law itself the horrible abomination of sins and the magnitude of the wrath of God against sin. Therefore Bernard says: "I would never have believed that the horribleness of sin and of the wrath of God is so great if God had not set it before me to contemplate in the most bitter death of Christ." Is there, then, need for the Law to set forth clearly sin and the wrath of God?*

To teach what [is] sin and what is not sin, likewise to pronounce on us sinners the sentence of divine wrath and eternal damnation is not the function of the Gospel, but of the Law. Ro 3:20; 4:15; 2 Co 3:6-9. But since the Gospel teaches that Christ has redeemed us and has reconciled [us] to God the Father, it at the same time shows from what Christ has redeemed us, namely from the condemnation of the Law, Gl 3:13. It likewise shows how and at what cost Christ has obtained reconciliation for us, namely, since he was made under the Law, He took upon Himself our sins and the righteous wrath of God against sins, and, according to the severity of the Law, made satisfaction for our sins by His obedience and death. And thus the Gospel, while it teaches that Christ, made under the Law, has fulfilled the Law for us, sets forth the doctrine of the Law, showing, namely, and setting before our eyes, in the passion of Christ, how grave and intolerable a burden sin and the due punishment for sin are before the judgment seat of God, and what it is to be cursed according to the Law. Gl 3:13. And yet the difference between Law and Gospel remains clear. For the Gospel declares that God made His Son to be under the Law for us, that He heaped our sins on Him, [and] that He poured out on Him His whole wrath and the curse merited by our sins, that we might have peace (Is 53:5), and that we might be made the righteousness of God in Him (2 Co 5:21). But the Law constrains our very selves, rebukes our sins not in someone else, but in our very selves, [and] pronounces the sentence of wrath and damnation because of our sins not against someone else, but against our very selves, unless we lay hold on reconciliation in Christ.

88   *Is the Law to be taught for this purpose, that men are justified and saved by it?*

By no means. Gl 3:10-11, 21.

89   *But what about Dt 30:19; Mt 19:17; Lk 10:28; Ro 2:13; 7:10?*

The law of God requires pure, holy, and altogether absolute and perfect righteousness; if one has and renders this, he shall doubtless be righteous thereby and saved in the sight of God, according to the promises of the Law. But that no one is justified or saved by the Law is not the fault of the Law, as though it teaches either wicked or imperfect works, but [it is] because the Law is weakened by the flesh, which cannot keep the Law perfectly. Ro 8:3; Acts 7:53; 15:10.

90   *But Paul testifies Ro 7:22 that a man reborn through the Holy Spirit renders not only outward but also inward obedience toward the law of God. Can the reborn, then, be justified by the Law?*

The divine law in the Decalog requires not incomplete, mutilated, or imperfect, but such pure and perfect, obedience, that it is rendered perfectly from the whole heart, from the whole soul, and without any evil lust, according to the first and last commandment, which two commandments, Augustine learnedly gathers, determine the limits of the perfection that the Law requires. But the complaints of Paul and David testify that also the saints and those reborn by the Spirit of God in this life are able neither to attain nor render that perfection. Ro. 7:14 ff; Ps 32:5-6;

130:3; 143:2. And the sentence of the Law remains unchanged. Ja 2:10; Gl 3:10.

91   *Why, then, is the Law to be taught, and what is its legitimate use?*

I. That people might learn from the Law seriously to acknowledge both their manifold sins and the judgment of God against sins, namely that they are subject to divine wrath and the curse or eternal condemnation, unless they are set free through Christ, so that they thus turn themselves away from sins, fear the wrath of God, and seek the true physician who alone can heal our weaknesses. Ro 3:20; 4:15; 2 Co 3:6-9; Eze 18:30-31; Mt 9:12.

II. That the Law, written by the finger of God, might be for the reborn a sure norm and rule, showing which works God has prepared, in which He wants the reborn to walk and serve Him. Dt 12:32; Eze 20:19; Ro 13:8; Cl 2:20-23.

Sin

92   *What is, or what do you call, sin?*

Whatever is contrary to the law of God, or against the precepts of the Decalog, namely not only what is done in very deed, either outwardly or inwardly, but also whatever in our nature is not in conformity with the law of God. 1 Jn 3:4; Ro 3:9-15; 7:23.

93   *Is sin, then, not that which is done against the laws of government?*

It is indeed sin, because the government, together with its laws that are in harmony with the Decalog, are included in the Fourth Commandment of the Decalog. Ro 13:1-2.

94   *Is therefore for the same reason also that sin, whatever is committed against the traditions and statutes of the bishops and prelates, because it is included in the Third Commandment?*

When bishops teach the Word of God pure and incorrupt and enjoin what Christ commanded to be observed, then their authority is sanctioned by Christ. Lk 10:16; Mt 10:40; 1 Th 4:8.

But when they teach or command anything that conflicts with the Word of God or without command and divine Word impose anything on consciences as necessary worship of God, then let us remember the precept of Christ and Paul. Lk 12:1; Mt 15:9; Cl 2:20-22; Gl 5:1.

95   *Why do you call only that sin which conflicts with the law of God?*

Because God claims for Himself alone in the church, as in His great house, the authority to command and to forbid and lordship over consciences; therefore He begins His commandments thus: I am the Lord thy God, etc. Ex 20:2; Eze 20:5, 19. He therefore prescribed a certain rule in the Decalog, according to which He wants it recognized and decided what is to be regarded as good and just and what [is to be regarded] as wicked and sin in the sight of God.

96   *What is the judgment of God against sins? or what is the wages of sin if the sinner is not reconciled to God in this life?*

God hates and abominates sin and is deeply angry at it. Ps 5:4-5; Dt 32:4, 19. And He not only threatens with words, but as a very zealous one He visits and punishes sins both in body as well as soul, with both temporal and eternal punishments. Ex 20:5; Ro 2:9; 6:23; Gl 3:10; Mk 9:48.

97   *How manifold is sin?*

Twofold: original and actual.

98   *Why do you not say that sin is fourfold, so that one might add that some sin is mortal, some venial?*

When we speak of sin as to what it is per se, no sin, according to the statement of the Law, [and] considered in its own nature, so to say, and per se, is venial; but all [sins] make one subject to eternal death and damnation. Therefore the distinction between mortal and venial sin is valid after a person has already been reconciled with God through faith in Christ; we will therefore postpone it to that place.

99   *What is original sin?*

Let the common definition be stated and other questions be added to its explanation.

100   *Whence is original sin?*

By one man sin entered into the world, and death by sin, Ro 5:12.

101   *But how? Only by the similitude and imitation of the sin of Adam? Or only by the guilt of the actual sin of Adam, while our nature is pure and innocent?*

Original sin is not simply actual imitation of the bad example of Adam, nor only bare guilt because of the fall of Adam, as an honorable son is often made to bear the disgrace of his mother with no fault of his own. But as the church sings, "Durch Adams Fall ist gantz verderbt menschlich Natur und Wesen; dasselb Gifft ist auf uns geerbt, etc." ["All mankind fell in Adam's fall, One common sin affects us all; etc."]. Original sin therefore passed through one man into all, by carnal propagation, namely because nature in its very origin is conceived and born sinful.

102   *Did God from the beginning make the nature of man thus corrupt?*

By no means. But God in the beginning created man exactly according to His image, so that in mind, will, and heart, in fact in the whole nature and in all the powers of man, truth, holiness, and righteousness, that is, an altogether lovely conformity with the divine mind and will, might shine forth. Eph 4:24. But, seduced by the wiles of the devil, [our] first parents of [their own] free will turned themselves away from God and His obedience; through this fall they lost those most outstanding and most beautiful gifts received at creation.

103   *But what harm can result for us from this, that Adam and Eve lost their gifts?*

Very much indeed. For Adam was made in such a way by God, that he might be the original root out of which the whole human race might be propagated. And God put in his nature as hereditary the good things that we have mentioned, so that, had he remained in that original integrity and righteousness, he should have transmitted them as hereditary righteousness to all his descendants by natural propagation. And thus he lost those good things by the Fall not only for himself but also for all of us his descendants. For we have been begotten according to his image and likeness. Gn 5:3. And we bear the image of the earthly. 1 Co 15:47, 49. For as he was made by the Fall, so are we now by nature. Eph 2:3; Ro 5:19.

104   *In what, then, does the nature of original sin properly consist, so that we might learn somehow to recognize that evil born with us and inherent [in] us?*

First, in the defect or lack of original righteousness, namely that our nature in and by [its] first birth does not have and does not bring with itself the conformity with the Word and will of God that Adam, made at the beginning in the image of God, had; it also does not have the faculties or powers either to begin or to effect that conformity, but it is now despoiled, denuded, and made destitute of those original gifts of righteousness. 1 Co 2:14; 2 Co 3:5.

Second, in the very corruption of nature, namely that in our corrupted nature there not only is that defect, but that in place of lost original righteousness there followed, and as poison pervaded our whole nature, a corrupt depravity, *ataxia* [disorder], destruction and corruption of all the powers of man. Hence it is, that man by nature is strange and averse to the things that the divine will requires, and cares either little or nothing for them, or certainly does [them] unwillingly, as it were, with weariness and a certain dislike; but on the other hand, he is drawn and carried by natural appetite, with all desire, the greatest pleasure, and ready will to the things that are repugnant to the will of God. Thus, out of such an evil root nothing but evil fruits can come forth. Gn 6; 8; Ps 51; Jer 17; Mt 7:18; 12:35; 15; Jn 3; Ro 5; 7.

Third, to the nature of original sin belongs also guilt, namely that, because of the fall of Adam and that hereditary or original evil, all men, propagated by human seed, are by nature children of wrath (Eph 2:3) and, besides other calamities, subject to death and eternal condemnation (Ro 5:12, 18).

105   *Which testimonies of Scripture show that original sin exists and what it is?*

At this place in the examination let there be required a recitation and true explanation of the chief passages of Scripture in which the doctrine of

58

original sin has, as it were, its seat, e.g., Gn 2:17; 3; 5:3; 6:5; 8:21; Ps 51:5; Jer 17:9; Mt 15:19; Jn 3:6; Ro 5:12, 14, 19; 7:18, 21, 23; 1 Co 15:21; 22, 49; Eph 2:3.

106 *Is it necessary to acknowledge original sin, and even to acknowledge it in such a way that it is truly and properly sin?*

The Holy Scriptures teach not only that actual sins conflict with the divine law and are truly sins, which human reason also acknowledges to some extent, but also that the hereditary evil of original sin, which all men naturally propagated bring with them beginning in [their] very conception and birth and by which their whole nature has been perverted and depraved, is, most of all, truly and properly sin, conflicting with the law of God and meriting eternal wrath; in fact, it is the chief sin (Ger. *Hauptsünde*), from which, as from a root, fount, and cause, all other actual sins go forth, as the proof texts of Scripture in the preceding question emphasize. Luther also had this in mind when he called that original evil a natural sin or a sin of nature, likewise a personal sin or sin of a person. He namely intended that in unregenerate man it signified not only that thoughts, desires, words, and deeds are evil or sin, but also that nature or the person itself, infected by that original sin as with poison, is corrupt and depraved.

107 *Is then a man's nature, person, or essence, or his body and soul original sin itself?*

In the Smalcald Articles original sin is thus described, that it is a very deep corruption or depravation of human nature. But what sane man will declare that what has been depraved is the same as that by which it was depraved? Just as the leprosy by which a body is infected and the leprous body of a man are, properly speaking, not the same.

And since Paul declares that sin dwells in the flesh, Ro 7:16-18, properly speaking, therefore, the flesh, in which evil dwells, and evil itself, which dwells in the flesh, are not the same.

108 *Does this passage, then, mean that the very nature of man after the Fall is per se, or in itself, still clean, good, unhurt, and uncorrupted [and] that only original sin in nature is evil?*

The church rightly sings and confesses that by the fall of Adam the whole nature and essence[8] of man has been completely depraved[9]; and Scripture says: "They have all gone aside; they have together become unprofitable; there is none that does good—there is not even one," Ro 3:12. And because of that corruption, the whole depraved nature of man is accused and condemned by the Law, unless there is remission for the sake of Christ the Mediator apprehended by faith.

109 *Is original sin such a light evil as some outwardly spattered spot that can easily be wiped off, so that nature meanwhile remains unhurt and good or at least in spiritual things it nonetheless of itself has and is capable of something good?*

Original sin, as we said [questions 104—106], is a most profound corruption by which the nature of man has been completely and utterly depraved in body and soul and in all powers, so that in the sight of God, especially in spiritual things, no good dwells in our flesh (Ro 7:18), but by nature every imagination of the thoughts of the human heart is only evil (Gn 6:5; 8:21; etc.). In fact, human reason can neither imagine nor understand how profound, horrible, and grave an evil original sin is, but that must be learned and known from the divinely revealed Word. For the heart of man is so evil, perverse, and shattered, that it is inscrutable (Jer 17:9-10). And so great is the magnitude of the original sickness that it cannot be healed but by the regeneration and renewal of the Holy Ghost; this healing, begun in this life, will be completed in eternal life to come.

110   *What good is it, or [why] is it necessary to distinguish between the nature or substance [essence] of man, that is, between the body and soul of man (depraved by sin) and sin itself, by which the nature of man has been depraved?*

Though original sin has so infected, corrupted, and depraved the whole nature of man as spiritual poison and leprosy (as Luther says) that nature as such cannot separately be shown to the senses and to the eye, and original sin as such likewise separately (for original sin is not something that exists of itself separately outside the nature of man, or exists by itself), yet the nature or essence (that is, the body and soul) of man, which is the creature and work of God, and original sin, which is the work of the devil, by which human nature has been corrupted and depraved, are altogether to be distinctly considered by the intellect and thought. The chief articles of our faith drive and compel us to establish, consider, and observe that distinction.

For, I. Scripture testifies regarding the doctrine of creation that God created human nature not only before the Fall, but also after the Fall, and that He is the one who gives shape and form to this our nature and substance (or this our body and soul), so that man according to his essence, which consists of body and soul, is also now the creature and work of God, though this creature of God has been miserably corrupted and depraved by sin, as testimonies of Scripture clearly show. Dt 32:6; Is 45:12; 54:5; 64:8; Acts 17:26; Jb 10:8; Ps 138:8; 139:15; Ro 12:1; Rv 4:11. So also Luther explains and sets forth the doctrine of creation in the *Small Catechism.* Since original sin is not of God (for God is neither the author nor the doer of sin), it is also not the creature or work of God, but the work of the devil. Therefore, in order not to blaspheme by either making God the author of sin, or the devil the creator and maker of our nature or essence (that is, of our body and soul), but in order that the creation and work of God in man be reverently distinguished from that which is the work of the devil, we must distinguish between the nature or essence of our body and soul (which is the creature and work of God, also now after the Fall) and sin (which is the depravity of our nature and a work of the devil himself).

II. Of the doctrine of redemption Scripture firmly declares that the Son of God assumed our human nature in conception by the Holy Spirit, cleansed and sanctified from the fall into sin, so that in all things, except sin, He could be made like to and consubstantial with (as the ancients put it) our[10] brethren. Heb 2:16-17. If, then, there were no difference at all between our human nature (which has been depraved by the Fall) and original sin (by which our nature has been corrupted and perverted), it would follow that Christ did not assume our human nature, or essence consisting of body and soul, because He did not take on sin, or that He also took on sin because He assumed our nature. But both conflict with Scripture. Therefore we must distinguish between human nature and sin.

III. In the doctrine of sanctification, Scripture teaches that God washes, cleanses, and sanctifies man from sin, first by free remission of sins, by not imputing sin to him, but covering [it]; then by the beginning of renewal and sanctification of the Holy Ghost. How, then, can sin either be called or be man himself? For God receives the person of man, or man himself, into grace for the sake of Christ [and] adopts [him] as a son and heir of life eternal. But sin itself, inasmuch as it is sin, he never received into grace or counted [it] among his children. Know rather that sin, by which man is weighed down, and which is sometimes covered in this life, will cease in the elect after this life, but body and soul will continue in eternal life.

IV. Of the resurrection of the flesh and life eternal the Holy Scriptures testify that the same substance[11] of our flesh (Job 19:26), but glorified, will also be raised without sin. And in life eternal we shall have this same soul, but likewise glorified and without sin. If, then, there were no difference at all between the nature or body and soul of man and original sin, it would follow, contrary to the articles of our faith that have now been stated, either that this our flesh would not come forth in the resurrection of the dead, and that in life eternal we would have not this our substance of body and soul, but another very far different from it, since it is clear from the Word of God that the elect will then be without sin—or that sin itself will be raised again in the resurrection of the dead, together with the flesh, and will cling to the elect also in life eternal, since the substance of our body and soul is not to be destroyed there.

Hence it is clear how, why, and in how far a difference is to be established and observed between the nature or substance of man, which has been depraved by sin, and sin, which has corrupted and perverted the substance.

111   *Is original sin essence[12] or accident?*

Since the philosophic and dialectic words "essence" and "accident" are unknown to the unlearned, common people not familiar with the arts,

61

and they cannot be instructed regarding the proper meaning of these words—in fact these very scholastic words of the arts cannot be adequately rendered in German—it is most prudent that simple and common hearers be not disturbed by those words of the arts and schools, since there are other known and common words in the form of sound speech by which this doctrine can be set forth and explained to the common people. But when the learned use the words of the arts or dialectic terms among themselves in these discussions, we know that they are commonly regarded as clear alternatives, so that, whatever it is, it is either essence or accident. And since Augustine rightly condemns that proposition as Manichaean, that sin is essence, or nature, it is clear that dialectic words fit the doctrine of original sin. For since that which does not subsist of itself, nor is part of another, but is changeably in another is commonly and by the people called accident, Augustine does not shy away from the word "accident" in this dispute. But since those philosophic words "accident" and "quality" are too light and cold to express the magnitude, gravity, and abomination of original sin, lest therefore through those Aristotelian words original sin is extenuated contrary to the position of Scripture, as scholastic writers have by their philosophic accident and dialectic qualities falsely extenuated the power of original sin, one must be diligently on guard, lest by philosophic disputes and arguments about essential forms [and] about accidents and qualities the simple doctrine of original sin taught in Scripture be muddled and distorted. One must therefore add the clear statement that original sin is not such a light accident or light quality as a dialectician makes it to be with reference to his "accidents" and "qualities." But it is so great a depravity of the whole nature of man that the mind cannot conceive it by thought nor the tongue express it in words. Thus Luther writes on Psalm 90 that whether you call original sin a quality or a sickness, it is certainly an extreme evil.

112   *When does original sin begin in us?*

Not then first when a man has come to the years of discretion (as we commonly say); in fact, also not then first, when he is born; but in that very moment when he is conceived in [his] mother's womb the mass is already contaminated and infected by original sin. Gn 8:21; Jn 3:6; Ps 51:5.

113   *How and through whom are we freed from original sin?*

Only through Christ, whose merit is applied to us by the washing of water by the Word, so that, regenerated, we are cleansed from sin and renewed through the Holy Spirit. Jn 3:6; Eph 5:25-26; Tts 3:5.

114   *Is original sin, then, remitted in Baptism in such a way that thereafter no remnants of it are left over in this life in those who are baptized?*

It is commonly and rightly said in the schools that the formal of original sin is taken away in Baptism, the material remains. For Paul, already washed and sanctified through Baptism, yet complains with all saints that that radical sin still dwells in his flesh, and that it does so in such a way that it begets in him all [kinds of] concupiscence in fact it takes him captive under the law of sin, which is in his members, so that he must continually through the Spirit fight with himself against that indwelling sin and pray without ceasing that for the sake of Christ God would not impute those natural[13] sins (as Ambrose says). Ro 7:8, 18, 23-24; Gl 5:17.

115 *What, then, is the efficacy of Baptism against original sin, if it remains in the reborn in this life also after baptism?*

Paul points out that the effect of Baptism is twofold, namely regeneration and renewal. Tts 3:5. For, first, sins are washed away in remission through Baptism by the Word, so that they are not imputed, if they who are baptized remain in Christ through faith; and thus guilt is taken away. Acts 2:38; 22:16; Ps 32:1-2; Ro 7:24-25; 8:2. And this remission is not half or partial, but full, perfect, and complete. Second, in place of lost original righteousness, the Holy Ghost begins renewal, by which he begins to crucify and mortify original depravity with its actions. But this benefit of renewal is not perfectly completed in this life so that that corrupt root of original depravity is completely taken away and uprooted out of our nature in this life. But the Holy Ghost works, continues, and increases that mortification and renewal, which has been begun, through this whole life in those who have been reborn. 2 Co 4:16; Ro 8:13; Gl 5:24.

116 *Are those remnants of original sin in the baptized truly and in themselves sins?*

Original sin is not sanctified by Baptism so that after Baptism has been received it is a good, holy, God-pleasing and accepted [by Him] thing in those who are sanctified; but it is and remains also in the sanctified truly and in itself not a good but an evil thing and in conflict with the divine law, that is, it is truly and in itself sin. So Paul also expressly calls it sin. Ro 7:17. And it is a thing damnable in itself and worthy of eternal death, if God would want to test it according to the statement of the Law, according to the strictness of His judgment, if it were not that it is not imputed for damnation to those who by faith are and remain in Christ Jesus. Ro 7:24; 8:1.

117 *When, then, will original sin finally be altogether extinguished in the reborn?*

When this body of sin (Ro 6:6) will be reduced to earth and ashes by natural death and this corruptible put on incorruptibility, 1 Co 15:53. For as long as we live in this flesh we bear the image of the earthly, 1 Co 15:49; and the struggle between the flesh and the Spirit[14] does not cease before death in the reborn, Gl 5:17.

118 *What are actual sins?*

Actual sins are the depraved fruits of original sin as of a corrupt root and evil tree, that is, they are actions in conflict with the law of God, both interior in mind, will, and heart, and exterior in attitudes,[15] words, and deeds, whether it be by commission or omission.

119 *List the various divisions of actual sins.*

 I. Some are internal sins, [some] external.
 II. Some are manifest, [some] hidden or concealed.
 III. Some are of commission, [some] of omission.
 IV. Some are done by thought, will, desires.
 V. It is also sin to give occasion to sin. To share in sins of others.
 VI. Some are done directly against God, [some against] the neighbor, [some against] ourselves.

All divisions like this are taught for this purpose, that we might somehow learn to acknowledge and consider with how many kinds of sins, various even to the point of [being] innumerable, we pollute ourselves. And yet that [statement] of David nevertheless remains, Ps 19:12: "Who understands [his] faults?"

120 *Is it enough so to set forth the doctrine of sin in general in the church?*

By no means. This doctrine must be applied to practice, that it might be catechetical instruction how everyone should know and consider in [connection with] each of the precepts of the Decalog how varied and manifold remnants of original sin he still has clinging to his flesh and how there arise and come forth thence innumerable actual sins against each precept. Pastors are therefore at this point to be examined whether and how they can and usually do point out to their hearers the application[16] of this doctrine in [connection with] each of the precepts of the Decalog. And they are to be instructed and exercised, so that they might point out to their hearers, in the doctrine of the instruction, in a simple way, in setting forth each precept, the purpose of distinguishing [between] original and actual sin and [between] mortal and venial sin, of which we will speak later, so that people might learn not only in general to say thoughtlessly that common [statement]: we are all sinners [and] we have many sins; but that they might be taught clearly to carry the acknowledgment of sins through each precept, namely what original, what actual, what mortal, [and] what venial sins they have in [connection with] each precept of the Decalog.

Contrition

121 *But what does it serve, to rebuke sin on the basis of the Law, threaten sinners with the wrath of God, and terrify them with divine threats?*

That they might repent, fear the wrath of God, and turn from sins.

122 *Is repentance or contrition necessary?*

By all means. For John the Baptist, Christ, Peter, Paul, etc. begin their sermons with that point: Repent. See also Lk 13:3, 5; Is 66:2. And Jer 5, when the people despised exhortations to repentance, continued in sins, and gradually heaped more of them up (verse 3), the Lord finally said, verse 7: "How then can I be merciful to thee?"

123 *What, then, is contrition?*

It is in a sinner a serious fear of conscience that recognizes the wrath of God against sins and is sorry that it has offended God by this kind of sins.

124 *Since it is necessary in conversion that some contrition come first, so that the pastor of a church might accordingly rightly know [how] to teach repentance, and [that] the hearers might be able to examine themselves, whether they have a penitent or impenitent heart—say, I pray, what the things are that are required for true and in no way false contrition.*

For true contrition there is required, first, acknowledgment of sins, so that a man instructed in the divine law might know what things God reckons and regards as sins in His judgment.

125 *Does one teach rightly and sufficiently regarding contrition when only a catalog of sins is set forth?*

By no means. For in an exhortation to repentance the matter is to be led to this point, that the Law works wrath (Ro 4:15), and that the ministry of the Law might be the ministration of death and condemnation (2 Co 3:7, 9). The second thing, therefore, that belongs to true repentance, is that the sinner seriously acknowledge the magnitude and abomination of sin in the sight of God; this takes place when the wrath of God is revealed from heaven against all ungodliness (Ro 1:18), namely that man might be shown by the Law that God is seriously and fearfully angered by sins and that He will avenge them with temporal and eternal punishments, unless the sinner is again reconciled to God by Christ the Mediator.

126 *If, then, one admits his ungodliness and knows that God is angry with him and offended thereby, but meanwhile, not concerned about this, continues in sins, is he truly penitent? Does he have true contrition?*

By no means. For Saul indeed confesses that he does wrong in persecuting David. 1 Sm 24:17; 26:21. David also was not unaware that murder and adultery are such sins as God abhors. Yet both indulge in their passions and nonetheless commit those sins and securely persevere in them. The third thing, therefore, in which the true nature of contrition chiefly consists is this, that by that revelation of sin and divine wrath the heart of a sinner is moved and affected, in fact, as Scripture says, is shattered, broken, and crushed, seriously considering for itself that by its sins it has drawn upon itself the wrath of God and eternal punishment. Therefore it no longer takes pleasure in its ungodliness, nor does it keep the intention to continue in it, but in sorrow over sins committed turns itself from them and in true concern and with all care follows and pursues this, that it be not left under the wrath of God and eternal damnation and perish. This, then, is true contrition and from this it can rightly be judged that the statement of Augustine is exceedingly true, that many are not penitent, but imagine [that they are].

Free Will, or Human Powers

127   *Can a man of himself and by his own powers begin and effect the things that are required for true contrition?*

Not at all. For true repentance, part and parcel of which is unfeigned contrition, is a gift of God. 2 Ti 2:25; Acts 5:31; 11:18.

128   *Does man therefore have no free will?*

We call free will the human powers or faculties in mind, heart, and will, namely when the human mind can understand, consider, and evaluate something that is presented or proposed. The will and heart can choose, desire, and pursue, or reject and flee that which has been pointed out by the intellect; [they can] command, or not command, the members [to take] or suspend certain action. Therefore one cannot rightly give answer to the proposed question without [making] a distinction, but the opposites must be recognized. For with regard to sins, in them natural man of himself, since he is the servant of sin, is exceedingly free of righteousness, as Paul says Ro 6:20. For in mind, thought, heart, will, and all powers he is inclined to evil continually, Gn 6:5. But it is a most miserable liberty to be the servant of sin. Jn 8:34-35. Then, with regard to outward and civil things, which are subject to the judgment of reason, likewise [with regard] to outward discipline, there also unregenerate man has some liberty or ability in mind, will, and heart. (Lk 16:8; Ro 2:14) and can live blamelessly according to the Law (Ph 3:6). But this liberty is very weak and limited and spoiled in various ways. But with regard to spiritual matters or actions, as those that belong to the true conversion of man, namely repentance, faith, new obedience, and the things connected with these, natural man of himself and by his first birth, before he is regenerated and renewed by the Holy Spirit, has no powers or ability at all to begin and effect them rightly and as the Word of God demands; in fact, he by nature opposes and resists those spiritual actions. For Scripture predicates two things of natural man. First, it simply robs and deprives him of all those powers and abilities. 1 Co 2:14; 2 Co 3:5; Ro 8:7; Jn 15:5. In fact, it asserts that in spiritual things such a man is darkness itself (Jn 1:5; Eph 5:8; Acts 26:17-18) and dead in sins (Eph 2:1; Cl 2:13). Moreover, it ascribes to natural man a heart of stone, hard and perverse, which fights against the Word of God and is enmity against God. Gn 8:21; Jer 17:9; Eze 36:26; Ro 2:5; 8:7.

129   *Is, then, true conversion there, and true contrition in conversion,* *where there is altogether no change, and [where] there are no feelings in the mind, will, and heart of a man?*

No. For repentance or contrition takes place and exists when a man acknowledges his sins, seriously considers in his heart the threats of divine wrath, truly fears the wrath of God, and is sorry for sins in such a way, that with unfeigned resolution he turns himself from them and with a troubled heart is concerned lest he be forever damned, etc. When, then, such a change does not take place in a man and there are no feelings of this kind, it is certain that no true conversion or contrition whatsoever is there either.

130 *But if that kind of feelings must be present in conversion, is, then, the will of man not idle in contrition, but does and works something?*

The issue of this controversy does not consist in the question regarding the formal cause of contrition or conversion, but [that] regarding the efficient cause; that is: the question is not whether such change and such feelings must take place and be present in contrition or conversion (for this is beyond controversy, since conversion itself is nothing else than that kind of change), but the question is about this, whence man has and acquires those feelings and changes. Whence does the mind, heart, and will of man obtain that power or ability, that he can begin and effect the things that are required for repentance or contrition according to the divine Word?

Now, to this question Scripture, as we have shown a little earlier, plainly and clearly replies: Man of himself, by the powers that belong to his nature or free will, can by no means have that ability or be able to call forth those feelings, but all this is a gift and work of God. Acts 5:31; 11:18; 2 Ti 2:25. For it is God who converts man, who takes away the heart of stone and gives a heart of flesh. Eze 11:19; 36:26; see also Jer 31:18-19.

131 *Can man resist this kind of divine operation, hinder it, drive [it] out, and counter with contrary action?*

Indeed he can and, alas, too often and [too] much does so. But people should be taught that this itself is a most serious sin. For thus they resist the Holy Spirit himself, whose operation in themselves they hinder, despise, and destroy. For when God through the Word arouses and works the beginnings of such feelings in man and by that very thing provides the powers and ability to begin and do what is required for repentance, He surely also earnestly requires of us that we do not receive that grace in vain or allow it to be idle or vain in us. 1 Co 15:10; 2 Co 6:1. But let us well and profitably invest the talent received from God and diligently put it to use. Mt 25:16-17. Let us not allow the Old Adam either to hinder or destroy that work of God in us. Ro 6:12; 8:13; Gl 5:24.

132 *Should one, then, neither hear nor meditate on the exhortation of the Law, but wait idle and secure till he is drawn and converted by God with violent force?*

No. He who hopes to convert himself in this way is all wrong. For God indeed wants to convert man, but not without means. For that reason He instituted, for repentance or contrition (of which we now speak), a certain means or instrument through which He wants to work it in man, namely the preaching of the Law, which Paul, 2 Co 3:7, 9, therefore calls a ministry of death and condemnation, namely because it is a ministry, means, and instrument by which God leads us to the acknowledgment of our sins, of divine wrath, and fully deserved damnation, so that thence the fear of God and repentance might be aroused in us by the working of the Holy Spirit. Men are therefore to be led to a diligent hearing and meditation of the Law by frequent exhortations. And they are to be reminded very often that those exhortations of the Law, by which sins are rebuked, are to be loved and exalted because God wants to work, preserve, and increase repentance in us through that means. Moreover, that the exhortation of the Law is effective in hearts—this does not depend on powers of our free will but on the operation of God Himself, who alone can change the heart of man and put one of flesh in place of one of stone.

The Gospel

133   *Are, then, hearts, frightened in repentance by the exhortation of the Law and contrite, to be left without comfort?*

By no means. For the Lord kills and makes alive, brings down to the grave[17] and brings back again. 1 Sm 2:6. And it is a mark of the New Testament to heal the contrite heart and comfort those that mourn (Is 61:1-2) and to forgive and comfort, lest those that are contrite be swallowed up with boundless sorrow (2 Co 2:7).

134   *What doctrine, then, is to be set before those that are contrite, whence they might seek comfort?*

They are not to be sent away to the doctrine of the Law, to seek comfort from its works. Ro 3:20; 4:15. But the doctrine of the Gospel is to be set before them, for from it they will be able to draw true comfort. Is 40:1-2; 61:1; Lk 4:18.

135   *What is the Gospel?*

The prophets designated the preaching of the New Testament with the special [Hebrew] word *basar* [tell good tidings], Is 40:9; 52:7; 61:1. The term [evangelize] has been taken from the Greek translation into the common use also of other tongues, so that it is commonly called Evangelium [Gospel], that is, a doctrine that announces good and joyful things.

Now the name Gospel is sometimes used in general for the whole doctrine that is to be set before the people of the New Testament. Mk

1:14; 16:15; Lk 9:6; Acts 20:24; Ro 1:16. So also by the name Law is often understood the whole doctrine of the divine Word. Is 2:3; Ps 19:7; Ro 8:2. And in this sense the general definition is true, that the Gospel is the preaching of repentance and remission of sins. For Christ and Paul include the whole doctrine of the entire ministry in those as the chief members or chief parts. Lk 24:46-47; Acts 20:21. Moreover, since the preaching of grace and of remission of sins is not to be set forth before either the proud Pharisees or the secure Epicureans, but the contrite or penitent; since also in the preaching of repentance—lest consciences be brought to despair, but that the sorrow of contrition might bring forth repentance unto salvation, not to be repented of (2 Co 7:10)—the preaching of the Law is not enough, but the preaching of the Gospel must be added, as the Apology says.[18] And finally, those who neither believe nor obey the Gospel are and remain under the wrath of God and eternal damnation, unless they are converted. Mk 16:16; Jn 3:36; 2 Th 1:8-9.

In this sense, then, it has often been said and is repeated several times in the Apology itself,[19] that the Gospel is the preaching of repentance and of remission of sins. For in the doctrine of repentance, which is taught on the basis of the Law, the Gospel profitably declares many things.

But when we speak especially and properly of the Gospel—observing the distinction between Law and Gospel, so that the proper ministry and work of each is attributed to it, so that namely the Law is the ministry of sin, of divine wrath, of death and damnation (Ro 3:20; 4:15; 2 Co 3:7; 9), but the Gospel is the ministry of righteousness, life and salvation (2 Co 3:9; Acts 13:26; 14:3; 5:20)—then the Gospel (as the Apology[20] says) is properly the promise of remission of sins and of justification for the sake of Christ, preaching the righteousness of faith in Christ.

136 *What are the chief parts in which the doctrine of the Gospel is comprehended and set forth?*

The Gospel is properly the doctrine of the person and office or benefits of Christ. But this doctrine consists most of all in these chief parts:

I. That the Son of God, before the world of time, was, by a wonderful decree made in the hidden counsel of the Trinity, appointed to be our Mediator, Redeemer, Reconciler, and Savior.

II. That this decree was revealed by the word of promise immediately after the Fall, and the promise of the coming Messiah gradually renewed and repeated to the fathers during the whole time of the Old Testament.

III. Likewise that the Son of God, according to the promise, was made man in the fulness of time and most perfectly completed the work of redemption and reconciliation by His obedience, passion, and death, and thus gained righteousness and life eternal, by His resurrection and ascension, for those who believe in Him.

IV. The Gospel does not only set forth the account of Christ in story form, but the proper doctrine of Him is the promise of grace, by which God, in the Word and the Sacraments, sets before and offers to miserable sinners—thoroughly terrified by the knowledge of sins and of divine wrath and damnation—grace, remission of sins, adoption, and the inheritance of life eternal freely and out of pure mercy or grace, without our merit, only for the sake of the obedience, passion, death, and merit of Christ.

V. The Gospel teaches that these benefits of Christ the Mediator are to be apprehended and applied by faith.

VI. The Gospel declares those who believe righteous and saved.

137   *Is the Gospel a new doctrine, which first began at the time of Christ and the apostles?*

By no means. For as there is one faith of the pious both of the New and of the Old Testament (2 Co 4:13), so also is it one and the same Gospel of both people, those of the Old as well as of the New Testament (Ro 1:1-2; Jn 8:56; 1 Ptr 1:10; Acts 10:43). For the doctrine of the Gospel was revealed by God immediately after the Fall and thereafter gradually repeated during the whole time of the Old Testament not less than in the New Testament. There is only this difference, that in the Old Testament it was the promise of the Messiah to come, who was to be a sacrifice for us; but in the New Testament it is truly Gospel, that is the joyful tidings of the Messiah who has been sent [and] who has completed the work of redemption. Ro 1:1-4. There is also a difference in the mode of revelation, which was more obscure in the Old Testament, but is clearer and brighter in the New. But just as we in the New Testament are justified and saved by faith in Christ [who is] now revealed, so the fathers in the Old Testament were justified and saved by faith in Christ [who was] to come. Ro 4:3, 6; Acts 15:11; Rv 13:8.

138   *Is the Law destroyed or abolished by the Gospel?*

God forbid, says Paul, Ro 3:31; but by the doctrine of the Gospel, or faith, the Law is rather established. See also Mt 5:17.

139   *But the Law and the Gospel appear to teach complete opposites. For the Law sets an angry and offended God before sinners, but the Gospel [presents] Him gracious and merciful. The Law threatens sinners with punishment and eternal damnation; the Gospel offers them remission of sins and life eternal. The Law promises mercy, life, and salvation, but with the condition of fulfilling the Law; but the Gospel promises those good things freely without our works. These things truly appear to be so contradictory that they mutually nullify and destroy themselves.*

This antithesis is to be carefully weighed and correctly stated on the basis of true foundations. For the true and sound understanding of the whole doctrine of the Gospel depends chiefly on this basis. And those profane and Epicurean fancies are to be completely taken away out of the hearts of men, that God in the Law only acts as if He is angered by sins, but that in the Gospel, with that statement of His mind and [with] His will changed, He thus nullifies and destroys the Law, that the statement of the Law concerning sin is now taken away and made invalid by the revealed Gospel, and that this is the position of the Gospel: God is now neither concerned about sin, nor hates nor abominates it, but loves and approves [it], and is so delighted by it that He wants to give the ungodly eternal life because of sins. For such opinions are not only false and ungodly but also blasphemous. For the divine law is and remains the serious, eternal, and unchangeable will of God, which the Gospel by no means either nullifies or destroys, but rather confirms and establishes, so that the rule might remain firm and unchangeable: Unless the law of God is kept with full and perfect obedience, God neither can nor wants to be merciful to any sinner. Mt 5:18; Ro 8:4; 10:5; Gl 3:10.

140 *But that kind of fulfillment or satisfaction is impossible for us. How then shall we obtain either righteousness or salvation?*

As far as we are concerned, we would absolutely have to perish in eternal damnation. For if the divine law is not fulfilled, it can in no way be abolished or taken away. And for us its fulfillment is impossible. Therefore God, in his secret counsel regarding the restoration of the welfare of mankind, planned and determined, and made a decree, to send His Son into the flesh, who was not to abolish or destroy the Law, so that fulfillment would no longer be necessary for us, but who, made under the Law and subject [to it], would in our place perfectly render and discharge His fulfillment and satisfaction for our sins—indeed required of us by the unchangeable judgment of God, but impossible for us—and thus, since the Law would plainly be fulfilled for us, merit and obtain [this], that because of His obedience and satisfaction God would deign to be merciful and compassionate toward penitent sinners. And in this way the Gospel does not abolish or destroy the Law, but points out and testifies that Christ has fulfilled the Law for us by completely perfect fulfillment. Ro 8:3-4; 2 Co 5:14; Is 53:6; Gl 4:4-5.

141 *But, someone may object, what [good does it do] me, that another has fulfilled the Law, since the Law makes its demands on me, and how can the satisfaction of one be enough and sufficient for all?*

Christ was made subject to the Law, was made sin and a curse, not because of Himself, but for us (Gl 3:13; 4:4-5; 2 Co 5:21), and that by the decree and good pleasure of the will of God for our redemption (Eph 1:5, 7; 2 Co 5:14; Is 53:6). And since this person is not only man, but God and man, that redemption is therefore so ample and great that it is sufficient propitiation for the sins of the whole world (1 Jn 2:2); since Christ accomplished it in the flesh it provides us highest and sweetest comfort (Ro 8:3; 34).

142 *But how does Scripture affirm that we are justified and saved freely, without merits, if the work of redemption cost Christ so much, namely*

His own blood and death?

With respect to us, this righteousness and salvation is and is called free grace, which comes to us without either our works or merits and without any payment or satisfaction from us.

But with respect to Christ the Redeemer it is and is called redemption, *lytron* [in Greek], or satisfaction, something bought or merited. Ro 3:24; 1 Co 6:20; 1 Ptr 1:18-19; 1 Ti 2:6; Acts 20:28.

143 *And what kind of satisfaction does the Law require that Christ had to render for us?*

I. The Law requires complete, holy, pure, and perfect obedience. This Christ rendered fully and perfectly for us. Ro 5:19; Heb 10:9-10, 14.

II. The Law requires satisfaction for sins, that by passion and punishment divine wrath might be satisfied. And Christ accomplished this satisfaction for us by His passion and death. 2 Co 5:14; Gl 3:13; Is 53:5-6.

And in this way Christ obtained this for us, that by His redemption we are justified freely, or by grace, without our merit. Ro 3:24.

144 *What is the difference between the Law and the Gospel?*

I. The Law is to some extent known by nature. Ro 2:14. But the Gospel is a mystery hidden to reason, which God has revealed only through His Word. Mt 16:17; 1 Co 2:7; Eph 1:9; Ro 16:25-26.

II. The Law is a mystery pointing out, censuring, and rebuking sins, and pronouncing all men worthy of eternal death because of them; but the Gospel is a ministry that points to true righteousness before God through Christ and through it offers and bestows life eternal to all that apprehend it by faith. 2 Co 3:7, 9; Ro 1:16-17.

III. The Law indeed itself also speaks of righteousness and salvation, but it has respect to us, and it seeks and requires to perfection that righteouness in us, in our nature, actions, and works, if we want to be saved by it. But since that cannot be rendered by us because of our corrupt nature, therefore the Gospel sets Christ before us, who by His obedience, passion, and death has purchased for us the true righteousness before God that is imputed and given to us freely, without our merit, solely for the sake of Christ and through faith. Ro 1:4; Gl 3:24.

Justification

145 *In what, then, does justification of man the sinner before God consist according to the statement of the Gospel?*

In this very thing, that God imputes to us the righteousness of the obedience and death of Christ the Mediator and thus justifies us freely out of grace, without our works or merits, alone by faith that apprehends the grace of God the Father and the merit of Christ; that is, He forgives us

[our] sins, receives [us] into grace, adopts [us] as [His] sons, and receives [us] to the inheritance of life eternal. Ro 4:24-25, 28; 4:5; 10:4; Gl 3:24; Eph 2:8-9; Tts 3:5-7.

146 *But to justify, by reason of etymology or composition, is the same as to make just; and since the Holy Ghost renews believers, so that they yield their members instruments of righteousness (Ro 6:13), surely justification consists in that renewal of the Holy Ghost, or in the new obedience of the reborn.*

One must not determine the true meaning of the word justify by Latin usage, for it is a special word proper to the Holy Scriptures. For when Scripture wants to say that someone is cleared of a charge that was aimed [at him] and of the sentence of damnation, it uses the word justify in a forensic sense and often in antithesis, opposing damnation with justification. Dt 25:1; Pr 17:15; Ro 5:18; 8:33-34. Now, at this point the Holy Spirit was pleased [to use] the word justification in a forensic sense. For the whole process or act of the reconciliation of man the sinner with God is simply and clearly represented, as it were, with the word justify. For this matter is not handled incidentally or lightly, but seriously and, what is more, before the court of God and God Himself the judge. For the Law summons us to the tribunal of divine judgment, where it not only accuses us of sin, but completely convicts us. And since before that just court of God every mouth is to be stopped and the whole world [is to be] subject to God (Ro 3:19), therefore Moses pronounces against us the sentence of death and condemnation. 2 Co 3:7, 9; Dt 27:26. Therefore when our conscience, now convicted of sins and therefore made subject to eternal death and damnation, anxiously looks about for something with which to oppose this just judgment of God, so that it might avoid and evade the broad sentence of damnation, it finds nothing at all. But finally God Himself, rich in mercy, sets His Son before us in the Gospel as atonement. Ro 3:25. And those who through faith take recourse to that Son the Mediator, and apprehend Him by faith—those the Father justifies from the charge placed by the Law and from the sentence of condemnation; that is, He absolves [them] for the sake of Christ, and, by imputation of the obedience and death of Christ, declares [them] righteous and awards them life eternal. Ro 8:33-34. And this is the process or act of the justification of a sinner before the judgment seat of God, so that he appeals from the throne of the strict justice of God to the throne of grace in the blood of the Son of God, as Gerson describes the matter of justification by the apt simile of forensic appeal.

147 *Does God, then, justify the sinner because of sins, so that in that justification no righteousness whatever need intervene in respect to which the sinner is pronounced righteous?*

God Himself calls that kind of justification abomination. Ex 23:7; Pr 17:15; Is 5:22-23. Therefore the judgment of God must be met with such righteousness—or there must be interposed between God, the angry judge, and man the sinner [such righteousness]—through which and because of which God justifies the wicked. For justification cannot take place without righteousness. Ro 3:22, 24.

148 *But what, then, is the righteousness that faith brings to the judgment seat of God, that God might justify the miserable sinner because of it?*

The new obedience of the reborn is indeed also called a kind of righteousness; e.g., Ro 6:16; 1 Jn 2:29. But it cannot be that righteousness through and because of which we are justified before God unto life eternal. For before anyone might render that righteousness of new obedience, it is necessary that the person be reconciled to God, that is, be justified by God. 1 Jn 2:29. Moreover, because of sin dwelling in our flesh, the new obedience of the reborn is weak, impure, and imperfect in this life, so that we can by no means be justified by it before God. Ps 143:2; 1 Co 4:4. Since, then, faith instructed by the Word of God knows that it cannot find such righteousness—either in the nature or in any of the most sanctified life of any man, or in any other creature—by which a man might be justified before God, it therefore apprehends, in the Word and the Sacraments, Christ the Mediator with His most holy obedience and most innocent death, by which He satisfied the Law for us, having formed the resolute conviction that this is the true and only righteousness that avails and stands before God. And faith meets the judgment of God with this righteousness, wishing, desiring, praying, and in true confidence believing that because of it a sinner is justified by God, that is, absolved of sins, received into grace, and given life eternal. And since this righteousness of Christ, rendered for us, is perfect, sufficient and abundant and can stand before the judgment seat of God, therefore God has promised that He would impute it to believers just as if they rendered it themselves. Ro 3:22; 4:23-25; 5:18. And thus believers absolutely have, not indeed in themselves, but in Christ, true and genuine righteousness, through which they are justified before God.

149 *Are all men justified and saved because of this righteousness of the Son of God?*

The way is broad that leads to damnation, and there are many that walk in it. Mt 7:13.

150 *What, then is the reason? Did Christ not make satisfaction for all? Or does the heavenly Father not want this benefit to be common to all?*

The cause or fault of damnation is by no means to be ascribed to God. For Christ is the propitiation for the sins of the whole world, 1 Jn 2:2. And the will of God is that no one should perish, but that all be saved. 1 Ti 2:4; 2 Ptr 3:9; Eze 18:23; Mt 18:14. But it is by the fault of men that not all are saved, because not all accept that benefit. Jn 1:5, 10-11; 3:19. For it is necessary that the benefit or merit of Christ become ours (Ro 8:32), that is, that it be applied to us, so that each one accept and apprehend it (Jn

1:12), and thus Christ be in us (Jn 6:56) and we be found in Him (Ph 3:8-9).

151 *By what means is Christ, or the merit of Christ, applied to us?*

For that application two things are absolutely required: First, that God, through the Holy Spirit set forth, offer, present, and give to us that benefit. For this purpose God has established a certain means or instrument, namely the word of the Gospel and the Sacraments. That means is, as it were, the hand of God, which He extends and opens to us, offering and presenting to us the merit and benefits of His Son for our salvation. Ro 10:17; 2 Co 5:19-20; Tts 3:5.

The other thing that is required for application is that we apprehend, receive, and apply to ourselves the benefit of the sons of God that is offered and presented to us in the Word and the Sacraments; this is done by no other means or instruments than faith. Ro 1:17; 3:28; 4:5; Jn 3:15-16; Gl 3:22, 24. For faith is, as it were, our hand with which we take, apprehend, and accept the benefits of Christ. Jn 1:12. And it is a kind of bond by which we are bound to Christ, that He might be and dwell in us (Eph 3:17) and that we might be found in Him (Ph 3:8-9).

Faith

152 *What is justifying faith, of which Scripture speaks?*

The definition of faith is well known; but to the unlearned it can most simply be explained thus: The object of faith in general is the Word of God; for we ought to apply faith to every Word divinely given and revealed. But justifying faith has its own and special object that it seeks in Holy Scripture and that it regards and apprehends, namely Christ our Mediator and the promise of grace, which is given for the sake of Christ. Ro 3:24-25; 4:13, 16; Gl 3:22.

153 *But how does faith apprehend and embrace the object that is proper to it?*

First, it learns from the Word of God to recognize the person, office, merit, and benefits of Christ; all these things it holds to be altogether true and certain. Eph 1:17; 4:13; Cl 2:2.

Second, justifying faith apprehends all those things not as simple history, nor only insofar as they are in themselves true in general, but in such a way that it specifically includes the person of the believer in that promise of grace, so that each believer apprehends and receives Christ in the Word and the Sacraments with true confidence of the heart as given personally to him, and applies them to himself individually. And though this faith is often attacked by various temptations and of itself is weak and languid, yet it surely is faith by which each one specially or warmly[21] believes and trusts that sins are forgiven him by God for the sake of

Christ, that he is received into grace, [and] that he is adopted into the sonship of God. Jn 1:12; 3:15-16; Ro 1:16; 3:22; 4:16, 23-24; 5:1-2; 8:35, 38-39; 10:4, 9; 1 Ti 1:16; Mt 9:22; Lk 7:50.

154 *What if a secure Epicurean, without repentance, holding fast to the intent to continue in sins, forms this conviction, that he nevertheless has a merciful God—is that kind of conviction true and justifying faith?*

By no means. For faith is not this kind of conviction, that it is immaterial before God to remain in sins or desist from sins, to love sins or detest them; true faith likewise does not seek this in Christ, that it dares to indulge in sins and give rein to them securely and freely, without any fear, in the hope of impunity. But the nature and property of true faith is seen and recognized in sincere repentance, namely when the heart acknowledges its sins in such a way that it seriously shudders in acknowledging the wrath of God, and no longer delights in sin, but is seriously and earnestly troubled, lest it fall into danger of eternal damnation. When faith, in such repentance or contrition, looks around for Christ, seeks [Him], looks to [Him] and apprehends [Him], desiring, seeking, believing, and trusting that sins are remitted to him for the sake of Christ, etc., this very thing is a very sure indication of true and justifying faith. Is 61:1; 66:2; Mt 9:12.

155 *But you may find many who boast that they have faith, though they neglect and despise the Word and the Sacraments.*

One departs from true faith also this way. Hearing the Word, and faith, are correlative, for faith is conceived, nourished, and increased thereby. He who wants to apprehend Christ by faith must know where he should look and [where] he can find Him, namely in the Word and the Sacraments. Likewise, if faith, as our hand, is to receive anything from God, we must not seek it outside the Word and without the Word, out of the air, as it were, but receive [it] from the hand of God, which He opens in the Word and the Sacraments, offering us the fullness of His grace. For God has determined to deal with us at this point through the Word of the Gospel and the Sacraments. Ro 10:17; Tts 3:5.

156 *Can man by his own free will or by virtue of his own powers acquire this faith?*

No. 2 Th 3:2. It is a gift of God, Ph 1:29, not of yourselves, Eph 2:8. By nature we are foolish and slow of heart to believe, Lk 24:25. God opens and enlightens the heart and mind and kindles faith in the heart. Lk 24:25; Acts 16:14; 2 Co 4:6; Eph 1:17-18. Faith is not wrought by our human powers, but according to the working of the mighty power of God, Eph 1:19.

157 *Are there, then, in the activity and exercise of faith no actions or feelings of the human mind, will, and heart whatever?*

The intellect, heart, and will of man (of whatever kind they are of themselves by the first birth, before they are illumined and renewed by the

Holy Spirit) cannot contribute anything or cooperate in beginning and establishing faith. 1 Co 2:14; 2 Co 4:4; Dt 29:4. For reason is by nature in conflict with faith. Lk 24:25; 1 Co 2:14. Therefore it is to be brought into captivity to the obedience of Christ. 2 Co 10:5. Yet faith does not exist without certain feelings or actions in the mind, will, and heart of man. For faith is nothing else than assent in the mind, and trust in the will, regarding, apprehending, accepting, and applying to itself the promise of grace. As for the rest, man cannot by his own natural powers conceive, begin, and perfect those feelings, nor does he have this of himself, but it is a special gift of God, who works that very thing in the intellect, heart, and will of man by the power and efficacy of the Holy Spirit.

158   *But how and through what means does God want to work and kindle faith in us?*

Surely not without means. Nor does He want us, with the enthusiasts, to await the bestowal of special revelations and violent raptures, beyond and beside the use of the Word and the Sacraments, by private speculations. But for that purpose He instituted and ordained a certain means, which He would have to be the tool,[22] organ, or instrument of the Holy Spirit, namely the preaching, hearing, and meditation of the Word. Ro 10:17; 2 Co 3:8; Ps 119:50, 130. Through this means God works and is efficacious in man, enlightens the mind, opens the heart, and thus stirs up and kindles faith by the power of the Holy Spirit. Lk 24:45; Acts 16:14; 2 Co 4:6; Ph 2:13; 1 Co 3:5-6; Jn 1:7.

159   *But does faith justify for this reason, that it is such an excellent gift of God and such an outstanding virtue in itself?*

By no means. For faith does not meet the judgment of God with either our works or any virtue in us, in respect of which a person is justified. Ro 4:6. Rather, faith itself acknowledges and confesses its own infirmity and imperfection. Mk 9:24; Lk 17:5. But it apprehends Christ and His merit, and the promised grace of God in Christ, and opposes [these] to the judgment of God; and trusting solely therein, it seeks, asks, and receives justification without any works or merits whatever on our part. Ro 3:28; 4:5; 10:4, 10. For that reason, therefore, and for that cause faith justifies, not because it is such an outstanding work of God and virtue in us, but because it apprehends Christ, who is our propitiation and righteousness, and relies and confides in Him. This is what the common statement means, [which says] that the proposition regarding justification by faith is to be understood correlatively.

160   *But why does Scripture ascribe justification to faith?*

First, to show that our righteousness before God is not to be built on our works and merits, but that we are justified freely by grace, alone for the sake of Christ apprehended by faith, that the promise might be sure. For this is what Paul means when he affirms that we are justified by faith, Ro 4:16; 10:4.

Second, since it is necessary that there be an application of the promise, therefore, that we might be sure how, when, and through what means it might be applied to us, so that it might be ours, and that we might be able confidently to rejoice in it and safely rely on it as on completely sure comfort—for this reason Scripture says that we are justified by faith. Ro 5:1-2; Eph 3:11-12.

161 *Is it right to say that we are justified by faith alone?*

Absolutely. For in this article Scripture from time to time uses, repeats, and emphasizes exclusive particles, which are, e.g., freely by grace, Ro 3:24; Eph 2:8; according to His grace and mercy, 2 Ti 1:9; Tts 3:5; freely, by free gift, [Ger.] *ohne Verdienst* [without merit], Ro 3:24; not of ourselves, not by works, Eph 2:8-9; without the Law, without works, Ro 3:21, 28; 4:6. All these exclusive particles are comprehended in that one proposition (we are justified by faith alone), and are thereby simply, clearly, and aptly set forth, whence also this proposition was used by nearly all the fathers.

Basil in a homily on humility: This is perfect and unspoiled glorying in God, when one is not exalted because of his own righteousness, but acknowledges that he lacks righteousness and that he is justified alone by faith in Christ.

Hilary on Mt 9: This was forgiven by Christ through faith, because the Law could not yield, for faith alone justifies.

Ambrose on Ro 3: They are justified freely who do nothing, neither give in return; they are justified by faith alone, a gift of God.

The same on the call of the Gentiles: This has been determined by God, that he who believes in Christ is saved without work, receiving remission of sins by faith alone.

Jerome on Ro 10: God justifies alone by faith.

162 *When Paul says that we are justified without the Law, or without the works of the Law, does he exclude from justification only Levitical ceremonies or works done without the Spirit and faith?*

Paul speaks of the whole Law, and chiefly, moreover, of the works of the Decalog. For he points out Ro 3 that he is dealing with the works of that Law by which sins are recognized, v. 20. But Ro 7 he ascribes that very thing to the moral law, v 7. Cf. Gl 3:10, 12. But the earlier statement of Moses refers to the whole Law, Dt 27:26. The other, Christ applies chiefly to the moral law, Lk 10:26-28.

Thus also he expressly excludes from justification the works of the reborn done out of faith, Ro 4:2-3; 1 Co 4:4.

163 *But if faith alone justifies, will then such faith as is without repentance, without good intent, and without subsequent works justify?*

Not at all. For where there is no repentance, but the intent remains to continue in sins, there true faith cannot exist, and faith that does not work by love but remains without good fruits, is not true, but feigned and dead faith. 1 Ti 1:5; 5:8; Ja 2:26; 2 Ptr 1:8.

164 *What, then, do the exclusive particles exclude?*

They exclude chiefly three things from the matter of justification.

First, neither repentance, nor good intent, nor renewal, nor virtues, nor good works, are a merit or efficient cause of our justification or reconciliation; but the merit is to be ascribed alone to Christ, and the cause alone to the free grace or mercy of God for the sake of Christ the Mediator.

Second, no good works whatever, but only faith is the means and instrument, ordained by God Himself, by which we apprehend, receive, and apply to ourselves the merit of Christ and the grace of God, promised through and for the sake of Christ and offered in the Word and the Sacraments.

Third, renewal, sanctification, virtues, and good works are not our justification and reconciliation, or form or part of it; but they consist completely in the free imputation of the righteousness of Christ and [in the] remission of sins for Christ's sake, whom we apprehend alone by faith, Ro 4:5-7. For our good works do not enter the circle (as Luther says) or article or act of justification; but there grace alone, Christ alone, faith alone, remission of sins alone rule. And thus, though true faith is never without good works, yet it justifies alone without works. Likewise, though making alive, or renewal, is always with justification, yet they are not to be mixed or mingled with each other, for justification is one thing, renewal another. And though they cannot be separated according to difference in time, yet, in the order of significance[23] or nature, justification precedes and renewal follows, which [latter] does not come in the nature of justification but is its fruit or consequence.

165 *Can the article of justification be rightly and aptly taught apart from the exclusive particles?*

As often as Paul teaches the fundamentals of this article and defends against adversaries he always sets forth the antitheses by exclusive particles and thus shows that the purity of the article of justification cannot be preserved if the exclusive particles are neglected or opposed.

166 *For what reasons is it necessary to retain the exclusive particles?*

I. That due and proper honor be attributed to Christ and to the grace of God.

II. That conscience might have sure and firm comfort.

III. That the distinction between Law and Gospel might be very clear.

IV. That prayer might have boldness and access with confidence to God, Eph 3:12.

167 *But most men abuse this doctrine of free justification, as though no good works whatever are to be done, and they receive the exclusive particles as license for all shamefulness.*

The form of sound doctrine is not to be rejected or changed because of abuse, but the abuse can and ought to be guarded against in teaching with the greatest diligence, on the example of the apostles, so that, namely, first, it be stated clearly and on the basis of the fundamentals in what sense those exclusive particles are to be received, what, how, and why they exclude, as has already been stated.

Second, that men might be constantly and diligently admonished to test themselves, whether they believe, lest they deceive themselves with a wrong idea of faith, that is, by a feigned or dead faith, 2 Co 13:5. This is the test: Where there is no contrition in the heart, but the intent remains to continue in sins, there certainly is no true faith. Likewise, faith that does not work by love or which is not followed by good works is surely dead. But faith justifies, not because of good intent, or because it works by love, or brings forth good works, but only because it apprehends Christ with His merit in the promise of the Gospel. If anyone nevertheless wants to abuse this doctrine, clearly and distinctly set forth and explained in this way, let him hear Paul, Ro 3:8: His condemnation is just. But because of abuse the true and necessary doctrine ought by no means to be neglected or mutilated.

168 *Is justification to be attributed to faith only at the beginning of conversion in such a way, that after the first conversion we are justified no longer by faith alone, but by faith and works together, as by a second justification, and then justification consists not only in remission of sins but in simultaneous reconciliation and sanctification or renewal?*

The manner of justification is one and the same in the beginning, middle, and end, namely that we are justified by faith alone, by the pure grace of God, solely for the sake of Christ. For Paul, Ro 4, citing a universal example of justification, does not cite Abraham when he was first converted, Gn 12, but Gn 15, when he had already rendered to God obedience in faith in various exercises for a number of years after his first call, Heb 11:8 ff. Midstream in good works, as it were, Paul puts the question: What is Abraham's justification or in what does Abraham's justification before God consist, when he no longer only believes God but is also eminent in many good works, not only now reconciled, but also sanctified and renewed? Now, Paul answers plainly and clearly that Abraham is justified freely, by faith alone and without works, also in midcourse of good works (that is, he is pronounced righteous before God and received to life eternal), and that his righteousness and blessedness also then does not consist in renewal, but only in free reconciliation or remission of sins. Ro 4:3; 5, 7. And Ro 5:2 Paul beautifully connects the beginning, middle, and end of justification and ascribes [it] alone to faith. For he says: By faith in Christ (1) we have access to the grace of God, (2) we stand in that grace, (3) we glory in hope of the glory of God; that is, when we meet Christ in the resurrection of the dead, we do not want to be found having our own righteousness, which is of the Law, but that which is by faith in Christ Jesus, Ph 3:8-9, 11. Paul therefore does not admit renewal, sanctification, and good works of the reborn to the beginning, middle, or end of the process and act of justification; he does not mix it in with it but wants the grace of God alone, the merit of Christ alone, to rule there by faith alone.

169 *But renewal, sanctification, and good works of the reborn are also works of God; why, then, are they excluded from the circle of justification (as Luther says)?*

Reasons for this exclusion are very weighty and compelling. For renewal in this life is only begun by us, and it is not complete or perfect, 2 Co 4:16. For, because of sin dwelling in the flesh, good works also of the reborn in this life are not perfect, but contaminated and impure in many ways. Ro 7:21; Is 64:6. In order, then, that the promise of righteousness, salvation, and life eternal might be firm and sure, and due honor be attributed to Christ, our whole justification—beginning, middle, and end—must consist solely in the free grace of God promised for the sake of Christ alone and apprehended by faith alone, Ro 4:16.

170 *Does he, then, who is justified in this way, freely for Christ's sake by faith, need anything more for salvation?*

Paul certainly denies that plainly, Ro 4:5-6. There he maintains that the way in which we are justified and in which we are saved is one and the same, so that he who has justification by faith, the same by that very fact has adoption, blessedness, or salvation and the inheritance of life eternal. Therefore, just as we are justified freely, by faith alone, for the sake of Christ, without our works—as Paul points out on surest grounds, so that namely the promise of both righteousness and salvation might be firm and sure, Ro 4:16—so it is therefore falsely taught that our good works are necessary for our justification and that no one can be justified without his good works, [and] so it is also not rightly said that good works are necessary for salvation and that no one can be saved without his good works. For though true faith neither can nor ought to be without good works, yet good works do not enter to join in[24] the act or circle (as Luther says) of either justification or salvation.

For Scripture adds the exclusive particles with no less earnestness to the article of salvation than to the article of justification, Ro 4:6; 11:5-6; Eph 2:8-9; 2 Ti 1:9; Tts 3:5. And for this reason Luther publicly declared those propositions regarding the necessity of good works for salvation off limits for the church.

171 *What is the difference between the evangelical and papistic doctrine in the article of justification and salvation?*

The basis of papistic doctrine is that man in this life can fulfill the law of God. Hence also some of them teach that by his good works man can earn and obtain righteousness and salvation before God; others, in order not to appear to lend support to such crass error, teach that Christ alone indeed earned righteousness and salvation for us, but if we want to partake of it we need faith and good works, by which together the righteousness and salvation procured by Christ is applied to us. There are also those among the papists who teach that our righteousness consists not only in free reconciliation, but at the same time also in renewal or sanctification. But the Gospel, on the other hand, teaches that also those who are made holy and renewed cannot in this life fulfill the law of God. Ps 32:6; 143:2; Is 64:6; Ro 7:21. Therefore righteousness and salvation is not of our works, but of the merit of Christ alone. Ro 3:24; 4:25; 10:4. Likewise it is the grace and free gift of God. Ro 6:23. But the means or instrument of apprehension and application is faith alone. Ro 3:22, 28; 4:5. Our righteousness and salvation does not consist either in our renewal or in our powers or good works, but in free reconciliation and adoption through, and because of, Christ. Ro 4:6-7. The bases of this doctrine have been pointed out in the preceding.

172   *What is the difference between the doctrine of the papists and that of the Gospel regarding faith?*

The papists teach that faith is only historical knowledge and general assent regarding the truth of the Word of God and that this faith justifies inasmuch as it is informed[25] by many and sufficient good works. But since no man can know whether and when he has enough good works, they teach that a believing man may indeed hope and promise himself various excellent things regarding the mercy of God, but he can be sure of nothing certain, but should perpetually remain suspended in doubt whether he truly and surely has a merciful God, remission of sins, and the inheritance of life eternal.

The Gospel on the other hand teaches that this is chiefly the nature, character, and function of faith—beyond that general assent—that it apprehends Christ and applies the general promise of the Gospel regarding the grace of God separately to individual believers, and it does not build righteousness on love, by which it works, but only on Christ, whom it apprehends in the Word and the Sacraments. And since the promise of God in Christ is firm, true, and trustworthy[26] (2 Co 1:20), faith does not look at its own weakness and imperfection, to doubt and hesitate because of it, but looks to Christ and the grace of God promised in Christ, and thus surely and firmly concludes that, by grace, for Christ's sake, it has a merciful God and remission of sins.

173   *But you will find many who, either imbued with false faith or bewitched by Epicurean persuasion, nevertheless harbor a certain assurance of salvation.*

We do not speak of heretic faith, which is presumed either without or contrary to Holy Scripture; for this doubtless neither justifies nor saves. And we also do not speak of Epicurean opinion, which promises itself impunity in hardened impenitence. For the sentence of divine judgment is: They that do such things shall not possess the kingdom of God, Gl 5:21. But we say of true and justifying faith, whose character and function we have described a little earlier, that it ought not hesitate, but conclude in firm trust, that it will be for it just as it believes according to the Word of God.

174 *But what bases and what sure and firm reasons does faith have for its confidence?*

I. The promise of divine grace is firm and sure for all to whom it is imputed by faith. Ro 4:16. And it was confirmed by divine oath for this reason, that all who flee to it and lay hold on it as a holy anchor might have firm, sure, and solid comfort. Heb 6:17-20.

II. It is the nature and character of faith, that it does not hesitate, but approaches God in strong *plerophoria* [full assurance] and firm trust. Eph 3:12; Heb 3:6; 10:22-23; 11:1; 1 Jn 3:14; 5:13, 19; Ro 4:20-21; 5:2; 8:33-39; 1 Ptr 1:13. And the faith of the saints in this name is commended in Scripture. Ro 4:18-19; Mt 8:10; Lk 7:9.

III. In order that this confidence might be made the firmer and surer, God himself sealed the righteousness of faith by His sacraments, Ro 4:11; 1 Ptr 3:21, and through His Holy Spirit, whom He for this reason pours out into the hearts of the believers, 2 Co 1:22; Eph 1:13-14; 4:30.

IV. Scripture clearly and expressly rebukes and condemns doubt. Mt 6:30; 14:31; Mk 11:23; Ro 4:20; Jas 1:6-7.

V. The doctrine regarding doubt is an old and damned error of the Pharisees. For Mt 9 the scribes accused Christ of blasphemy because He commanded the paralytic *tharsein*, to take heart, or to be of good and serene mind, v. 3. Thus Lk 7, when Christ forgave the woman and commanded [her] to go in peace, the Pharisees muttered that it was blasphemy, v. 49. And it is the same error later revived by the Novatians.

175 *But many statements of Scripture are raised in objection which seem to attribute justification to the renewal and good works of the reborn; therefore point out the sources and bases of the explanations.*

The chief objections can be simply and thoroughly explained and refuted, when this distinction is observed and applied, namely that some Scripture statements properly speak of free justification and some deal with related matters.

For, first, there are certain Scripture passages in which there is, as it were, the seat of the doctrine of free justification (for example, those that speak of the merit and cause of justification, which is solely the obedience of Christ and the grace of God; likewise, those that speak of application, how and by what means this grace of God and obedience and merit of Christ is applied, apprehended, and received, namely through faith in the promise; and [those that tell us] that righteousness or justification consists in free reconciliation and the forgiveness of sins, solely for Christ's sake). We have spoken above of these passages. The true, proper, and genuine statement of the doctrine of free justification is to be drawn and established on the basis of these passages.

Second, some Scripture statements speak of the perfect and complete righteousness of the Law; if a man render it with the perfection that is prescribed in the Law, he shall without doubt be justified and saved by it, as Christ and Paul grant. Mt 19:17; Lk 10:28; Ro 2:13; 10:5. But since we cannot attain that perfection in this life, we need another righteousness, which is revealed in the Gospel.

Third, many passages of Scripture do not teach how we are justified before God, but describe the nature and character of those who have already been justified by faith, namely that they bring forth good works. 1 Jn 1:6-7; 2:3, 6; 3:3, 6; 4:7; 5:3; 2 Ptr 1:5, 8; Eph 4:17-24; Ro 12:2 ff.

Fourth, elsewhere in Scripture the signs or outward marks are described, namely love and good works, which attest true faith a posteriori, as it were, and by which those who are truly justified by faith are distinguished and discerned from those who, persevering in sins in the Epicurean conviction of impunity, fashion for themselves a false notion of faith and righteousness; this is the thrust of the whole Epistle of John, likewise of James and of Peter. And here belong Mt 5:3-9; 20:6 ff; 24:46; 25:34 ff; Jn 5:29; Ro 6:13, 19; Gl 5:24-25; Ps 15:1 ff; and similar passages.

Fifth, some passages of Scripture teach not how, [or] through or because of what, we can obtain salvation and life eternal, but that God wants to reward and compensate, both in this life and in that which is to come, the good works of those who have now already obtained justification and the inheritance of life eternal freely, through faith, for Christ's sake. Mt 5:12; 19:21; 2 Co 5:10; 2 Ti 4:7-8.

Sixth, some statements of Scripture do not properly speak of the remission of guilt and eternal punishment, which is given alone by grace, through faith, for Christ's sake; but they deal with remission or reduction of temporal punishments, which comes for Christ's sake to those who are truly and earnestly penitent. Dn 4:27; Tob 4:11; 12:9; Ps 41:1-3; 1 Co 11:31.

Finally, some Scripture passages include exhortations to repentance and assurances that God is merciful to the penitent and wants to forgive sins. Mt 6:14; Is 1:16-18. But on what propitiation depends and why God forgives sins, likewise by what means the promise of remission is apprehended and applied, namely by faith alone for Christ's sake, that is to be drawn from, and set forth on the basis of, the doctrine of the Gospel.

At this point in the examination let the superintendents put a number of Scripture passages like that before the pastors, form arguments based on them, and test their explanations and solutions.

Predestination or election of those who are to be saved

176   *Is this doctrine to be set before the hearers, or necessary to be known?*
Since most holy Scripture touches the doctrine of this article, namely
that God before the beginning of time and the creation of the world
predestined the elect in Christ unto salvation and life eternal, etc. not only
once, and that lightly or in passing, but teaches, emphasizes, and explains
[it] thoroughly [and] often in many places, it is truly by no means to be
passed by in silence and indifference,[27] as though that is useless,
whatever it may be, which cannot be set forth without offense and loss of
faith, provided it is taught and explained thoughtfully and according to
the pattern of divinely inspired Scripture, namely as much as it has
revealed to us about this puzzling mystery. And the chief passages that
are found in Scripture regarding this article should be familiar to pastors,
e.g., Mt 20:16; 22:14; Lk 10:20; Jn 13:18; 15:16; Acts 13:48; Ro 8:29-30;
9:11; 10:12-13; 11:5, 7, 29: 1 Co 1:26-29; Gl 1:15; Eph 4:1-5, 11; 2 Th
2:13-14; 2 Ti 1:9; 2:19; Rv 20:12, 15.

177   *But some at times speak about and discuss this article less circumspectly and not without offense, whereby pernicious thoughts are stirred
up in the minds of many, which [thoughts] give occasion for security and
impenitence or despair.*
Doctrine divinely revealed and taught in the Scriptures is by no means
to be abandoned or rejected because it is abused or misunderstood; but
corruptions are to be prudently separated from sound doctrine and
rebuked, and abuse is to be guarded against by earnest and diligent
warning. But if some who are admonished nevertheless want to abuse
true doctrine, their damnation is just, Ro 3:8. Many conceive fanciful
thoughts from this article about predestination and fabricate the
conclusions: Since God predestinated His elect before the foundations of
the world were laid (Eph 1:4), and the predestination and purpose of God
can neither fail nor be hindered or changed for any reason (Is 14:27; Ro
9:11, 19), therefore, if God has predestined me to salvation and life
eternal, nothing shall hurt me, even if I persevere without repentance in
sins and transgressions, despise the Word and the Sacraments, [and]
concern myself little about contrition, faith, and piety; I will be saved,
since the foreknowledge and predestination of God never fail. But if God
has not predestined me to salvation, nothing will help me, even if I hear
the Word of God, repent, and have faith, since I cannot hinder or change
God's foreknowledge and predestination.
Pious minds are also often disturbed by this kind of temptations, so
that even if, by the grace of God, they had repentance, faith, and good
intent, they nevertheless sometimes fall into these thoughts: If you are not
predestined to salvation from eternity, everything you do is in vain for
that reason. These speculations often increase when we look at our own

weakness and the example of those who did not continue in the way of piety they began but, fallen headlong into sins again, have fallen from grace.

That false view and [those] pernicious thoughts are to be countered with this firm and immovable principle: Since all Scripture, divinely inspired, was not given to stir up, nourish, or strengthen security and impenitence in us, but to be profitable for reproof, rebuke, and correction, 2 Ti 3:16, [and] since, likewise, the doctrine of the divine Word was not written aforetime for us, in order that faith might be disturbed or be led to despair, but that through patience and comfort of the Scriptures we might have hope, Ro 15:4, therefore that is beyond all doubt neither the sound meaning nor the proper use of the doctrine of predestination, when by it occasion is either given or seized for security and impenitence or for doubt and despair. And Scripture itself does not teach the doctrine of predestination in any other way, sense, and purpose than that by it [i.e., this doctrine] it [i.e., Scripture] might lead us to the divinely revealed Word (Eph 1:9; 1 Co 1:21), exhort to repentance (2 Ti 2:19), incite to piety (Eph 1:4; Jn 15:16), stengthen faith by consolations, and make us sure of our salvation in Christ (Eph 1:7, 13-14; Jn 10:17-28; 2 Th 2:13-17).

178   *Yet is it true that God foreknows and foresees all future things, and this His foreknowledge and foresight cannot fail, nor can anything take place without or contrary to His will?*

The ancients taught the true and profitable distinction between the foreknowledge or foresight of God and predestination or election, and on that basis this whole matter can be simply and clearly explained, understood, and elucidated. For proper distinctions are by all means to be applied in the explanation of this article, lest the doctrine, otherwise difficult in itself, be more involved and obscured in perplexing confusion. Therefore God, to whom all things, future as well as past, are equally and presently open, foreknows and foresees all things that will come to pass, good as well as evil. And this act of God is called foreknowledge or foresight. But He foreknows and foresees evil things in one way, good things in another. He foreknows and foresees evil things not [in such a way] that He wants them to happen by the good pleasure of His will. Ps 5:4-5. Nor is such foreknowledge and foresight of God a cause that effects, works, promotes, or aids evil; but the sole cause of that is the depraved and perverse will of the devil and men. But God foreknows and foresees the evil which that depraved will of man will attempt and effect out of its own wickedness, contrary to the command and revealed will of God. And He does not only foresee, but at the same time, in a hidden way and order, He sets bounds and determines how far He will permit the evil things (Acts 14:16; 17:26), likewise when and how He would restrain and punish them (Gn 15:16; 1 Th 2:16; Mt 23:32; Ro 2:5; 2 K 19:27-28).

But God did not only foreknow and foresee future good things, but He is their cause and He effects, works, promotes, and aids them in us according to the good pleasure of His will. And in the church this act of God is called predestination, election, or preordination, with regard to salvation and life eternal.

179   *How, then, can the doctrine of eternal predestination or the election of the children of God to salvation be grasped in a sure way, according to the analogy of Scripture, and set before the uninstructed, that they be not offended or disturbed thereby, but rather draw comfort and be improved?*

That kind of method is not only necessary for a minister of the church but also very useful for any pious man, to adopt a pattern according to which to conform his thoughts regarding this deep mystery and keep [them] within proper limits. For if someone approaches the article of predestination a priori, that is, from the hidden and inscrutable will of God and believes that nothing else or more is to be considered in it besides these bare fancies, that God, in the hidden counsel of His predestination, preordained and decreed only who and how many are to be saved, likewise who and how many are to be damned, or that He determined thus by some selection as of a military nature, "This one I want to be saved, that one is to be damned," various absurd as well as dangerous and pernicious thoughts will surely arise thence. That is what happens if the human mind puts together a line of argument like this: If you are predestinated, no matter what you do, you will nevertheless be saved; but if you are not predestinated, you will certainly be damned, etc. Christ in the parable Mt 22:1-14 and Paul Ro 8:29-39 [and] Eph 1:4-11 teach that one must begin a posteriori, that is, from the divinely revealed Word. For when that article is considered, they set it before us not simply in the arcane and hidden counsel of the Trinity, but as that mystery has been revealed to us in Christ, who is the true book of life, through the Word, in such a way, that in the doctrine of this article are embraced the whole counsel and decree of the Trinity regarding the redemption of mankind through Christ, regarding the holy call through the Word, [and] regarding the justification and eternal glorification of the elect, as that counsel of God has been revealed to us in Scripture. Therefore he that wants to think and speak piously and circumspectly, according to Scripture, about the purpose, predestination, and election or preordination of God to life eternal—he must together embrace with mind and thought these chief things, which we have now set forth, as being each included in the article of predestination. For thus the mystery of this difficult article can be most simply understood and most correctly explained. Therefore God, foreseeing the fall of the first parents and the evils that were to follow as a result of it, decreed and determined, in His hidden counsel, out of free mercy and love toward mankind

I. That, and how, He wanted to redeem and reconcile mankind to Himself through the incarnation, obedience, passion, and resurrection of [His] Son [as] Mediator.

II. That He wanted to offer to mankind that grace of His, the merit and blessings of Christ, through the ministry of the Word and the Sacraments, and invite guests to the wedding of His Son through His ministers, and thus in this world to the end of time gather for Himself out of lost mankind an eternal church, in which He would offer and distribute those blessings of His through the Word.

III. That by the preaching, hearing, and meditation of that Word He wanted to work effectively in us, by enlightening hearts through the Holy Spirit, by turning [them] to repentance, and by kindling, increasing, strengthening, and preserving faith in them.

IV. He determined to justify all those who in earnest repentance and true faith embraced and received Christ offered in the Word and the Sacraments; that is, absolve [them] from sins, receive [them] into grace, [and] adopt [them] into sonship and the inheritance of life eternal. But those who reject, despise, blaspheme, and persecute His Word (Acts 13:45-46), who harden their hearts when they hear the Word (Heb 4:7), who resist the Holy Spirit (Acts 7:51) and persevere in sins without repentance (Lk 14:18), who do not want to receive Christ in true faith (Mk 16:16), who choose for themselves other ways, outside of Christ, by which they might be justified and saved (Ro 9:31-32), or who imitate the form of piety by outward hypocrisy, to which there is no foundation (Mt 7:15)—those, I say, He has also determined, according to His long-suffering and much patience, to call and invite to repentance through the ministry (Lk 15; Ro 2:4; Jer 3:12). But if they persist and continue in ungodliness, He determined to consign them to eternal damnation, since they loved darkness rather than light (Jn 3:19).

V. He determined that He would also sanctify in love those who have been justified by faith (Eph 1:4) and to renew [them] unto new obedience through His Holy Spirit.

VI. That He would also graciously defend those who have been called to that way, justified, and sanctified, against sin, death, the devil, the world, and the flesh, guard [them] against all evil, lead and direct [them] through the Holy Spirit in the way of His commandments, raise the fallen [and] sustain and preserve [them] under the cross and temptation with strong comfort, and as the faithful God not permit them to be tempted beyond their ability, but make the outcome such that they can bear [it] (1 Co 10:13), and finally bring it about that for those who have been called according to [His] purpose all things, also cross, temptations, and tribulations, result in good (Ro 8:28).

VII. That if only those whom He has called rely firmly on the Word, continue in prayers without ceasing, and remain in the goodness of God

(Ro 11:22), hold the beginning of [His][28] confidence[29] firmly[30] to the end (Heb 3:14) [and] properly and faithfully administer the gifts [they have] received (Mt 25:21, 29)—I say that He wants to strengthen them to be faithful to the end (1 Co 1:8-9; Ph 1:6). But those who grieve and vex the Holy Spirit (Eph 4:30; Is 63:10), [who] turn themselves impudently away from the knowledge of Christ and [from] the holy commandment, and are overcome, having freely become entangled again in the filth of this world (2 Ptr 2:20-21), who sweep and prepare their hearts for Satan, who walks about (Lk 11:25), or who also because of confidence in their own holiness before God begin to boast proudly (Mt 20:12)—[I say] that He wants to recall them also to repentance and, when they have been converted, receive [them] into grace (Lk 15 on the prodigal son). But if they neglect to repent while it is called Today, and persist in impenitence in such a way, that [their] latter state becomes worse than the former (2 Ptr 2:20; Mt 20:16)—[I say] that in them He wants to set up, also in this life, to show His wrath and power, a fearful example of desertion, hardening, blindness, and being given over to a reprobate mind, to do things that are not convenient (Eph 4:18; Ps 81:12; Acts 28:27).

VIII. Finally, God resolved in His eternal counsel to save and glorify in eternal life those—those, I say, whom He has called and justified, if they endure to the end (Mt 24:13), that is, if they hold fast their first trust in Him, confidence, and the glorying of hope firmly to the end (Heb 3:6, 14; Ro 8:30). Scripture relates all these things with each other, and they ought to be thought of and considered together when the purpose, decree, predestination, election, or preordination of God to salvation is discussed. And in that way the doctrine of predestination can be salutarily set forth and most clearly understood.

180   *But does predestination include only the work of salvation itself and not at the same time the persons of those to be saved?*

In this article Scripture includes at the same time also the persons of the elect. For one must not believe that God has by His predestination prepared only salvation in general, but gave no thought to the very persons of those to be saved, but left this whole matter to them, so that they try to obtain and attain that salvation by their own natural powers and endeavors. But God graciously foreknew the elect, one and all, who are to be saved through Christ, in His eternal counsel of predestination and gracious purpose, and predestinated and chose [them] to salvation, at the same time preordaining how He would call, bring, and preserve them through His grace, gifts, and power to the salvation prepared in Christ.

181   *Does that election take place then first, when men repent and believe the Gospel, or was it made because of their holiness, foreseen from eternity?*

Paul declares, Eph 1:4: He has chosen us in Christ, not in time, but

89

before the foundations of the world were laid. [See also] 2 Ti 1:9. For the election of God does not follow our faith and righteousness but precedes it as efficient cause (Ro 8:30). Augustine carefully considered what Paul writes Eph 1:4: He chose us, not because we were holy or were made holy, or because He foresaw that we would be holy, but: He chose us in Christ, he says, and [He did] that before the foundation of the world, that we might be holy and blameless before Him. For the election or purpose of grace is the efficient cause of all those things that belong to salvation (Eph 1:11-12, 19).

And this election was made before this world began, not in view of our works, either past or present or future, but according to the purpose and good pleasure of the grace of God (Ro 9:11; 2 Ti 1:9).

182 *But since it is certain that only those who are predestined or elected are saved, and those whose names have been written in the book of life, how then can it be known who the elect are? Or how can I be sure that I am in the number of those that are predestined and that my name is found written in the book of life?*

Regarding this question one must judge not on the basis of the judgment of our reason, nor on the basis of the statement of the divine law, nor by any outward appearance whatever; and much less should we take recourse to this, that we look for the answer by peering into the secrets of the hidden counsel of the Trinity; but we must look to the word of the Gospel, in which God has revealed to us His counsel and will in Christ. For Scripture leads and sends us back to it in this question (Eph 1:9; 2 Ti 1:9-10). But that hidden counsel of God is revealed to us in this way (Ro 8:29-30): Those whom God has foreknown, predestinated, elected, and preordained according to His purpose before the foundation of the world, those He also called in time. And those whom He wants to be guests at the marriage of His Son, those same ones He also calls through servants sent out by Him (Mt 22:3), namely each one at his time, one at the first hour, another at the third, the sixth, the ninth, or even at the eleventh hour. (Mt 20:1-7). And truly God, who thus calls men through the Word, earnestly wants them to be saved and come to the knowledge of the truth (1 Ti 2:4). Likewise He wants to be effective in them through the Word, so that they be illuminated, converted, justified, and saved. For let us not think that the call of God is child's play, or a joke, or something like that, but let us firmly believe that God truly wants to reveal His will to us through it. And what the will of God toward us is, is to be learned and judged on no other basis than alone from the word of the call. And that word by which we are called is truly the ministry of the Spirit (2 Co 3:8) and the very power of God unto salvation to everyone that believes (Ro 1:16). And this is the highest and necessary comfort for pious minds and troubled consciences, that I can, in fact, I should firmly and confidently believe and hold that God, who calls me by the Word, by that very fact makes His will known and revealed to me, that He wants to save me, that is, confer the Spirit and His grace on me through the Word, that I might be enlightened, converted, justified, and saved. In this way such a description of the elect can be drawn out of Eph 1: They that have been predestinated and elected to salvation and life eternal have, hear, and follow the Word of God (Jn 10:27), repent, believe in Christ, call upon God, [and] are justified and sanctified. And though all these things in themselves are still tenuous and weak, yet they hunger and thirst after righteousness (Mt 5:6). And in this way the Spirit of God bears witness to the elect that they are children of God, and though they do not know what they should pray for as they ought, the same Spirit makes intercession for them with groanings that cannot be uttered (Ro 8;16, 26). And he gives the very sweet comfort that God is so faithful that He wants to confirm, continue, and complete the good work begun in us (1 Co 1:8; Ph 1:6; 1 Ptr 5:10), unless we turn ourselves away from Him (2 Ptr 2:21). Hence Paul also says 2 Ti 2:19 that this very thing is a sign: to depart from iniquity and call upon the name of Christ. Hence we know for sure that none of the elect remains in final impenitence, as it is called, and unbelief. Therefore he that neither hears nor follows the voice of Christ but persists in sins without repentance and does not seek to be reconciled with God in Christ through faith, who likewise does not obey the Holy Spirit but resists—let him neither think nor say that he is among the elect (Jn 8:47; 10:26), though one should not finally despair of the salvation of such a person, since God can call and convert him even at the sixth, or ninth, or even the eleventh hour. Therefore let us never cease to exhort and admonish such through the Word, in the hope that perhaps God will give them repentance to acknowledge the truth, that they may recover themselves from the snares of the devil, by whom they are held captive at his will (2 Ti 2:25-26). But he that perseveres in sins unto the end without repentance is certainly not elect but is among the rejected and damned.

183   *But it is written that many are called, but few chosen (Mt 22:14; 20:16). Many likewise receive the Word with joy, who for a while indeed believe but fall away in time of temptation (Lk 8:13). How then can the call and beginning of conversion be a sure sign by which God reveals the mystery of His will to us?*

The reason why not all who are called are chosen is not this, that the sense and meaning of God calling us through the Word is this: I indeed call you outwardly through the ministry to salvation and participation in my heavenly kingdom, but in truth I have something else in mind; for I do not want all whom I call through the Word to be enlightened and converted, but that most of them be condemned and perish, though in My word I profess something else, etc. Surely God Himself earnestly abominates and condemns in us that kind of levity and wickedness by which we say one thing, [but] hide another in the heart (Ps 5:6; 12:2-3).

91

Nor can this be said, that God does not call all to whom He sends His Word. For God does not call without means but through the Word preached and heard (2 Th 2:14), and He Himself exhorts through the ministers of the Word that they be reconciled to God (2 Co 5:20). And He wants repentance and remission of sins to be preached not only to a few but to all nations and the whole world (Mt 28:19; Mk 16:15; Lk 24:46-47). For the preaching of repentance and the promise of universal grace are to be set before all people everywhere. But Scripture gives this as the reason why few are chosen, though many are called: Mt 23:37; Acts 7:51; 13:46. And Christ states this as plainly as possible in the parable Mt 22:5-6. They that were called, He says, did not want to come, but despised the Word, treated the servants shamefully, and slew [them]. But that it was not the will of God that they spurn the call that was brought [to them] and resist the Holy Spirit is gathered from this in that parable, that the king was indignant that those who were called were unwilling to accept the grace that was offered. And this is the reason why such, though they are called, are nevertheless not chosen, because they resist the Holy Spirit about to work salvation in them. For this is not the nature of divine predestination or election, that anyone should obtain salvation, even if he do not hear the Word of God or harden [his] heart against hearing the Word. But those who have been predestined and chosen to salvation and life eternal, they hear the voice of Christ and follow Him (John 10:27). And since the Holy Spirit wants to work and effect in them, through the Word, the things that belong to their salvation, it is therefore the will of God that they do not reject but receive and rightly use and piously exercise the workings, grace, and gifts of the Holy Spirit, especially since the Holy Spirit Himself enables them to do this. but those who do not hear the voice of Christ, or do not follow when they hear it, but resist the Holy Spirit and persevere in such wickedness, it was pointed out in the preceding that they are not among the elect. Thus indeed many are called, but few chosen, because the minority of the called receive and follow that word; the reason for disobedience is not divine predestination but the will of man, perverse and turned away from God; in obstinate wickedness it is not willing to allow or suffer the working of the Holy Spirit through the Word, but by impudent resistance repulses and rejects it.

In the same way many who began will, having fallen again, defect and fall from grace, not because God denies them grace and the gift of perseverance, but because of their own will they turn themselves from the holy commandment (2 Ptr 2); they insult the Spirit of grace (Heb 10:29); they vex Him (Is 63:10) and grieve [Him] (Eph 4:30); they adorn the house anew for Satan (Lk 11:25); and for them the last state becomes worse than the first (2 Ptr 2:20); and their damnation is just (Ro 3:8).

184 *What, then, is the true and proper use of this doctrine of predestination? And what [is] its fruit or usefulness?*

Paul declares that all Scripture, divinely inspired, is profitable for doctrine, correction, instruction, and comfort (2 Ti 3:16). Since, then, also this doctrine is of Scripture and founded in it, it will surely also serve the same purpose. Now, for the sake of teaching, these chief parts may be set forth for the uninstructed.

I. This article excellently confirms the doctrine of free justification by faith, namely that we are justified and saved without our works and merits, freely through grace, for Christ's sake. For before we were born, in fact, before the foundations of the world were laid, before this world began, when we were still nothing, much less could do anything good, we were predestined and chosen to salvation according to God's purpose, on the basis of grace, in Christ, not on the basis of works, or according to our works, as Paul strongly emphasizes that matter Ro 9:11 ff; 2 Ti 1:8-9.

II. This article overturns all the opinions by which something is ascribed to the natural powers of our will in spiritual things and actions. For God, before the times of this world, in His eternal counsel, decreed that He Himself wanted to effect and work in us, through His Spirit, all the things that belong to our conversion. And man, without this working of God and left to himself, is, per se and of himself, with all the powers of his natural will in the spiritual things that concern our conversion, nothing but enmity against God. Ro 8:7; Gn 6:5.

III. This doctrine supplies very sweet comfort. For it teaches that our conversion, justification, and salvation was so much in the mind and heart of God, that before the foundation of the world He took counsel and determined and preordained how He wanted to call, lead, and preserve us unto that salvation.

IV. Though Satan stalks our salvation in baffling ways, and the world abounds in infinite offenses, our flesh likewise is both weak and evil, the doctrine of predestination gives us the infinite comfort, that the things that pertain to our salvation are built on the sure and immovable foundation of the eternal purpose of God. For our salvation does not lie in our hand, whence it might be easily taken from us, but rests in the overruling hand of our Lord and Savior Jesus Christ, out of which no one will be able to snatch us, provided we steadfastly and faithfully cling to Him and remain in Him. Jn 10:28-29; 15:4. Thus Paul draws those most beautiful and sweet consolations from the article of predestination, Ro 8:30-39; 2 Ti 1:7, 9; Ro 11:29.

V. How much comfort one may draw under the cross and [in] storms of temptations from this doctrine Paul teaches Ro 8:28 ff., namely that God, in His purpose before the foundation of the world, predetermined and predestined by what afflictions and tribulations He wanted the individual elect to be conformed to the image of His Son, and that for each one his cross would be for a help to good, namely because they have been called according to the purpose of God. That is, that God, in His eternal counsel, before the foundations of the world were laid, graciously foreknew and determined what and how much of cross and salutary afflictions it was His will to lay on each one, and at the same time He determined the result of temptations before this world began and arranged them to serve this purpose, that all things work out for good and salvation for those who love Him. And hence Paul finally concludes with resolute and confident mind: I am therefore sure that neither affliction, nor distress, nor height, nor depth, etc. can separate us from the love of God which is in Christ, but in all these things we overcome through Him who loved us etc. And this is the very sweet and great comfort of the pious under the cross, drawn from the doctrine of predestination.

VI. Many earnest admonitions and exhortations are also drawn from this article, e.g., when we despise the Word of God, and do not follow it, and reject the guidance and direction of the Holy Spirit (regarding which Luke says, 7:30: The Pharisees rejected the counsel of God against themselves), likewise, if one is carried away by the vain opinion that he will be saved even without the Word, neglecting and rejecting it, or, when he finds in himself, on the basis of the call and the beginnings of conversion, the signs of election, he believes that he will now henceforth be out of danger of [losing] salvation, even if he freely indulges and gives free rein to sins against conscience. Against those false and harmful opinions this article teaches that God in His counsel, before the foundations of the world were laid, decreed regarding those that indeed were called but refused to come, that none of them would taste of His supper (Lk 14:24); likewise that the latter state of those who turn themselves away from the holy commandment and again involve themselves in sins would be worse than the former (2 Ptr 2:20).

And in this simple way that difficult article regarding the mystery of the eternal predestination of God can be profitably set forth and taught without disturbing consciences, as also Christ Himself, over against highflying speculations of reason, summarized the whole doctrine of predestination in a simple parable, Mt 22:2 ff.

185   *But what will you reply to these objections: With God there is a certain and definite number of elect, to which none can be added and from which none can be subtracted; likewise, that the Word of God is preached purely in some places, in others not; and that some are hardened against hearing the Word but others are converted, and of the fallen some are raised again, others are given over to a reprobate mind.*

The simplest and soundest way of all to respond is this, that we should distinguish between the things that God has revealed to us, in the Word, of His secret counsel, and [that] He wants us to know (Eph 1:9) and the things that He wanted to be unsaid and hidden regarding that mystery and that He has reserved for His knowledge and understanding alone. Let us learn, embrace, and follow the things that have been revealed in the

Word; thus far we have spoken of those things. But we ought not curiously try to look with our speculations and reasonings into the things that God wants to be hidden and [that] He has reserved for Himself alone, but leave them to the knowledge of God and simply and firmly cling to the revealed Word.

Doubtless, then, God from eternity most certainly foresaw, foreknew, and still knows who of the called would believe, [and] who not, [and] who of the converted would persevere, [and] who not. Their definite number is doubtless also very well known to God; and divine foresight and foreknowledge cannot fail. But since God wanted to reserve that mystery to His wisdom, and did not reveal any of it in His Word, and much less commanded that it be explored by our thoughts, but rather earnestly forbade [it] (Ro 11:33), it is not for us to go into this matter with curious speculations and cunning conclusions of reason, but obediently and reverently rest in the revealed Word of God, to which He Himself directs us.

In the same way God knows, without all doubt, in fact, He has determined for each one the time and hour of both call and conversion. But since He did not make that known to us, it behooves us constantly to continue in the Word and commit to God the specific details of timing (Acts 1:7). Likewise, when we see God give His most holy Word to some kingdom or province, but at the same time not bestow [it] on another people, likewise take it away from one people but grant it longer to another, and that this one is hardened, blinded, and given over to a reprobate mind, but that one, fallen into the same fault, is converted to God, etc., it is not that[31] we should try to pry into and ferret out the reason for that with our reason. And Paul has set certain limits for us in that kind of questions, how far we ought to go, while he wants us, on the other hand, namely in considering those that perish, to acknowledge the just judgments of God and just punishments of sins. For God makes some nations and persons a just example of His severity, showing what we, collectively and individually, have deserved by reason both of our nature, corrupted by sin, and of ingratitude toward His most holy Word, and that for this purpose, that the rest should live the more carefully in the fear of God and learn to acknowledge and praise His pure and undeserved grace in vessels of mercy. For though we all fall into that same filth of sins, no injustice is done to those who suffer the just punishment of wickedness. In others, whom God gives the light of His Word, enlightens, converts, preserves, and saves, the Lord commends and makes known His great grace and mercy, which reaches us without, in fact, despite, all our merit.

If we proceed so far in meditating on this article and stop within the stated limits, we shall walk in the altogether sure and truly royal way. For it is written regarding this mystery, Hos 13:9: Israel, your destruction is of yourself; in Me alone is your help.

But if some things are loftier and range beyond those Pauline bounds, we should remember, with Paul, to lay a finger on the lips and exclaim: O man, who are you, that you answer back to God? Ro 9:20. For that great apostle teaches us by his example that we neither can nor should investigate everything in this article.

For when he had spoken at length, on the basis of the revealed Word of God, about this mystery [and] when he finally came to the things that God has reserved for His hidden wisdom, he cuts the discussion short and concludes with such an exclamation, Ro 11:33-34: O the depth of the riches of the wisdom and knowledge of God; how unsearchable are His judgments, and how past finding out [are] His ways; for who has known the mind of the Lord? etc. Or who has been a counselor to Him? namely beyond and above that which He has revealed to us in His Word, etc.

Good Works, or New Obedience

186   *Now then, with sin forgiven us, as has thus far been said, does God want us thus to persevere and continue in sin without renewal?*

By no means. On the contrary, though sins are and remain in the saints in this life (Ro 7:17-18; Ps 32:6), yet God bestows on those who are justified by faith His Holy Spirit, who transforms and renews them (Ro 12:2; Eph 4:23-24; Cl 3:10). Hence he is called back-to-back the Spirit of regeneration and renewal (Tts 3:5). For the Son of God did not redeem us for so great a price, in order to procure for us the privilege of shamefulness and the license to live in disgrace freely and with impunity (Ro 3:8; 6:1-2; 1 Th 4:7), but to purify unto Himself a particular people, one that follows good works and that, with all ungodliness denied, would serve Him in holiness and righteousness, and in newness of life and [in] good works, which He Himself has prepared that it [the people] should walk [in them] (Tts 2:11-14; Lk 1:74-75; Ro 6:4; Eph 2:10; 2 Co 5:15).

187   *In what does this renewal consist?*

Scripture summarizes it under two heads, namely that we mortify the passions or works of the flesh and walk in the Spirit (Ro 8:13; Gl 5:16), that we might abstain from evil and do good (Ps 34:14), that, being dead to sin, we should live unto righteousness (Ro 6:2, 18; 1 Ptr 2:24), that we might put off the old man and put on the new (Eph 4:21-22,24; Ro 13:12), that we might bring forth not evil but good fruits (Mt 3:10; 7:19).

188   *Is this proposition true: "Good works are necessary"?*

It is true both with regard to sense and with regard to the form of sound words. For in the Augsburg Confession and the Apology these propositions are common and accepted: that good works are necessary; that it is necessary to do good works; that good works should necessarily follow reconciliation; that we necessarily ought to do divinely commanded good works. And the position of Scripture is, that good works are to be done because they are necessary on the basis of the command of God, and we are debtors. For the will and command of God is that believers should not be idle (Mt 3:10; 7:19; 20:6), but that they walk and exercise themselves in good works (1 Th 4:3; Jn 15:12; 1 Jn 4:21). Hence Scripture also uses this terminology, that the new obedience of the reborn is not arbitrary, but necessary and required. Ro 8:12; 13:5, 8; 15:1; 1 Co 9:16; Lk 17:10; 1 Jn 4:11.

189   *But Paul nevertheless teaches that good works ought not to be done by constraint. 2 Co 9:7; Phmn 14; 1 Ptr 5:2.*

The word "necessity" is sometimes used for constraint or for that which is done unwillingly and is wrung from the unwilling without the approval of the mind. And in this sense Paul says: not of necessity. For the outward work that is rendered by constraint, or unwillingly and with aversion, without a ready heart and mind according to the inner man, is not truly a good work. 2 Co 9:7; Phmn 14. For God requires the obedience that is rendered from the mind or heart, though it is not perfect in this life. Ro 6:17; 1 Ti 1:5.

But Paul also calls that necessary which is not arbitrary but is required by reason of the command and divine will. Ro 13:5; 1 Co 9:16. And in this sense it is rightly and well said in the Augsburg Confession and the Apology, that good works are necessary, or that it is necessary and required to do good works.

190   *Are good works necessary to justification or to salvation?*

By no means. For, as has been pointed out above, justification and our salvation does not depend on our works, but alone on the obedience, passion, and death of Christ; and it is apprehended and applied to us by faith alone and thus consists only in free reconciliation and remission of sins. Ro 4:7, 16. Therefore, as it is not to be taught in the church of God, because of the exclusive particles, that good works are necessary for justification, so since Scripture determines and protects the article of salvation with equal diligence (Ro 4:6; 11:5-6; Eph 2:8-9; 2 Ti 1:9; Tts 3:5), Luther also rightly and properly rejected and excluded that proposition (good works are necessary for salvation) from our churches.

191   *Will one, then, obtain and retain righteousness and salvation, even if he indulges in his corrupt lusts against conscience and brings forth no good fruit?*

By no means. For these most earnest statements and threats of Scripture are to be diligently and earnestly impressed on men: Ro 8:13, If you live according to the flesh, you shall die; Gl 5:21; Eph 5:5, They that do such such things shall not possess the kingdom of God; 1 Jn 3:14, He that does not love remains in death. When David therefore took a strange woman he was surely neither just nor saved in the sight of God, and that

97

not for this reason, that something else and more is necessary for justification and salvation besides Christ apprehended by faith (for righteousness and salvation must be present first, before good and God-pleasing works can be done, or, as Scripture says, a tree must first be good, before it can bear good fruits. Mt 7:18) but because good fruits necessarily follow where true faith, righteousness, and salvation are present. Therefore, where no good fruits are brought forth, it is a very sure sign that no true faith is present there, but that righteousness and salvation have been lost. 1 Ti 5:8; 2 Ptr 1:9; 1 Jn 3:6.

192   *What, then, are the reasons for which good works are to be done by believers or those who are justified?*

The Augsburg Confession and the Apology set forth the reasons thus: It is necessary to do good works commanded by God, not that we may trust to earn grace by them, but because of the will and command of God, likewise to exercise faith, and for the sake of confession and giving of thanks. Urbanus Rhegius, in the booklet *De formulis caute loquendi,* summarizes the reasons in this way:

I. Because our good works are due obedience commanded by God which we creatures owe the Creator, and they are as it were thanksgiving for the favors of God and sacrifices pleasing to God because of Christ.

II. That our heavenly Father might be glorified thereby.

III. That our faith might be exercised and increased by our good works, so that it may grow and be stirred up.

IV. That our neighbor might be edified by our good works and spurred to imitation and be helped in need.

V. That we might make our calling sure by good works and testify that our faith is neither feigned nor dead.

VI. Though our good works do not merit either justification or salvation, yet they are to be done, since they have promises of this life and of that which is to come. 1 Ti 4:8.

In *Loci communes* Philipp Melanchthon lists in this order the reasons why good works are to be done:

I. Because it is God's command, and we are debtors.

II. Lest faith be lost and the Holy Spirit grieved and driven out.

III. To avoid punishments.

IV. Since our works, though they do not fulfill the law of God and not merit eternal life, are nevertheless called by God sacrifices that both please and serve Him for the sake of Christ.

V. Since godliness has promises of this life and of that which is to come.

Luther sets forth the reasons why good works are to be done in such a way that, if they were briefly summarized, the list would be about this: First, some have regard to God Himself, namely since it is the will of God (1 Th 4:3) and the command of God (1 Jn 4:21). And since He is our

Father, it therefore behooves us children to render obedience to the Father (1 Ptr 1:14, 16-17; 1 Jn 3:2-3). And as He loved us and graciously forgave [our] sins, so we also should love the brethren, forgiving them [their] sins (Eph 4:32; 1 Jn 4:11), that God might be glorified through us (Ph 1:1; 1 Ptr 4:11; Mt 5:16). Christ also redeemed us, that, being dead to sins, we might live unto righteousness and serve Him (1 Ptr 2:24; 2 Co 5:15; Tts 2:10; Lk 1:74-75; Gl 5:25). Nor should we grieve the Holy Spirit (Eph 4:30; 1 Th 4:8).

II. Some motivating reasons for good works have regard to the reborn themselves. For since we are dead to sins, we ought therefore no longer walk in sins but live unto righteousness (Ro 6:2, 18; 2 Co 5:17; Eph 5:8, 11). Likewise, that we might have sure testimony that our faith is not false, feigned, or dead, but true and living [faith], which works by love (1 Jn 2:9-10; 3:6, 10; 4:7-8; 2 Ptr 1:8; Mt 7:17; Gl 5:6). And that we might not drive out faith, grieve the Holy Spirit, [and] lose righteousness and salvation (1 Ti 1:19; 5:8; 6:10; 1 Ptr 2:11; 2 Ptr 1:9; 2:20; Ro 8:13; Gl 5:21; Cl 3:6; Eph 4:30). And that we might not draw divine punishments on ourselves (1 Co 6:9-10; 1 Th 4:6; Mt 3:10; 25:30; Lk 6:37; Ps 89:31-32).

III. Some reasons have regard to the neighbor, namely that the neighbor be helped and served by good works (Lk 14:13; 1 Jn 3:16-18). That [our] neighbor might be drawn to godliness by our example (Mt 5:16; 1 Ptr 3:1). That we be not an offense to others (1 Co 10:32; 2 Co 6:3; Ph 2:15; Heb 12:15). That we might stop the mouths of adversaries (1 Ptr 2:12; 3:16; Tts 2:7-8). And it is unimportant in what order the reasons are listed because of which good works are to be done, provided the Scripture basis of this article is retained complete and pure.

193 *But what are the good works that are to be taught and performed in the church?*

Only those that God Himself has prescribed and commanded in His Word, whose sum is briefly contained and set forth in the Decalog rightly understood, that is, according to the interpretation of Scripture, which [Decalog] Scripture therefore calls the law of deeds or of works (Ro 3:27). And David describes the whole obedience of the pious in this way, Ps 119:32: I have run the way of Thy commandments.

194 *But why are not a monastic life and similar things good and God-pleasing works, since they were instituted by holy fathers and are done with good intent?*

[They are] not, for this reason: Because God wants to rule, Himself and alone, in His great house, which is the church, by commanding and forbidding consciences, as He expressly says Dt 12:8, 31.

And of self-appointed works He says: Is 1:12; 29:13; Mt 15:9; Eze 20:18-19. And Paul clearly rejects self-appointed acts of worship, though they have the appearance of wisdom (Cl 2:20).

195 *Yet Paul preached the Gospel to the Corinthians freely and without* *pay and vaunts this very thing as a notable work (1 Co 9:12, 15) even though it was not commanded by God.*

Paul had a general commandment from God to preach the Gospel in such a way as not to obstruct its way by any offense, but that he might rather by all means gain the weak (1 Co 9:22). And on the basis of this divine command, and to that end, for the sake of the church at Corinth, he taught the Gospel without pay, not in order by that very thing to establish a special *ethelothreskeia* [man-made religion] without commands of God, as he himself declares in the passage cited [cf. Cl 2:23]. This work of Paul therefore belongs to the general command of God regarding the faithful administration of the apostolic ministry, just as also the example of David playing before the ark (2 Sm 6:5) and of Mary anointing Christ (Mt 26:7) is included in divine commands.

196 *But now we are no longer under the Law, but free from the Law and dead to it (Ro 6:14; 7:4, 6). Why, then, after we have now been justified by faith, are we again subjected to required good works, contrary to the Christian freedom from the Law (Gl 5:1)?*

We are free from the Law. First, with regard to justification; namely, that good works are not to be done in this opinion, [and] to this end, as though we need them for justification and salvation, which are favors of Christ alone and are received by faith alone.

Second, with regard to curse and condemnation, because the works of believers, though they are by no means pure and perfect in this life by reason of sin dwelling in them [i.e., in the believers], yet they are not, for that reason, subject to the curse and condemnation of the Law. Ro 8:1.

Third, with regard to constraint, namely, that the Law, with the rod of its demand, ought not to extort from believers, as from unwilling people, only the outward appearance of obedience, out of harmony with inward feelings, but with the will unwilling and opposed, which Paul calls the oldness of the letter (Ro 7:6). For God requires ready obedience (Ro 6:17; 1 Ti 1:5; 1 Ptr 5:2; Ps 54:6; 100:2).

And to that extent we have indeed been made free from the Law. But when the question is asked, which the works are that God has ordained that we should walk in them (Eph 2:10), then God Himself leads us to His commands and precepts (Dt 12:32; Eze 20:19; Ro 3:27).

And as Paul is about to point out what the well-pleasing and perfect will of God is with regard to good works (Ro 12:2), he leads us to love, which is a brief summary of the Law, and then he expressly lists the commandments of the Decalog (Ro 13:9; Gl 5:14).

197 *Why is this doctrine regarding good works, which have been divinely commanded by the Law, so necessary?*

I. That all self-chosen and man-appointed acts of worship might be rejected.

II. That believers might be reminded that new obedience is not optional, but divinely commanded; it is required of us.

III. That the good works of believers might be sanctified by the Word of God, in which they are prescribed, and by the Holy Spirit, by whom they are prepared in us.

IV. That in the exercise of good works the believers might be continually reminded of their imperfections by the law of God. For in self-appointed works men easily get the idea of perfection or supererogation.

198 *Can man do truly good works by the powers of his free will?*

An unspiritual man can to some extent avoid outward sins and exercise outward discipline (Ro 2:14; 10:3; Ph 3:6). But by his own powers he can neither begin nor render true spiritual obedience. For the law of God is spiritual, and true good works consist in this, that love is out of a pure heart and a good conscience and faith unfeigned (1 Ti 1:5), that obedience is not under pressure and of necessity, but voluntary and spontaneous, out of the heart (Ro 7:22; Ps 119:14). But the Law can neither form nor give that kind of heart by urging, driving, and compelling. Nor is man's free will able to render such obedience by its own natural powers. But such works are and are called fruits of the Spirit (Gl 5:22; Eph 5:9).

199 *But how can good works be done by us, when the devil stalks us with his snares, the world is full of offenses, and sin itself dwells in our flesh?*

First of all it is necessary that the person be reconciled to God through faith for the sake of Christ. For thus the Holy Spirit is given in reconciliation itself (Gl 3:2, 14; Tts 3:5-6); He purifies and renews hearts (Acts 15:8-9; Ps 51:10; Eph 4:23; Eze 36:26); He will kindle new affections in [your] heart, that it submit itself to the Law and divine obedience (Ro 6:17; 7:22). For a tree must first be good, before good fruits come forth from it (Mt 7:18; 12:33). But after the Holy Spirit has already begun in us that work of renewal, we also can and should add our effort, by following the leadership of the Holy Spirit and mortifying the works of the flesh through the Spirit (Ro 8:13; 12:2; 2 Ptr 1:5; 2 Ti 1:6). For through these exercises God wants to preserve and increase in us His gifts by the grace, power, and help of the Holy Spirit (1 Co 15:10; Mt 25:21, 29). And what is more, for this the Holy Spirit uses as ordinary means the preaching, hearing, and meditation of the divine Word (Ps 119).

200 *Are the good works of believers welcome, acceptable, and pleasing to God?*

Of the works of the unregenerate, unbelievers, and hypocrites, no matter how good they seem, Scripture says, Heb 11:6: Without faith it is impossible for anything to please God (cf. Ro 14:23; Is 1:13; 66:3; Ps 109:7).

But of the works of the reborn and believers Scripture says, Cl 3:20: Children, obey [your] parents in all things, for this is well pleasing unto the Lord (cf. 1 Ti 5:4; Ro 12:1; Heb 13:16; 1 Ptr 2:5; 1 Jn 3:22; Eph 5:10; Ps 119:108).

201   *Are the good works of believers in this life so clean and perfect that they please God for this reason?*

With the help and operation of the Holy Spirit the reborn indeed render some inward and outward obedience, but since the Law requires complete and altogether absolute perfection from the whole heart, without any evil desire (Dt 5:21; 6:5), therefore all the saints complain that because of sin clinging to the flesh they can by no means attain that perfection in this life. Ro 7:18; Gl 5:17. For though, by God's favor, they have the will and pious intent to do good things, yet, because of sin dwelling in the flesh, evil lies near them and is fastened on them. Ro 7:18, 21; Is 64:6; Ps 143:2; Lk 17:10.

202   *Since the good works of the reborn are neither pure nor perfect, how then can they please God?*

They do not please God by reason of worthiness or perfection; but because the person has already been reconciled with God through faith, for Christ's sake, therefore to Him as to a father, the inchoate obedience of His children, such as it is, is acceptable for the sake of that same Christ, no matter how weak, imperfect, and soiled by the filth of sin still clinging to the flesh. For that which our obedience lacks in that respect is supplied and covered by the completely perfect obedience of Christ, namely in those (Ro 8:1) who are in Christ Jesus, who walk not after the flesh, but after the Spirit and acknowledge their imperfections. 1 Ptr 2:5; Ph 1:11; Heb 11:2: By faith all the saints obtained a testimony (namely regarding their deeds or works and sufferings, etc.).

The Difference Between Mortal and Venial Sin

203   *Do the remains of sin exist and remain in the reborn in this life?*

They by all means are and remain. For though [the reborn] are ruled by the Holy Spirit, yet they complain that nothing good dwells in their flesh, in fact also when they want to do good, evil is connected [with it] (Ro 7:18, 21), and that the flesh wars against the Spirit (Gl 5:17). And even also when they are holy and serve God and are not conscious of any evil, yet they confess that they are sinners. 1 Co 4:4; Ps 32:6; 130:3; 143:3. In fact, he that does not acknowledge and confess this, but says that he has no sin, deceives himself. 1 Jn 1:8. Therefore all the saints have need in this life daily to repeat this: Father, forgive us our sins.

204   *Is then David, committing adultery, nevertheless righteous and holy, and does he remain so?*

By no means. For Scriptures distinguishes between sins, namely that in the saints or reborn there are some sins because of which they are not condemned, but at the same time retain faith, the Holy Spirit, grace, and the forgiveness of sins. Ro 7:23—8:1; 1 Jn 1:8-9; Ps 32:1. But Scripture testifies that there are also some other sins in which also the reconciled, when they have fallen, lose faith, the Holy Spirit, the grace of God, and life eternal, and render themselves subject to divine wrath and eternal death unless, turned again, they are reconciled to God through faith. Ro 8:13; 1 Co 6:10; Gl 5:21; Eph 5:5; Cl 3:6; 1 Jn 3:6, 8; 1 Ti 1:19; 2 Ptr 1:9. And the useful distinction between mortal and venial sin is drawn from this basis. Paul speaks of sin ruling against conscience or with conscience put away, and sin that indeed dwells in the flesh but does not rule. 1 Ti 1:19; Ro 6:12, 14; 7:17.

205   *What is the use of retaining and earnestly inculcating this difference between mortal and venial sin in the church?*

I. That we might learn to acknowledge and earnestly avoid mortal sins.

II. If we are caught in that kind of sins, that we do not obstinately persevere and continue in them impenitently.

III. That we try the more to restrain and control sin that dwells in us, lest it become mortal. For, when this distinction is neglected or not rightly understood and used, Christians also often fall into security and impenitence. Pastors are therefore to be reminded and trained in examinations not only to list the 7 mortal (or deadly, capital) sins,[32] but to be able to point out to their hearers, in each Commandment, which sins are mortal, which venial.

Let definitions as to what is venial sin, what mortal sin, be sought from Philipp [Melanchthon's] examination and for the sake of declaration be added to these questions.

206   *Is, then, original sin, which still remains in the reborn in this life, in itself such a light little sin, or, so to say, peccadillo, that God neither can nor wants to be angry against it?*

All sins are not equal; some are more grievous and greater than others (Jn 19:11; Mt 11:22; Lk 12:47-48); yet if one judges according to the sense of the divine law, no sin per se and by its own nature deserves forgiveness; that is, none is so small and insignificant, but that it makes [one] subject to divine wrath and worthy of eternal damnation if God enters into judgment with him. Dt 27:26; Gl 3:10; Ja 2:10. This error regarding the least commandment of the divine law is condemned by Christ in the Pharisees. Mt 5:19. Paul sadly complains also about sin still dwelling in his flesh. Ro 7:24; Gl 5:17.

207   *Are some sins so great and horrible that they cannot be forgiven in the Gospel to those who repent and believe in Christ?*

No. Christ made satisfaction for all sins. 1 Jn 2:2. He wants to save also the greatest sinners. 1 Ti 1:15. He commanded repentance and remission of sins to be preached in His name to all sinners. Jn 20:23; Mt 9:13; Lk 15:7; 24:47. Grace abounded more than sin. Ro 5:20.

208   *Now, then, since it is clear that no sin per se deserves forgiveness, likewise that no sin is so horrible that it cannot be forgiven to those who repent and believe in Christ—why, then, are some sins in the reborn called venial, some mortal?*

This should be well and carefully explained, so that each Christian can know and determine if he is living in mortal or venial sin. The explanation consists essentially in this, that everyone examine himself as to whether or not he has true repentance and faith. Ro 2:4-5; Jer 5:3; 2 Co 13:5. Original sin, which still dwells in the flesh of the reborn, is not idle, but is the restless law of sin in our members, enticing, tempting, driving to sin with various suggestions and evil lusts. Ja 1:14; Ro 7:8; Gl 5:17. Since, then, one who is reborn does not delight in this kind of carnal lusts, and is neither led by them nor follows [them], but earnestly represses and crucifies them as sins and mortifies [them] through the Spirit, lest they rule or be performed (Ro 6:12; 7:15; 8:13; Gl 5:24), this very thing is a very sure sign of true and earnest repentance. And when the reborn pray that God would not impute these weaknesses to them but forgive for the sake of Christ, and at the same time believe and trust that Christ, as the true propitiation, would, in the sight of God, cover this their uncleanness with His innocence and obedience (Ro 4:7; Ps 32:1; 1 Jn 1:7; 2:1-2), this also is a sure sign of true and justifying faith. And where true faith, in earnest repentance, apprehends Christ in the Gospel, and relies on Him and is supported [by Him], there is no condemnation, but the pure grace of God, forgiveness of sins, and eternal salvation (Ro 8:1; 1 Jn 1:9; Ps 32:2). In this way there are and occur these venial sins in the reborn, for which they are not condemned, because, as Augustine says, they live under grace.

209   *But what if we indulge and delight in evil lusts and seek occasions to give them free rein (Ro 6:12; Mi 2:1; Ja 1:15)?*

Then they become mortal sins (Ro 8:13; Ja 1:15), because there surely is no room for true repentance and faith where the lusts of the flesh are served and given rein, so that they break out into action. 1 Ti 1:19; 5:8; 2 Ptr 1:9. It is the nature and particular character of true faith that it does not seek how to commit, continue, and heap up sins freely, but rather hungers and thirsts after the righteousness that releases and frees from sins. Therefore, where there is no true repentance, the Holy Spirit pronounces a very solemn sentence. Jer 5:3, 9; Ro 2:5, 9; Lk 13:3; Rv 2:5. And where there is no true faith, there is neither Christ, nor the Holy Spirit, nor the grace of God, nor forgiveness of sins, nor any salvation. Therefore what? Doubtless the wrath of God, death, and eternal condemnation, unless the fallen are turned to God again. Cl 3:6; Ro 8:13. As a result of this, therefore, and for this reason mortal sins occur in the reborn, namely when repentance, faith, Christ, and the Holy Spirit are driven out and lost.

210 *How, then, should one deal with those who have fallen into this kind of sins?*

Their sins are not to be disguised by silence, camouflaged, excused, or defended, but solemnly and earnestly censured and rebuked. Is 56:10; 58:1; Eze 13:10, 18; 2 Ti 4:2; Tts 1:13: "Reprove them sharply," in such a way that the fearful judgment of God is threatened on them; 1 Co 6:10; Gl 5:21; Cl 3:6; 1 Jn 3:15; Mt 11:21; 2 Ptr 2:10. For he that regards those people as true Christians, and charms and misrepresents them, not only miserably misleads them, but also makes himself partaker of their damnation. Is 3:12; Jer 8:11; 23:17; Eze 3:18; 33:8.

Now, the preaching of repentance, rebuking sins, is the instrument and means by which God wants to lead fallen sinners back to the way and convert them. Jer 26:2-3. But if the wicked, neglecting this means, will persevere and continue in his wickedness, he indeed shall perish, but the word of the minister shall deliver his soul. Eze 3:19.

211 *But what if the fallen rise again by the grace of God and earnestly repent?*

Then they are indeed to be received with joy and are to be restored and supported with the declaration of the forgiveness of sins. Jer 3:12; 18:8; Eze 18:21; 33:15; Mt 18:13, 27; Lk 15:7. This is what the examples of Scripture testify, e.g., Peter, David, the prodigal, the Corinthians and Galatians. And this indeed not only seven times, but seventy times seven times, Mt 18:22.

The Sin Against the Holy Spirit

212 *Since Christ solemnly declares Mt 12:32; Mk 3:29; Lk 12:10 that there is a sin or blasphemy against the Holy Spirit that is forgiven neither in this world nor in that which is to come, ought one judge or speak lightly of that kind of sin?*

In this question we must be careful not to diminish the universal promises of the Gospel, as though some sins are so great and horrible that they cannot be forgiven to the sinner, though he repent and truly believe in Christ. For this would be to deny blasphemously that Christ has made satisfaction for all sins by His passion and death; by this very thing troubled consciences are faced with a situation that easily leads to despair.

Various profane and pernicious opinions regarding this question were advanced and promoted in the ancient church. Some held that absolutely no hope of forgiveness remains for those who have fallen after baptism. Paul clearly refutes this opinion by the example of the

Corinthians and Galatians who, having fallen after baptism, again obtained forgiveness and were reconciled to God. 2 Co 2:6-8; Gl 4:19. And Christ says: If thy brother, that is, one who is a Christian, sin against thee, and repent, forgive him, not only seven times, but seventy times seven times, Mt 19:21-22; Lk 17:3-4.

The Novatians sharply contended that he who denied acknowledged truth at the time of persecution could not obtain forgiveness of sins, no matter how much he repented and sought to be reconciled to God by faith in Christ. The orthodox church condemned this opinion as false and harmful, solidly refuted on immovable grounds of Scripture, as also the example of Peter denying Christ clearly shows.

Some have also dangerously held that sins committed out of weakness are against God the Father, [and] those done in ignorance are against the Son, and those can be forgiven; but [sinful] works done deliberately, consciously, and willingly are sins against the Holy Spirit, which cannot be forgiven, even if the sinner who has fallen comes to his senses, moved by repentance, and believes in Christ. But this view conflicts with the whole doctrine of the Gospel. For the Gospel teaches

First, that Christ is the propitiation not only for our sins, but for the sins of the whole world. 1 Jn 2:2.

Second, that Christ commanded that repentance and remission of sins be preached universally to all sinners; and Mk 1:15; Mt 11:28 is a universal command.

Third, that the promise of the Gospel is universal, that everyone who repents and believes in Christ shall not be condemned but obtain eternal life. Jn 3:16.

Fourth, that the keys of the kingdom of heaven are also attached to this universal promise: Whosesoever sins ye remit, they are remitted unto them, Jn 20:23. Finally there are found in Holy Scripture the examples of Adam and David, who indeed sinned consciously and willingly, and yet the way to repentance was open to them and they obtained remission of sins by faith.

Now, then, it is clear from these reminders with what danger it is fraught to speak too discretely and minutely of that sin which, in the judgment of Christ, shall be forgiven neither in this world nor in that which is to come. And these expressions of the ancients have namely been listed here for this purpose, that pastors be warned against which views in this question they should be on their guard, and if it ever happen that afflicted consciences are disturbed by that kind of thoughts, that they might know from what sources and grounds comfort is to be drawn.

213 *But how can the sin against the Holy Spirit that is unforgivable be simply, yet truly and thoroughly described?*

The simplest and safest way is that which Augustine pointed out to us and himself followed. For he noted that since that sin is called blasphemy

106

against the Holy Spirit, it is committed against the ministry, gifts, and works of the Holy Spirit. But since repentance unto remission of sins is preached also to them that resist the Holy Spirit (Acts 7:51; Lk 24:47), and Stephen also prays for them (Acts 7:60), Augustine points out that for that sin to be so against the Holy Spirit that it cannot be forgiven, final impenitence must be added, since, namely, a man perseveres and dies in it without repentance (Book 1, Retract. ch. 19; Serm. 11[33] on the words of the Lord; in Enchirid. ch 83; and Epist. 50). Therefore we can thus judge a posteriori very correctly and surely regarding that sin against the Holy Spirit that is not forgiven, namely since God makes known His righteous judgment against the man that goes astray in such sin and dies without any repentance.

And from this the ancients drew useful and salutary doctrines, warnings, and exhortations, namely, that not all sins that are committed against the ministry and operations of the Holy Spirit are by that token unforgivable. For many of those who have resisted the Holy Spirit, and have grieved and vexed Him, have later been converted and saved by the grace of God. Yet by and large the sins by which one resists the ministry and work of the Holy Spirit are much more serious and dangerous than other sins, and that for this reason, that we can be set free from other sins by the power of the Holy Spirit, namely when He, through His ministry and operation, arouses and kindles true repentance and faith in our hearts, by which we obtain forgiveness of sins; but as long as those who resist the ministry of the Holy Spirit and His work persist in that stubbornness, no way to obtain forgiveness of sins can be open to them. Moroever, the sins that oppose the ministry and work of the Holy Spirit are listed by the ancients in this order, that we may learn to avoid and beware of them:

I. Presumption regarding the mercy of God or regarding impunity to sin[34]; e.g., when someone, relying on mercy, sins freely, falsely persuaded that he will not lose his salvation, though he impudently continues indefinitely in sins without repentance and conversion and perishes in his stubbornness.

II. Obstinacy, when a man, with a hard and impenitent heart, rejects and despises exhortations to repentance and admonitions from the Word of God, in obstinate malice willing neither to hear nor to obey, [but] rather the more he is admonished, the more he is hardened and made worse. Likewise, when he does not acknowledge sins as sins but rather excuses, defends, and glories in them.

III. Attack on acknowledged truth, when someone who knows the acknowledged truth of the divine Word and knowingly violates, injures, and opposes conscience, and in Pharisaic hatred ascribes the work of the Holy Spirit to the devil.

IV. Despair, if one altogether despairs of the grace of God and his salvation, no matter how much it be offered to him in Christ through the Word and sealed through the Sacraments.

V. Envy of brotherly grace, when someone, out of ill will and violent hatred, envies his neighbor and brother the grace of God, the gifts of the Holy Spirit, and salvation in Christ.

VI. Final impenitence, when a man, obstinately persisting in sins, dies without conversion and repentance.

In short, since the Holy Spirit works repentance, faith, and renewal through the ministry of the Word, if someone, then, despises, abuses, blasphemes, and persecutes the Word of God, or impudently hinders and destroys the work of the Holy Spirit, who wants to arouse repentance, faith, and new obedience in us, he sins against the ministry and work of the Holy Spirit. And that kind of people are to be solemnly and sharply rebuked and warned with how much danger these sins are connected. And if some of these repent and are converted by the grace of God, one must by no means hold or say that sins cannot be forgiven them. Moreover, since the sins by which one resists the ministry and work of the Holy Spirit have this special and characteristic [mark], that they harden the heart of man and make it obstinate, as Scripture testifies of Pharaoh; and God, in His just judgment, usually censured them for the most part, by forsaking, hardening, [and] blinding them, and giving [them] over to a reprobate mind (Ro 11:8; Jn 12:40), it happens that few, after they have persisted in these sins, return to a sounder understanding and are converted. Cf. Tts 3:10-11. Yet since God, according to His boundless mercy sometimes leads also these back to the way and converts [them], and it is not for us to prescribe limits to His most gracious will, surely as long as there is time and it is the day of salvation, we neither ought nor can lightly charge anyone with the sin that is unforgivable. But if someone remains in this kind of sin to the end of life, unmoved by repentance and dies thus, the sentence of divine judgment revealed in the Word declares that it was a sin or affront against the Holy Spirit, and that of such a kind that it is forgiven neither in this world nor in that which is to come; that is, (as Chrysostom says), which is to be avenged in this life by hardening, in the other with eternal fire. Cf. Heb 6:4-6; 10:26-27, 29. These passages mean: For those who, after they once have been enlightened and made partakers of the Holy Spirit, knowingly and in obstinate wickedness again deny the acknowledged truth and completely fall away from Christ, and so persevere therein that, as it were, they crucify Christ anew, regard [Him] as a joke, and tread [Him] underfoot, and insult the Spirit of grace—for those, I say, there remains no remission of sins, but the prospect of the judgment of God and of eternal fire. For they do not return to repentance, and without Christ there remains no offering for sins. For thus are these rather difficult passages of the Epistle to the Hebrews explained by the context itself.

The Sacraments of the New Testament in General

214   *What is a Sacrament in the New Testament?*

Philipp Melanchthon gives this definition: It is a divinely instituted rite, added to the promise given in the Gospel, so that it becomes a testimony and pledge of the promise of grace that is set forth and applied.

215   *What things are required, as essential parts, to make a Sacrament in the New Testament?*

Two. First, an outward or visible element or sign in a certain outward ceremony or act, ordained and instituted in the New Testament by Christ by a special word and express command and committed to the whole church to the end that it be used to the end of the world.

Second, the word or promise of grace joined to the element in that act—namely that the Sacraments were instituted by Christ for this purpose and use, that through them as outward means and visible testimonies He wants to set forth, apply, give, confirm, and seal individually to those who use them in true faith, the promise of grace which is at other times proclaimed and offered in the Gospel to all in general.

216   *For what reasons did Christ add the Sacraments to the Word?*

So that our weak faith be sustained and preserved in this way. For our mind cannot so easily assent to the sole and bare Word and firmly rely on it. For though, when the general promise of the Gospel is heard, one indeed in general does not mistrust it, yet in the matter of a conscience troubled, and disturbed by temptations, one usually falls into doubt as to whether that general promise belongs and pertains also particularly to him and whether he can and should also apply it personally to himself. Therefore Christ, who is rich in mercy, instituted outward and visible sacraments to help our infirmity on this point; through them, as testimonies that are open and strike the eyes, He Himself wants to deal with us and thereby, as by a very sure seal and pledge testify that He truly applies, confirms, and seals the promise of the Gospel individually to those who use these sacraments in true faith. Doubtless the Son of God works effectively through these His sacraments in believers, strengthening and preserving faith in them. The error of the Sacramentarians is therefore properly rejected; they hold that the Sacraments are only mere signs that do not present but only signify or remind.

217   *Is our faith also necessary for a Sacrament?*

As to the essence of the Sacraments, the faith or unbelief of those who administer or those who use the Sacraments adds nothing to them and takes nothing from them, since they are acts of God that rest on His word. For not our faith but the Word, institution, ordination, and power of God creates and makes a Sacrament. But when one asks how and whom the Sacraments profit, so that as we use [them] we might receive not only their substance but also [their] fruit, usefulness, and efficacy unto salvation, there our faith is absolutely necessary; it apprehends, accepts, and applies to itself the grace offered also in the Sacraments as it is in the Word, as Scripture testifies Mk 16:16; 1 Co 11:29.

218   *How many sacraments of that kind are there in the New Testament?*

Properly speaking there are only two, Baptism and the Lord's Supper. These two have the essential parts required for a Sacrament, namely an outward sign or element instituted and commanded by Christ and the promise of grace, namely that it should be applied and sealed to believers through these sacraments.

219   *Is absolution also a sacrament of the New Testament?*

Absolution indeed has one mark characteristic of the Sacraments, namely that the universal promise of the Gospel is applied and sealed individually to each believer through absolution. And in view of this mark, some are not wrong in that they number absolution among the sacraments of the New Testament. But since no outward sign or element was ordained and instituted by Christ for its administration, it cannot properly be called a sacrament in the way in which Baptism and the Lord's Supper are called sacraments. Yet *logomachiai* [wars about words] are not therefore to be stirred up, provided the thing itself, taught in Scripture, is kept pure, as the Apology of the Augsburg Confession teaches.

220   *Why do we not count seven sacraments with the papistic church?*

Because most of those called sacraments by the papists lack the essential parts that properly belong to the essence of a Sacrament in the New Testament. Thus matrimony is indeed divinely instituted and ordained, but does not have such an outward sign added by command of God as the nature of a Sacrament demands. Nor is matrimony such a means and instrument by which the promise of salvation is applied. But you say that Paul calls matrimony a sacrament, and even a great sacrament, Eph 5:32. I reply: Paul does not call matrimony such a sacrament as Baptism is, and the Lord's Supper, but a mystery, and that in Christ and His bride, the church, namely that conjugal union is a figure of that mysterious union of Christ and the church.

221   *But at the laying on of hands of the apostles the Holy Spirit fell on the believers (Acts 8:17; 19:6). What, then, keeps confirmation from being a Sacrament, since it has an outward sign and the promise of the Holy Spirit?*

Besides the other gifts of miracles the apostles had also this one, that at the laying on of their hands they not only healed the sick (Mk 16:18), but the Holy Spirit was also conferred on the believers under the outward and visible form of such gifts as tongues and prophecy (Acts 19:6). But this prerogative given to the apostles to confirm doctrine was only temporary. In the divine Word we have neither any command by which we are enjoined to follow that example of the apostles nor divine promise that God wants to send, give, and confer the Holy Spirit by the laying on of our hands. In fact, the chrism of the papists rests much less on either such a word or command or promise.

222 *But why is ordination of ministers of the church not a Sacrament, though the apostles laid hands on those called to the ministry and through that laying on of hands necessary gifts were conferred on ministers (1 Ti 4:14; 2 Ti 1:6)?*

No doubt the legitimate call and ordination of ministers of the church is established by the Word of God and confirmed with the promise of divine blessing; and that affords very sweet comfort. But ordination does not have this promise, that he who wants to obtain the grace of God and eternal salvation must be invested with the holy priesthood. For also many who have prophesied will hear this fearful sentence of Christ on that day: I never knew you; depart from Me, etc. (Mt 7:23). And besides, the laying on of hands has no express command in the Word of God, but the apostles used that ceremony as a thing indifferent, for the sake of public prayers.

And unction, which the papists practice in ordaining elders, has neither any command nor promise in the Scripture of the New Testament; but, contrary to the Word of God, it reduces the ministry of the New Testament to the shadows of Levitical ceremonies. Since, then, the ordination of ministers of the church lacks both the element and the promise of grace, both of which are required for the essence of a Sacrament in the New Testament, it neither is nor can be called a true sacrament.

223 *But what do you hold regarding extreme unction, whose element is set forth in the Word of God (Mk 6:13; Ja 5:14) and which has the added promise of forgiveness of sins (Ja 5:15)?*

The apostles and others in the primitive church were equipped with that gift, that they might heal the sick by miracles (1 Co 12:9). And for that purpose they sometimes used the laying on of hands (Mk 16:18) and sometimes anointing with oil (Mk 6:13). But since that miracle, as also the rest, has now ceased in the church after the doctrine of the Gospel was confirmed, we lack both command and promise regarding that extreme unction on the basis of the Word of God. And James does not ascribe forgiveness of sins to the oil, but to the prayer of faith (Ja 5:15). The papists also do not anoint with their consecrated oil the sick who they hope can recover, but those that are already about to die, and that not to the end that they might be restored to health, but that by that extreme unction sins might be forgiven to those that are about to die. This, which is not only beyond but also contrary to the Word of God, is both said and taught.

Baptism

224   *What is Baptism?*

Luther answers: It is not simple water only, but that which is included in the divine command and connected with the Word of God.

Philipp Melanchthon: Immersion[35] in water was instituted by the Son of God with the declaration of the words: I baptize thee in the name of the Father, and of the Son, and of the Holy Spirit, testifying that since this testimony was divinely instituted, he who is immersed with the declaration of these words is reconciled to God for Christ's sake and is sanctified by the Holy Spirit to life eternal.

225   *What are the essential parts of Baptism?*

I. The element of water (Jn 3:5; Eph 5:25-26; Acts 10:47).

II. The Word of God (Eph 5:26: Cleansing with the washing of water by the Word—namely the command of Christ regarding the conferring of Baptism, Mt 28:19, and the very promise of grace, Mk 16:16). For that word of the command and promise of God is a true consecration or sanctification by which Baptism becomes a clean water (Eze 36:25), in fact a water of life (Eze 47:9; Zch 14:8) and a washing of regeneration (Tts 3:5).

226   *Is it also Baptism when the words of institution are spoken over the element of water, and yet there is no one who is baptized?*

By no means. For when Christ says, Baptize them, He surely wants and commands that Baptism be an act in which someone is baptized with the water that is connected with the Word of God. And therefore Paul also calls Baptism a washing (Eph 5:26; Tts 3:5). But Baptism was not instituted that either bells or other creatures but that nations (Mt 28:19), that is, those who have been born of flesh (Jn 3:6), be baptized for remission of sins (Acts 2:38).

227   *In the administration of Baptism, why is not the general statement (baptize all nations) used, but: I baptize thee?*

For this reason, namely, that this is distinctive of the Sacraments, that by them everyone is dealt with personally and specifically (Acts 2:38), so that in this way everyone of the believers might have in his heart as a sure testimony, pledge, and seal that the promise of grace is specifically offered and applied to him (Gl 3:27; 1 Ptr 3:21; Acts 2:38).

228   *What is the meaning of these words: I baptize thee in the name of the Father, and of the Son, and of the Holy Spirit?*

First, [this] is signified, that Baptism is administered in the name, that is, on command, of God the Father, and of the Son, and of the Holy Spirit.

Second, [this] is indicated, that we are baptized in the name, that is, in, or with, invocation, of the true God, or as the Greek words say, into the name, that is, into the knowledge and invocation, of the true God, who is the Father, Son, and Holy Spirit.

Third, this above all is the thrust of those words, that in the administration of Baptism a minister does not function in his own name, but that God the Father, Son, and Holy Spirit, Himself present, deals through the outward ministry with the one to be baptized, so that God the Father, because of the merit of the Son, receives him into grace and sanctifies [him] by the Holy Spirit unto righteousness and life eternal, so that in the name is the same as in the stead and place of God the Father, Son, and Holy Spirit, as Paul says in that same passage regarding the preaching of the Gospel and absolution (2 Co 2:10; 5:20).

229 *Is God the Father present in Baptism?*

He certainly is present. And that not only in the mode of presence by which He is present everywhere and fills all things, but in such a way that through this washing, He saved us according to His mercy, that, being justified by His grace for Christ's sake, we might be made heirs of eternal life through the Holy Spirit (Tts 3:5; 7). Likewise, God the Father is present in Baptism in such a way that in it He establishes a covenant of a good conscience between Himself and us through Christ (1 Ptr 3:21).

230 *Is the Son of God present in Baptism?*

Paul clearly affirms that, saying in very beautiful words, Eph 5:25-26: Christ gave Himself for the church, that He might sanctify it, cleansing it with the washing of water by the Word. Likewise, he says that we are baptized into the death of Christ (Ro 6:3) and into the resurrection of Christ (1 Ptr 3:21). In fact, in Baptism we put on Christ (Gl 3:27). And this is what is said in Acts: to be baptized in the name of Christ.

231 *Is the Holy Spirit also present in Baptism?*

We are born again of water and the Spirit, that we might enter into the kingdom of God (Jn 3:5; Tts 3:5-7).

And on this basis people are to be instructed and taught, so that they do not consider and regard Baptism as only a human work, but as the work of God, namely that in it the entire holy Trinity is present and deals with the poor sinner through that outward ministry, so that He cleanses him from sins, delivers [him] from death, Satan, and eternal damnation, and instead gives [him] righteousness and eternal salvation.

232 *What is the benefit, power, or efficacy of Baptism?*

The words of institution of Baptism and many other passages of Scripture show us this, e.g., Mk 16:16; Acts 2:38; 22:16; Eph 5:25-26; Tts 3:5, 7; Jn 3:5; 1 Ptr 3:21. Hence Luther rightly says in his Catechism: Baptism works forgiveness of sins, delivers from death and the devil, and gives eternal salvation to all who believe this, as the words of divine promise declare.

233 *But these benefits certainly depend on the merit of the obedience and passion of Christ. Are men, then, to be diverted from Christ and brought to Baptism instead of to Him?*

If Christ is separated from Baptism, or Baptism from Christ (as the Sacramentarians do), then indeed the washing of water can of itself work or confer none of these things, but it is and remains only a simple sign. But since Christ is in and with the act of Baptism, so that we are baptized into His death and resurrection (Ro 6:3; 1 Ptr 3:21), in fact, in Baptism we put on Christ (Gl 3:27), and He Himself cleanses us by this washing (Eph 5:25-26), likewise, since God the Father imparts, presents, and seals to believers the merit of Christ through His Holy Spirit in Baptism and through Baptism (Tts 3:5-6), therefore neither water nor the act of the minister performs and works the things that are predicated of Baptism, but God the Father, Son, and Holy Spirit Himself, through Baptism, as through the ordinary means ordained and instituted by God Himself for this purpose. Therefore, far from being diverted from Christ by Baptism, we by it, as by the ordinary means, are led to Christ and grafted in [Him] (Ro 6:4-5; Mk 10:14). For salvation has indeed been procured and accomplished by Christ on the cross, but in Baptism and through Baptism it is distributed, applied, and sealed to believers (Mk 16:16).

234 *How long does that salutary effect of Baptism and fruit of comfort last?*

Through a man's whole life on this earth, in fact unto life eternal (Mk 16:16). Likewise, we are born again in Baptism, that we might be made heirs of eternal life according to hope (Tts 3:7); cf. Eph 5:26-27; this is indeed begun in this life, but finally completed in the life to come. And it is indeed a very sweet comfort that through all of this life Baptism becomes for us the figure of a very firm pact and public testimony that we have been made partakers of the merit of Christ in such a way that we can at all times seek and draw continual comfort from it, as Paul comforts the Galatians on the basis of Baptism once received, when they repented after falling (Gl 3:27).

235 *But what if one who is baptized rejects repentance and loses faith?*

The salutary fruits of Baptism, of which we have spoken, are apprehended, retained, and preserved by faith. Mk 16:16. Therefore, where there is no repentance, and no good but only evil fruits follow, there certainly is no true and saving faith, as was pointed out above. Likewise, he that either does not seek or does not retain the grace of God in Christ, but spurns and rejects it, he does not have true faith. And though such have been baptized, yet they are under this sentence of divine judgment: He that does not believe shall be condemned.

236 *If, then, someone falls away from the covenant of Baptism and later is converted anew, is there no longer any comfort left for him on the basis of Baptism?*

The papist teach that the ark of Baptism is so dashed to pieces and completely destroyed by sin against conscience that it cannot be repaired, and therefore those who repent are not to return to the covenant of

Baptism, but are to seize a second plank, namely of repentance and our works, by which we might escape the depth of perdition. But God forbid that our unbelief make the faith of God of no effect (Ro 3:3-4; 2 Ti 2:13). And God does not want the basis of grace, entered with us by Baptism, to consist in this, that if we break faith He also will not keep faith, even if we repent and return to it. But, as the ancients have well said, Baptism is rather the door by which we are admitted and received to fellowship and participation in the merits of Christ, so that we might continue therein, or if we fall therefrom, that we might have access and a way back to that covenant of grace, in true repentance, through faith, continually, while it is still today. And Jeremiah describes in very comforting words in all of Jer 3 how much God commends His grace to us in this very thing.

237   *Is Baptism, then, to be repeated as often as we fall?*

By no means. For the covenant that God made with us in Baptism is an everlasting covenant (Is 55:3). And Baptism is a seal that testifies that God will continually keep the covenant of grace once made with us whenever and as often as we return to it. It is therefore not necessary to repeat Baptism as often as we are converted after a fall, as also in the Old Testament those who fell did not repeat circumcision at conversion but returned in earnest repentance through true faith to the covenant of grace that God had made with them in circumcision. Thus Paul did not rebaptize the Corinthians and Galatians who were again converted to God after a fall, but directed them to the covenant and comfort of Baptism once received. 1 Co 6:11; 12:13; Gl 3:27. It is indeed written regarding the Lord's Supper: As often as ye do this, etc. But no commandment like this is connected with Baptism: As often as ye are baptized, etc.

238   *Does Baptism, because of the comfort regarding forgiveness of sins and salvation, also have more effects and benefits?*

The chief benefit and comfort of Baptism is that of which we have spoken so far. But Paul mentions in addition also another effect of Baptism. For he says, Tts 3:5: Baptism is a washing, first, of regeneration, namely that we, who by nature were children of wrath, are reborn of water and the Spirit, so that, for Christ's sake, we might be children of God. Second, he says that it is a washing of renewing of the Holy Spirit.

239   *In what, then, does this renewal consist?*

Paul indeed briefly but thoroughly covers and describes this whole process of renewal Ro 6:4 ff., where he says, first, that we, being planted by Baptism in the death of Christ, are also buried with Him into death, namely that the power and efficacy of the death of Christ not only forgives us sins, but also begins to crucify, mortify, and bury sin in the flesh, in the baptized, by the Holy Spirit, that it should not reign in our body, and we should not obey its lusts, but that the body of sin might be destroyed. Second, he says that through Baptism we are also made partakers of the resurrection of Christ, namely that through it the Holy Spirit renews the mind, that we put on the new man, who is created according to God in righteousness and holiness of truth (Eph 4:24).

240   *How are exhortations to newness of life to be drawn from Baptism?*

By the example of Paul, Ro 6:3-4, 6, 11-12. For just as God made with us a covenant of grace and a good conscience in Baptism, so we also, on the other hand, promised Him that we would die to sin and live to righteousness. for this reason the renunciation in the act of Baptism was given this form of question and answer: Do you renounce the devil? Answer: I renounce, etc. It is therefore a horrible sin impudently to violate that covenant. For thus we hinder and destroy the work of the Holy Spirit, who works renewal in us. But all believers can, in fact should, confidently implore and entreat the Holy Spirit by a certain right of Baptism, as it were, to mortify the works of the flesh in them and cleanse and renew their hearts more and more.

241   *Are the effects and benefits of Baptism immediately complete and finished in the baptized?*

Regeneration indeed, that is, adoption and the forgiveness of sins is complete and finished in believers immediately after Baptism, and yet it nevertheless extends through the whole life of a man. But renewal is indeed begun in Baptism and grows daily, but is finally completed in the life to come. For in this [present] life renewal is still imperfect and should grow and increase from day to day. 2 Co 4:16; Eph 4:22-23; Cl 3:10; 1 Ptr 2:1-2.

242   *Are infants to be baptized?*

Yes. For baptism of infants was always observed in the Christian[36] church from the time of the apostles and was defended and approved against heretics on the basis of the Word of God, as the very ancient writers Irenaeus, Cyprian, Origen, Ambrose, Augustine, and Chrysostom testify.

243   *Does infant baptism have basis in the Word of God?*

Yes. For Christ declares regarding little children, Mt 19:14; Mk 10:14: Of such is the kingdom of heaven, or the kingdom of God. And no one who is born of flesh can enter the kingdom of God unless he is reborn, Jn 3:3. And this regeneration and rebirth takes place by water and the Spirit, Jn 3:5. For Baptism is the washing of regeneration of the Holy Spirit, Tts 3:5. Since, then, Christ wants little children to become partakers of the kingdom of heaven, and that must take place through Baptism, it is surely Christ's meaning, will, and command, that little children be baptized. For the promise of the kingdom of God must be applied through a certain means or instrument instituted by God Himself. For the promise without application profits no one. Therefore also the promise of the kingdom of heaven, which is given to infants (Mk 10:14) must be applied to them through a certain means. Now, Scripture declares that this means is

Baptism. Jn 3:5; Tts 3:5.

Second, Christ also wants infants to be saved, for He says: It is not the will of the heavenly Father that one of these little ones should perish, Mt 18:14. But the heavenly Father saved [us] by the washing of regeneration, Tts 3:5. It is therefore the will of God that infants be baptized and that they do not perish, but be saved.

Third, infants are conceived and born in sins, so that by nature they are children of wrath, Ps 51:5; Eph 2:3. Therefore they must obtain forgiveness of sins, so that they do not perish but be saved, Lk 1:77; Ro 4:7. But Baptism is the divine means by which sins are forgiven and washed away, Acts 2:38; 22:16.

Fourth, Christ wants and commands little children to be brought to Him, that He might bless them, Mk 10:14, 16. Now, one asks: How is this done? And Scripture declares that they who are baptized put on Christ in Baptism, Gl 3:27. For they are baptized into His death and resurrection, Ro 6:3; 1 Ptr 3:21. Christ cleanses and sanctifies the church, for which He gave Himself, through the washing of water by the Word, Eph 5:26. And this very thing is true blessing, Gl 4:14; Eph 1:3. It follows, therefore, that Christ's command is that infants be baptized.

Fifth, Baptism of the New Testament succeeded circumcision of the Old Testament, Cl 2:11-12. Therefore, just as in the Old Testament the covenant of divine grace was applied and sealed through circumcision not only to adults but also to infants, Gn 17:10, 12, so also now in the New Testament that grace should rightly be applied and confirmed as by a seal both to infants as well as adults through Baptism, since the grace of God was made not less but rather more abundant and richer in the New Testament.

Sixth, Is 49:22 prophesies that in the New Testament not only adults would be implanted in the church, but behold, he says, they shall bring your sons in [their] arms and your daughters shall they carry on [their] shoulders. And Peter says Acts 2:39 after he had baptized adults: This promise was made to you and to your children. In this way also the apostles baptized entire households, Acts 16:33; 1 Co 1:16. But where a household or family is mentioned infants are surely not excluded.

It is therefore clear and manifest from this that the doctrine of infant baptism is not only orthodox but also altogether useful and necessary and gives very sweet comfort to parents and children.

244 *But Christ joins teaching and baptism, saying: "Teach and baptize." Are infants, then, not to be baptized because they cannot be taught?*

It is apparent from the Gospel account that the apostles were also offended and disturbed by this question. For when little infants without bodily infirmity were brought to Christ, they [the apostles] thought within themselves: "Wait! Those little children are too young to receive either Word or teaching; what, then, can Christ do with them in the

117

matter of salvation?" They therefore did not want to let those little children annoy Christ by being brought [to Him], but they held that for them one should wait until they have grown up and become teachable. But Christ deals indignantly with their presumption and says with an oath that He can and will deal also with that kind of children brought to Him, so that they also can become partakers of His blessing and of the kingdom of God. Mt 19:14-15; Mk 10:14-16; Lk 18:16-17.

By Mt 29:19 ("Teach and baptize") He therefore did not mean what the Anabaptists imagine, but He meant this, that the Word and the Sacraments should be associated in the church. For it is a washing of water by the Word, Eph 5:26. Where the Gospel is not taught, there Baptism should also not be administered. But where the Gospel is proclaimed, parents are taught that that promise of grace is intended also for their children, Acts 2:39. So, then, sons in arms and daughters brought on shoulders[37] should be brought to Christ; Christ wants to confer His blessing and the kingdom of God also on them. Mk 10:14-16.

Therefore, just as in the Old Testament both was commanded, to teach and to circumcise, and adults were first taught, then circumcised (Gn 17), but infants were circumcised first (Gn 17:12) and taught later, at a time when they were old enough to understand and ask questions (Dt 6:20; Ex 12:26), so also does the whole ministry of the New Testament consist in the Word and the Sacraments. And when adults are first converted, teaching precedes and Baptism follows. Acts 2:41; 8:12, 35-38; 10:44-48. And regarding the infants of Christians, the same order of teaching and baptizing is observed as was of old followed in the Old Testament in teaching and circumcising. For what circumcision was in the Old Testament, the same is now Baptism in the New Testament. C 2:11-12. Thus John, writing to children of believers, that they might know the heavenly Father, gives [them] this comfort first, that they have forgiveness of sins through His name, 1 Jn 2:12-13; this applies to them since they are baptized in the name of Christ for the remission of sins, Acts 2:38; for that promise pertains also to little children, Acts 2:39; Is 49:22.

245   *But it is written: He that believes and is baptized, etc. Now, since faith is by hearing, how then can infants believe?*

Christ expressly says that infants that are brought to Him obtain and receive the kingdom of God, that is, forgiveness of sins, grace, and eternal salvation, Mk 10:14; Lk 18:16. And He adds: "Verily I say to you, Whosoever shall not receive the kingdom of God as a little child, he shall not enter therein." But they that receive and possess the kingdom of God, these are properly in the number or assembly of believers. For without faith no one can please God, Heb 11:6; and he that does not believe shall be condemned, Mk 16:16. Hence also circumcision, which was performed also on little children, is called the seal of the righteousness of faith, Ro 4:11. Therefore there is no doubt that the Holy Spirit is given also to infants in Baptism. He works and effects this in them, that they receive the kingdom of God, though we cannot understand and conceive the nature of that divine work. For Baptism is a washing of regeneration and of the renewing of the Holy Spirit, who is shed abundantly on the baptized, that, being justified, they might be made heirs of eternal life, Tts 3:5-7. And the example of John the Baptist in [his] mother's womb shows that the Holy Spirit can perform His work in infants also before the use of reason. Lk 1:41.

246 *Do the Sacramentarians teach correctly that the children of the baptized and believers are children of God and heirs of life eternal also before Baptism and without Baptism?*

This is an ancient error that Augustine condemned in the Pelagians and refuted *De baptismo parvulorum,* Book 2, ch. 25 and 26; in defense of their error they misapplied the same passage as the Calvinists vaunt, 1 Co 7:14, even though in that passage only this point is made, that a believing wife can in good conscience live with an unbelieving husband and bear him children. For to the pure all things are pure, Tts 1:15. But Paul roundly and without distinction declares regarding all things that we bring with us when we are born into this world, Eph 2:3: We were by nature children of wrath; namely, not only they that are begotten of heathen parents, but also we, says Paul, who have been born of circumcised parents. For that which is born of the flesh is flesh and cannot enter into the kingdom of God, unless it is born again of water and the Spirit, Jn 3:5-6. The promise of grace surely applies also to little children, Gn 17:7. But there must be an application of that promise, so that little children are brought to Christ, Mk 10:13; Is 49:22. It has been shown above that this very thing takes place in Baptism and through Baptism.

247 *Are, then, the children of believers who die before birth or in birth damned?*

By no means, but since our children, brought to the light by divine blessing, are, as it were, given into our hands and at the same time means are offered, or it is made possible for the seal of the covenant of grace to be applied to them, there indeed that very solemn divine statement applies: The man-child, the flesh of whose foreskin is not circumcised on the eighth day, his soul shall be blotted out from [his] people (Gn 17:14). Hence the Lord met Moses on the way and wanted to kill him, because he had neglected to circumcise [his] son (Ex 4:24-26). But when those means are not given us—as when in the Old Testament a male died before the eighth day of circumcision—likewise when they, who, born in the desert in the interval of 40 years, could not be circumcised because of daily harassment by enemies and constant wanderings, died uncircumcised, Jos 5:5-6, and when today infants die before they are born—in such cases the grace of God is not bound to the Sacraments, but those infants are to be brought and commended to Christ in prayers. And one should not doubt that those prayers are heard, for they are made in the name of Christ. Jn 16:23; Gn 17:7; Mt 19:14. Since, then, we cannot bring infants as yet unborn to Christ through Baptism, therefore we should do it through pious prayers. Parents are to be put in mind of this, and if perhaps such a case occur, they are to be encouraged with this comfort.

The Lord's Supper

248   *What is the Lord's Supper or the Sacrament of the Altar?*

It is the true body and the true blood of our Lord Jesus Christ under the bread and wine, for us Christians to eat and to drink, instituted by Christ Himself for His remembrance.

249   *What are the essential parts of this Sacrament?*

One usually and rightly answers: Word and element. But these must be rightly explained. For, first, to the essence of this Sacrament belong the outward elements of bread and wine (for in the cup that Christ took there was the fruit of the vine, Mt 26:29). These elements are taken according to the institution and are separated from common use for the purpose of this Sacrament. Second, the word of institution of this Sacrament is added to those elements. And by virtue of that Word that which is present, offered, and received in the use of this Supper is not only bread, not only wine, but the body of Christ, which was given for us, and the blood of Christ, which was shed for us for the remission of sins. And what is more, the Word is added to the elements not only in the way in which Christ spoke it once at the first Supper, but as Paul says, 1 Co 10:16: The cup of blessing which we bless, namely through the words of Christ which we repeat in the administration of the Lord's Supper and thus connect the bread and wine with the word of institution, so that in that Sacrament we have neither the element alone, nor the simple Word, but, as Luther says, the word is clothed in the element, and the element connected with the Word.

250   *Is the bread changed into the body of Christ, so that it altogether loses its own substance?*

The particular character of this Sacrament requires that there be two distinct things or substances which, joined by sacramental union, make one complete Sacrament, even as in the one person of Christ there are two complete and distinct natures. For all antiquity uses this comparison. But Paul mentions bread and wine also after the blessing, 1 Co 10:16; 11:27. Likewise the fathers also taught the same. In order to testify that they do not approve the papistic transubstantiation, they also usually used these terms, namely that in, with, and under the bread and wine the body and blood of Christ are present, offered, and received.

251   *But when consecration has been performed, as they say, or the words of institution have been recited over the elements, are the body and blood of Christ present, even if the elements are neither offered nor received, but are laid up, enclosed, or carried about?*

Christ did not institute this Sacrament in such a way that, even if no one uses it, or if it is changed into something else than He Himself commanded, it nevertheless is His body and blood, but in the very words of institution He prescribed the form of that which was commanded, how it is to be observed and used, and that not only for a time but to the end of the world, 1 Co 11:26. And use surely does not make a Sacrament, but the Word, ordinance, and institution of Christ. And there is a difference between the essence of a Sacrament and its use. But Christ so ordered and arranged the words of institution in the form of a testament, as He wanted this Sacrament to be an act in which bread and wine are taken, blessed, or consecrated, as they say, then offered, received, eaten, and drunk. And Christ says of that which is blessed, which is offered, received, eaten and drunk: This is My body; this is My blood. Therefore when the bread is indeed blessed but neither distributed nor received, but enclosed, shown, and carried about, it is surely clear that the whole word of institution is not added to the element, for this part is lacking: He gave [it] to them and said, Take and eat. And when the word of institution is incomplete there can be no complete Sacrament. In the same way it is also not true Baptism if the Word is indeed spoken over the water, but if there is no one who is baptized.

252   *How is this Sacrament to be offered and used, under one or under both kinds, as they say?*

Christ certainly instituted not only one kind. But first He took bread. Then, after the same manner He also took the cup, after He had supped. And that command (this do) was attached with equal force by Christ to the cup, 1 Co 11:25, and to the bread, Lk 22:19. In fact, with regard to the cup the universal clause is added: Drink ye all of it, Mt 26:27; likewise, And they all drank of it, Mk 14:23.

253   *But perhaps Christ granted His church this power, that it might be allowed later to change this His institution and arrange it in a different way, as Paul seems to refer to it, 1 Co 11:34: "The rest will I set in order when I come."*

Paul expressly says that he had received a command from the Lord, that the act of the Lord's Supper be celebrated in the way in which the institution ordered it, by eating, drinking, and showing forth the Lord's death until the Lord Himself would come to judgment at the end of the world. And he adds that it is not the Lord's Supper if it is not celebrated according to this prescribed order, 1 Co 11:20-21. Therefore when he says: "I will arrange the rest when I come," it does not mean this, that he wanted to change or mutilate the Lord's institution, but he speaks of adiaphora and things indifferent. For since Christ instituted His Supper in the form of a testament, it is also not allowed at another time to distort even a man's covenant, if it is confirmed, by adding or subtracting. How much greater sin it is, therefore, to change or mutilate the testament of the Son of God, Gl 3:15.

254 *But to be sure Christ did not have the seventy disciples, or His mother, or the rest of the women, as laymen, at His first Supper, but only His twelve disciples, whom He was to appoint priests.*

Paul says that he had received of the Lord that he was to give the ordinance and command regarding the use of both kinds not only to priests but to the whole church of God, men and women alike, 1 Co 11:23. What is more, he wrote that epistle not only to the Corinthians, but to all that in every place call upon the name of the Lord, 1 Co 1:2. This is the true and sound explanation which Christ wants understood when He says: "All of you eat [and] drink of this."

255 *But Paul, 1 Co 11, does not use these words: "All of you drink of this."*

Paul did not think it necessary to repeat those words, because they are set forth with greatest care by the rest of the evangelists. But he specifically says of both kinds, 1 Co 11:26: "As often as ye eat of this bread and drink of this cup etc." And lest anyone think that it is optional for us to use either one or both kinds, he immediately adds a command, 1 Co 11:28: "But let a man examine himself, and so let him eat of that bread and drink of that cup." He directs this command not only to priests but says: "Let a man examine himself." Perhaps the papists want to deny that laymen are men.

256 *But the Christian[38] church, which is the pillar and ground of truth, ordained that only one kind be offered to laymen.*

This is falsely ascribed to the true church. For the true Christian[38] church hears the voice of its chief shepherd and follows it, Jn 10:27. The primitive church of old always offered the Lord's Supper to laymen under both kinds, and it sharply rebuked those mutilators who introduced the use of one kind, as the accounts show. But in very late times also that decree about forbidding the other kind was established and thrust on laymen, besides other abuses and abominations of the papistic church at the Council of Constance, against the express command of God and the practice of the whole ancient and primitive church.

257 *But the body of Christ, as being alive, is not without blood. Therefore, when the body of Christ is received under the bread, isn't His blood also received, even if the use of the other kind is omitted?*

We should not, on the basis of the judgment of our smart-aleck reason, which Scripture declares is not only blind, but blindness itself, in divine things, take the testament of the Son of God to ourselves to reform and change [it], as though, in the night in which He was betrayed and instituted His Supper, He was not rational enough to know that a living body does not exist without blood; but we should rather take our foolish reason captive to the obedience of His infinite wisdom, and in simple obedient faith we should believe His word and obey [His] command. He does not say and command that we should eat His blood, but that we should eat His body, but drink His blood from the cup of blessing; if we very simply obey that command, there is no danger of any error to fear.

258 *Are the body and blood of Christ present in the Lord's Supper?*

Yes. For the Son of God, the Truth itself, says of that which is offered and received in the Supper: "This is My body; this is My blood."

259 *But are there various opinions regarding this question?*

Some say that the body of Christ is present there only as in a sign.

Others hold that only the power or efficacy and merit of the absent body of Christ are present.

But others affirm that the true and essential body of Christ is present there.

260 *What, then, is the true position? Or is everyone free to believe what he wants regarding this question, without risking [loss of] salvation?*

In the night in which He was betrayed, Christ instituted and ordained His most holy Supper in the form of His last will. Now, it is a violation of civil law, in fact a crime, if someone wrests and twists the testament of a good and honest man beyond and contrary to its meaning. It is a very much greater and [more] grievous offense to do anything to the testament of the Son of God by changing or perverting its words, especially since Paul says: "He that does not discern the body of the Lord," of which the words of the Supper speak, "eats and drinks judgment[39] to himself," 1 Co 11:29. The words of the Supper are known, plain, and clear in their natural and true sense. When I ask, "What is present in the Lord's Supper and offered by the hand of the minister and received by the mouth of those who use it? Is it only bread and wine?" He, who is Truth itself, answers: "This is My body; this is My blood." Thus Paul says, 1 Co 10:16, that a breaking and communion, that is, distribution and partaking or receiving takes place in the Lord's Supper, and that it takes place by outward eating and drinking with the mouth, for he says, "Eat and drink." Now, if I ask: "What is distributed and received when the bread is distributed and received in the Lord's Supper?" Paul answers that it is *koinonia*, that is, distribution and reception of Christ's body, etc.

261 *But many Scripture passages must be interpreted and understood differently than the words sound. Why, then, is it not permitted to explain and take also those words of the Supper differently than they sound, either as of a sign or of the power of the absent body of Christ, or of spiritual eating?*

Holy Scripture is not of any private interpretation, 2 Ptr 1:20. But it explains and interprets itself. For this reason the same statement or teaching is repeated for the sake of explanation in various passages of Scripture, either in the same or in other words. Thus the institution of the Supper is set forth not only in one Scripture passage, but is repeated in four passages. If, then, Christ had wanted those words to be taken and understood differently than as they sound in their proper and natural meaning, He would surely have given some indication of that in one of the stated passages. But the words of institution are found repeated in those individual passages in such a way, that it is clear that eating and drinking are to be understood of the reception that takes place with the mouth of the body. And which body and which blood He means He Himself explains by repeated statement, saying: This is My body (namely that one), which is given for you, and, This is My blood (namely that), which is shed for you. Now, Christ gave not a sign, or power and efficacy of [His] absent body for us, but the same true and substantial body that was conceived by the Holy Spirit and born of the Virgin Mary. If, then, you want to know from Christ Himself, who instituted this Supper, who is Truth itself, and whom the Father commended to us from heaven to hear, what it is that is present in the Supper in, with, and under the bread and wine, and that is offered by the hand of the minister and received by the mouth of the body, He answers expressly, clearly, and plainly: This is My body, which is given for you; this is My blood, which is shed for you.

262   *But how can the body of Christ and His true blood be present at the same time in those countless places where the Lord's Supper is celebrated, and be received by us with the mouth?*

If in matters of faith only the things are to be received and believed that we can either conceive with our mind or perceive with the senses, our whole faith would immediately collapse on all points. But faith is of the things that are revealed and taught by the clear Word of God, though they seem impossible to us (Lk 1:34, 37), though they seem foolish in the eyes of the world and our reason (1 Co 1:18, 23; 2:14), and though they are not seen (Heb 11:1), things, in fact, in which our mind is to be brought into captivity (2 Co 10:4-5). Since, then, the Lord's Supper is a great mystery, and is not to be judged on the basis of our reason, but is rather to be received by faith in the fear of the Lord according to His Word (whence the ancients call this Sacrament a great and tremendous mystery), we should simply accept in faith what Christ, the mouth of Truth, unable to lie or deceive, says and declares. But how it can be we commit to Him who instituted this Supper, to whom is given all power in heaven and on earth (Mt 28:18).

263   *But Scripture testifies that Christ, according to His human nature, was in all things except sin made like unto [His] brethren (Heb 2:17). And it is not the natural and essential character of a true human body to be present at the same time and at once in many places.*

It is without all doubt very true that Christ, according to [His] human nature, was made like unto [His] brethren in all things. But certainly, if according to that nature He is capable of nothing beyond or more than the extent of the natural or essential properties of a human body, surely His blood also will not be able to cleanse us from our sins (1 Jn 1:7). Nor will we have redemption and righteousness in His blood (Cl 1:14; Ro 5:9). Nor shall we be healed with His stripes (1 Ptr 2:24). And, in short, His passion and death will also not be satisfaction for our sins. One must therefore believe both, even as Scripture attests both: first, that Christ, according to the human nature, was in all things, like unto us His brethren; second, that, because of the personal union with the divine nature, His human nature is so exalted above all things that can be named (Eph 1:20-21), that to Him, also according to the human nature, is given all power in heaven and on earth (Mt 28:18), and that all things are given into His hand (Jn 3:35; 13:3) and all things are made subject under His feet (Eph 1:22). Therefore, since He said, This is My body, this is My blood, though the natural and essential attributes of a human body cannot do this, yet He can, to whom is given all power in heaven and on earth, also according to the human nature (Mt 28:18).

264   *But doesn't this teaching conflict with the articles of our faith: He ascended into heaven, from whence He shall come etc.?*

No. For Christ indeed, in His body, according to the true and natural way and particular character of [His] body, visibly and locally ascended to heaven, even as He shall return thence in the same way to judgment (Acts 1:9, 11; Mt 24:30). But that He did not know or have at His disposal another, heavenly mode, by which He might be present in the Supper in His body and blood—this specific thing the articles cited above do not declare, but rather teach and confirm the opposite. For the articles of our faith declare that Christ ascended to heaven in His body not like little birds, leaving the surface of the earth, sit in the top of a tree, nor like Elias was taken up into heaven, but in such a way that He sat down at the right hand of God the Father almighty. Now, the right hand of God is not a circumscribed place, or a particular seat or region in heaven by which Christ is limited, circumscribed, and enclosed. But Scripture calls it the right hand of the majesty and power of God, which fills all things (Ps 139:7-10) [and] to which Christ is exalted according to the human nature, above every principality, power, dominion, and every name that is named, not only in this world, but also in that which is to come (Eph 1:21; 1 Ptr 3:22), so that all things are subject to Him also according to the human nature (Ps 8:6; Eph 1:22; Heb 2:8; 1 Co 15:27; Mt 28:18; Jn 13:3). Should He, then, not be able to do with His body and blood what He declared and ordained in express and clear words in His testament? In fact, the articles cited above completely attest the true and essential presence of the body and blood of Christ in the Supper, according to the natural and essential attributes of a human body, yet since He declares

[it] who ascended into heaven with His body in such a way that He sat down at the right hand of the majesty and power of God the Father Almighty, it would be horrible blasphemy either to say or think that it is impossible for Him and cannot be in any way. And on the basis of this consideration one can see the nature of the sect of the Sacramentarians.

265   *Is the body of Christ to be offered to God the heavenly Father as a sacrifice in the Lord's Supper?*

Christ offered Himself to the Father once (Heb 7:26-27; Eph 5:2). But in His Supper He did not institute an offering or sacrifice, in which we offer something to God, but a Sacrament, in which He wants to offer, give, and bestow on us the highest and most precious treasure, namely His body and blood, with all the benefits obtained by their giving and shedding.

266   *What, then, is one to hold regarding the sacrifice of the papistic mass?*

That is is the greatest abomination of abominations.

267   *How so? On the other hand many by no means impious things are sung and said in the papistic mass.*

That they sing and read some things from the Psalms [and] from the writings of the prophets, evangelists, and apostles in the papistic mass, likewise that the Introit, Tracts, Sequences, [and] Collects that are genuine are used in its performance, and that Prefaces, the Patrem,[40] Sanctus, Agnus, etc. are sung, is neither impious in itself nor is that the abomination of the mass of which we speak, though also in these parts the papists have their abuses, namely, first, that they sing and read those things in the presence of uneducated people in a language not known [to them], contrary to the statement of Paul 1 Co 14:19; second, that they are done in the opinion of *opus operatum*,[41] as though they are worship pleasing and acceptable to God, though they are done without all feeling of piety and devotion, whereas Scripture teaches to the contrary (Mt 15:8-9; Jn 4:24); finally, that they often intermingle with and insert into that action the invocation of saints, contrary to the express word of God.

But the real abomination of the papistic mass consists above all in the canon, by which the Lord's Supper is transformed into a propitiatory sacrifice for the sins of the living and the dead.

268   *But nearly all the fathers call the action of the Lord's Supper a sacrifice.*

The true use of the Supper, and that which was instituted by Christ Himself, is, that it be celebrated in memory or commemoration of the only propitiatory sacrifice, which Christ accomplished once on the cross, that is, in thanksgiving and praise of the Lord's death; and that we use it worthily, in true faith, with penitent heart, and fruits of love that follow; and for this very thing ardent prayer is necessary. Scripture calls all these things spiritual offerings, or spiritual sacrifices (1 Ptr 2:5; Heb 13:15-16; Ps 4:5; 50:14, 23; 51:17, 19; 116:17; 141:2; Ph 4:18; Ro 12:1). And Paul calls the ministry of the Gospel, to which also the act of the Lord's Supper belongs, a spiritual sacrifice (Ro 15:16). And in that sense and respect the fathers well call the act of the Lord's Supper a sacrifice.

269 *Of what nature is the sacrifice of the papistic mass?*

The papists are not very much concerned about true and spiritual sacrifices, of which the fathers speak, as has just been pointed out. But this it is, for which they contend so greatly, namely, that when the officiating priest in the very act or canon of the mass carries on with various gestures, with elevating and lowering the blessed bread and wine and moving it here and there throughout the words of the canon—that this very action of the officiating priest is the kind of work by which Christ is offered anew to His heavenly Father in a propitiatory and expiatory sacrifice by which divine grace, forgiveness of sins, and every kind of benefit are acquired and obtained not only for those who are present at the mass, but also for the absent, in fact also for the dead for whom those masses are usually celebrated.

270 *Why, then, is that action of the mass so great an abomination?*

I. Because there is only one propitiatory or expiatory sacrifice, which Christ alone offered to the Father by giving [His] body and shedding His blood once on the altar of the cross for a sweet-smelling odor, in such a way that it might be a perfect and complete sacrifice to all eternity (Eph 5:2; Heb 7:27; 9:12, 26, 28; 10:10, 14).

II. Because Heb 10:1-2 affirms that if one and the same sacrifice is repeated from time to time, this is a testimony and evidence that the former sacrifice was insufficient.

III. Because a propitiatory sacrifice cannot be made without passion, death, and shedding of blood (Heb 9:7, 22, 25-26). And hence it is clear how great and how execrable an abomination the officiating priest performs in the work and sacrifice of his mass, over against which a pious and Christian man ought properly shudder wholeheartedly in horror.

271 *But since we sin daily, have we also need of daily reconciliation?*

That single expiatory sacrifice, which Christ brought once on the altar of the cross, is a perfect, sufficient, and complete propitiation for all sins of all time, 1 Jn 2:2; Heb 9:12; 10:14. We therefore have no need of another or new propitiatory sacrifice, but this only is required, that that one sacrifice of Christ is applied to us, so that we be made partakers of its fruit and power. But for this there is no need of some special outward sacrifice, but the Gospel and the institution of the Supper show us in what way that application and sealing takes place.

272 *What, then, is the true and salutary use of the Lord's Supper?*

When the ordinance and command of Christ are observed, namely that we eat His body and drink His blood, and do that in remembrance of Him, that is, with a penitent heart and in true faith. For a twofold eating and drinking is required for the salutary use of this Supper, namely sacramental and spiritual, and it is prescribed for us by Christ Himself. The sacramental is that which is done with the mouth of the body and is expressed in these words of Christ: Eat, this is My body; drink, this is My blood. But the spiritual is, and is called, that which takes place in solemn repentance, through true faith, by which we apprehend and apply to ourselves all the benefits that Christ merited and purchased by giving His body and shedding [His] blood for us. And Christ speaks of this spiritual eating when he says: This do in remembrance of Me.

273   *How often is the use of this Sacrament to be repeated by Christians?*

Christ did not want the use of this Sacrament to be bound either to a certain time or to certain days, except that Paul says that the Lord's Supper is to be celebrated when the church gathers to commemorate the death of the Lord, 1 Co 11:18-26. But it is certain that God wants us to use this Sacrament not only once, as we are baptized once, but often and frequently, 1 Co 11:26. For Paul has this in mind, that the Lord's Supper followed in place of the paschal lamb of the Old Testament. And the paschal lamb was indeed eaten on a certain day and that only once a year. But on the other hand Paul says of the Lord's Supper: As often etc.; with this term he wants to indicate that the use of this Sacrament is neither bound to a certain day, nor yet should it be only annually or by way of anniversary, like the eating of the paschal lamb, but often and frequently.

Therefore, you ask, how often would be enough to have been a guest of this Supper? It is not for any man to give a specific answer to this, either with a number or with a certain measure, other than as often as a troubled conscience feels and recognizes that it needs those benefits that are offered in the Supper for comfort and strengthening. Consciences are therefore not to be forced but aroused to frequent use of this Supper by earnest admonition and by consideration of how necessary [and] likewise how salutary and profitable the use of this Supper is for us. But he that does not attend this most holy table thereby clearly shows that he is a Christian in name rather than in fact, namely that he is one who neglects and despises the command of his Savior, who says: Eat, drink, and do this as often etc.

274   *What benefits or fruit does the true use of this Sacrament confer?*

One can reply briefly: It is profitable for strengthening of faith. But this must be explained more fully, and it cannot be done better than with the words of institution, thus:

I.   Remission of sins and salvation consists in this, that we are partakers of the merit of Christ and are included in the New Testament covenant of grace. Christ offers us the greatest token and surest seal of this in His Supper, namely that very same body of His, by whose offering these great benefits have been bought, and that very same blood, by whose shedding the New Testament was confirmed, so that we might be made sure and strong against all temptations by this most precious pledge, that the communion of the good things accomplished by the death of Christ most certainly applies also to us.

II. The promise of the Gospel in general offers grace to all believers, so that everyone might surely conclude that this universal promise applies specifically also to him and that this grace is offered and presented to him in such a way that he can safely rely on it and rejoice in it. In the true use of this Sacrament, Christ Himself offers and gives to every individual His body and blood, by the means ordained for this, beamed at every individual with this personal invitation: "Take, eat and drink; this is My body given for you; this is My blood [shed] for the remission of your sins."

III. Remembrance of the death of Christ, which consists in true repentance and faith, must be preserved, strengthened, and increased in us. But it is easily weakened, quenched, and lost as a result of manifold wiles of Satan, stumbling-blocks of the world, and the weakness, security, and wickedness of our flesh. Therefore Christ, in order from time to time to renew and strengthen it in us, ordained a salutary and very efficacious remedy in this His Supper, namely the reception of His body and blood, adding, "Do this in remembrance of Me."

IV. Since, alas, we often fall from the covenant and pact of grace through sins against conscience, therefore, so that in true conversion we might have sure and special evidence, besides the general Word, that God, [who is most gracious,] is willing to receive us anew into that covenant of grace, Christ says in His Supper: Take and drink, this cup is the New Testament in My blood. And these very same words (This is the New Testament) are a kind of very sure pledge that this will come to pass, that we are firmly kept and preserved by the power of God in that grace unto salvation.

V. Since nothing good, but only sin, dwells in our flesh, whence extremely many evil fruits continually sprout and come forth, therefore Christ, in His Supper, offers us His most holy body and blood, so that, engrafted by this communion as branches in Him who is the true vine, we might draw thence new, good, and spiritual sap. Thus we are also joined most closely by this communion with other Christians as members of the one body of Christ (1 Co 10:17), so that mutual love toward the neighbor is kindled, increased, and preserved in us.

All these things are thoroughly and aptly set forth in the words of institution. He that rightly and seriously considers these things will experience in deed how much comfort a troubled conscience will receive from the frequent use of this Sacrament.

And if this doctrine is constantly and earnestly emphasized, constraint will not be necessary, but believers in Christ will stir themselves up to a frequent use of this Sacrament. But he that has no concern or care for these things, he, by that very fact, bears witness that he is not a Christian.

275   *But do all that use this Sacrament receive and obtain the salutary fruit that we have now set forth?*

Paul says, 1 Co 11:27 and 29: They that eat and drink unworthily, eat judgment[42] to themselves and become guilty of the body and blood of Christ.

276   *Therefore much depends on the kind of heart and attitude with which one approaches this Sacrament?*

Absolutely! For it is a crushing verdict, to become guilty of the body and blood of the Lord. Therefore Paul says: "Let a man examine himself," namely [as to] how he eats of this bread and drinks of this cup. And people are to be diligently admonished regarding this examination both in public discourses and in the private conversation of confession.

277   *Who, then, are they that eat and drink unworthily in the Lord's Supper, so that we might learn to guard the more carefully against that unworthiness?*

That unworthiness does not consist in this, that we miserable sinners are unworthy of that heavenly food. For that food is prepared and intended especially for sinners. But the following are they that eat unworthily, as one can very clearly gather from Paul, 1 Co 11:

I. They that do not discern the body of the Lord, that is [they] that do not hold that the very sacred food of this Supper is the body and blood of Christ, but handle and use it with no greater reverence and devotion than other common foods.

II. They that continue in sins without repentance and have and retain not the intent to lead a better life, but rather to continue in sin, as Paul rebukes this very thing in some Corinthians. For such people make a mockery of the very bitter passion of our Lord, as though sin were, as it were, something trivial, and not so great an abomination, by reason of which the Son of God suffered such an ignominious death. In fact, he that comes to that holy table in this spirit regards Christ as a patron of sin, as though in the Supper He supplies fuel for the fires of sin with His body and blood and wants to nourish and strengthen it. And therefore they eat unworthily.

III. They that come to this Supper without true faith, namely they that either seek the grace of God, forgiveness of sins, and eternal salvation elsewhere than alone in the merit if Christ, or who, steeped in Epicurean security, hunger and thirst, with no true desires, after righteousness, that is, the grace of God in Christ, reconciliation, and salvation. For he that does not believe will be condemned, though he uses the Word and the Sacraments.

278   *What, then, do the unworthy eat and drink in the holy Supper?*

Just as our worthiness does not make or constitute a Sacrament, so does no man's unworthiness nullify, or invalidate, a Sacrament. For a Sacrament is not based on our faith but on the Word and divine institution. Since, then, the same Word speaks in the same way to Peter and to Judas, Take, eat, this is My body; drink, this is My blood—it follows very surely that Judas, though unworthy, yet just like Peter, received not only simple bread or wine, but at the same time also the body and blood of Christ, Peter indeed to salvation, but Judas to judgment.[43] And Paul declares that the unworthy become guilty not only of bread and wine alone, but of the body and blood of the Lord. And he adds that they become guilty of it because they do not discern, but eat unworthily. It follows, therefore, that also the unworthy take and eat the body of the Lord, but unworthily, and so become guilty of the body of the Lord, because they eat it unworthily. In this sense also Augustine says: The faith to which an individual is disposed does not affect the completeness or truth of a Sacrament, but it is very important for the way of life.

279 *But since life itself dwells in the body of Christ, what kind of cause of death can then exist for those that eat unworthily?*

That does not result from this, that the Lord's body per se is a deadly poison, but that they who eat unworthily sin against the body of Christ by Epicurean security and impenitence, and do it wrong by their unworthy eating, and, as it were, tread [it] underfoot. For thus they become guilty of that body in which life itself dwells, like Judas, who betrayed that body—like the Jews, who tried to bury it with stones—like Pilate, who condemned it with a death sentence—like the soldiers who scourged and crucified that body of life. For life is indeed in the flesh of Christ, but it does not work life in unbelievers but only in believers, just as also the Gospel is an odor unto life for believers, but for unbelievers [an odor] unto death (2 Co 2:15-16). And power is given to Christ not only to quicken believers, but also to judge unbelievers (Jn 5:21-22).

280 *How, then, should a man examine or look into himself, so that he might eat and drink worthily in the holy Supper?*

This worthy eating does not consist in a man's purity, holiness, or perfection. For they who are healthy do not need a doctor, but they who are not healthy (Mt 9:12). But, by way of contrast with the unworthy, one can understand very easily how that examination or exploration is to be undertaken, namely:

First, let the mind consider of what nature the act of this Supper is, who is present there, [and] what kind of food is offered and taken there, so that one might prepare himself with due humility and piety for its reception.

Second, let a man about to approach the Lord's Table be endowed with the kind of heart that seriously acknowledges his sins and errors, and shudders at the wrath of God, and does not delight in sin, but is troubled and grieved [by it], and has the earnest purpose to amend [his life].

Third, that the mind sincerely give itself to this concern, that it might not perish in sins under the wrath of God, and therefore with ardent desire thirst for and long for the grace of God, so that by true faith in the obedience, passion, and death of Christ, that is, in the offering of [His] body and shedding of His blood it seek, beg, lay hold on and apply to itself the grace of God, forgiveness of sins, and salvation. He that examines and prepares himself in this way, he truly uses this Sacrament worthily, not unto judgment,[44] but unto salvation. And though all these things are still weak, infirm, and sluggish, yet one should not for that reason abstain from the holy Supper. Rather on the contrary, this very reason will rouse and impel us the more to partake of it more frequently, especially since we know that the Son of God gradually kindles, increases, and strengthens repentance and faith in us more and more through this means. For this medicine has been prepared and provided for the sick who acknowledge their infirmity and seek counsel and help.

281   *With what outward reverence is this Sacrament to be observed in [its] true use?*

Since bread per se is and remains bread, and likewise wine, surely divine honor is not to be conferred on the elements. But if the heart truly believes according to the words of institution that Christ is present in that action and offers and distributes to us His body and blood, [then] outward rites joined with all reverence and honor, as is proper and as it becomes Christians, will follow of themselves. But let the chief concern be with what kind of heart we come to this Table of the Lord. For otherwise it is Pharisaic hypocrisy if we simulate reverence with outward rites, but the heart is far away (Mt 15:8).

Absolution

282   *What does Christ call the keys of the kingdom of heaven?*

The ministry of the Word itself, in which and through which, by divine command and power, sins are bound and retained to the impenitent and unbelieving (Mt 16:19; Jn 20:22-23).

283   *Why does Christ attach to the ministry the name keys of the kingdom of heaven?*

To indicate that the preaching of the Word is not a vain and useless babbling of words, but that the Holy Spirit is present in this ministry, is efficacious through it, and wants, by this means as with a kind of keys, the kingdom of heaven to be unlocked and many to be brought into it. Therefore ministers of the Word should, by this term, since they hear that the keys of the kingdom of heaven have been given and entrusted to them, bestir themselves to speak the doctrine of sin, repentance, faith, forgiveness of sins, new obedience, etc., not coldly and lightly, nor only in general or superficially, as a story, but set it forth and apply it to their hearers faithfully and diligently, sure that the Holy Spirit wants to kindle,

132

increase, strengthen, and preserve repentance, faith, and new obedience in the hearts of the hearers through this their ministry. This name also encourages their spirits, that their labor is not in vain in the Lord (1 Co 15:58). But if ever in the ministry they bind and retain sins to the impenitent, according to the Word of God, with threat of divine wrath and curse, they should know that this is regarded as valid and certain also in heaven. In the same way, if they loose and forgive sins by proclaiming the grace of God to the penitent and believing, they should be sure that it is not only good words (as is commonly said), but that the same is also certain and confirmed in heaven (Mt 16:19). Similarly the name keys should admonish the hearers not to despise the Word and ministry and regard it as a vain sound of words by which only the ears are struck, but that they might know and be firmly persuaded that if they want to enter the kingdom of heaven, the approach and entrance is not given and granted to them except through these keys. And if they notice that something is lacking in repentance, faith, new obedience, etc. in themselves, they should remember that the Holy Spirit wants to supply and increase the things that are lacking in them by this means and instrument. So also, when they are censured and rebuked by the exhortation of the Law, let them not think that they are vain warnings that can be shaken off, like dust from a garment; but let them know, if they continue in impenitence and unbelief, that whatever is bound in this way on earth, the same is also bound and retained in heaven. On the other hand, when they hear the promises of the Gospel set forth for believers on the basis of the Word of God, let them not think that they are only words, and that of a man; but let them consider and firmly believe that it is the voice of the Holy Spirit Himself, bringing comfort to our hearts through this means, and that whatever is loosed on earth in that way is loosed and forgiven in heaven by God Himself, because it is done through the keys of the kingdom of heaven. It should therefore be earnestly set forth and often considered why Christ wanted to speak in this way about the ministry: "I will give unto thee the keys of the kingdom of heaven."

284   *How, then, are sins bound and loosed? Only in general? or only privately or in particular?*

Scripture testifies that this is done in two ways:

I. In public address, when, on the basis of the Word and according to the Word of God, sins are rebuked in general and the wrath of God and eternal damnation threatened to them who continue in sins without repentance. For though a minister of the Word does not know who is guilty of which sins, and does not rebuke them in particular and by name, yet they are bound and retained in the sight of God by that general address to the impenitent and unbelieving (Lk 10:10-12; 13:3, 5; Acts 13:46, 51; Eph 5:5-6; 2 Th 1:8-9). In the same way, when, after a preceding exhortation to repentance, the promise of the Gospel is set forth in general and to all, one apprehends it in his heart in true faith and applies it to himself, let him surely believe the more firmly that God forgives and remits sins to him in this way. Thus we read of the use of the key that unlocks in general: Acts 3:19; 4:12; 10:43; Lk 10:6.

1. But since the wicked are often not at all moved by that general use of the binding key, God ordered and ordained that the binding key be used also in particular and applied to individuals who clearly are impenitent or obstinate, but with this order observed, that the sinner first be privately reminded of his wickedness and the judgment of God and called to repentance. Then the same admonition should be repeated with some witnesses drawn in. But if this course leads to no effect, let it be told to the church, and let the binding key be used against such a person in the name of the whole church (Mt 18:15-17; 1 Co 5:1-5). Let this be done in order that the spirit may be saved, the sinner become ashamed and repent, and the rest fear to commit such great sins (1 Co 5:5, 2 Th 3:14; 1 Ti 5:20). Thus we read of the binding key used against Cain (Gn 10:4-12), Canaan (Gn 9:25), Simon Magus (Acts 8:20-21, 23), Elymas (Acts 13:10-11), the incestuous one (1 Co 5:1-5); likewise against others (e.g., 2 Th 3:14; 1 Ti 1:20). In the same way also that general preaching of the Gospel often does not satisfy a troubled and disturbed conscience, nor does it give that comfort that suffices to strengthen weak and feeble faith; therefore that [conscience], troubled and hesitant regarding individual application because of its unworthiness, is troubled above all by this doubt in temptations: perhaps those blessings and divine promises are not intended for you, since [you are] unworthy and defiled by many sins, but God passes another sentence on you in heaven. In order, then, that consciences might have thorough, sure, and strong comfort in temptation, Christ not only taught the Gospel in general but also proclaimed forgiveness of sins privately to individual penitents (Mt 9:2; Lk 7:48, 50; 19:9; 23:43). And Christ committed this private or special use of the unlocking key also to His ministers, with the added promise: Whatsoever ye shall loose and forgive on earth shall be loosed and forgiven in heaven (Mt 16:19; 18:18; 10:22-23). And this use of the unlocking key is commonly called private absolution.

285 *What, then, is private absolution?*

When a minister of the church, or, in case of necessity, any Christian, sets forth the comfort of the Gospel not in general, but proclaims forgiveness of sins on the basis of the Word of God privately in particular to a sinner who seeks the grace of God in Christ in earnest repentance and true faith, so that he absolves him of his sins in the name of Christ and pronounces him forgiven; Christ has promised to be present with His Spirit in this act (Mt 18:20; 28:20; Jn 20:22-23). He Himself [i.e. Christ] also through this means truly offers, gives, applies and seals forgiveness of sins to a troubled conscience, with the added promise that whatever is forgiven and loosed on earth in this way is forgiven and loosed also in heaven (2 Co 2:10; Mt 16:19).

But if one should diligently explain how much comfort comes to a troubled conscience from this, namely that I might know from this where I ought to seek and might find Christ my Lord, so that He might deal individually and separately with me, a very vile sinner, through the Word, and I may be allowed to hear that very sweet statement and comfort as immediately from Him: Son, be of good cheer, thy sins are forgiven thee; go in peace (Mt 9:2; Lk 7:50). Moreover, private absolution also effects this, that I have no need to dispute anxiously and with concern within myself what God thinks or decides about me in heaven, inasmuch as I can become the more sure about that matter through private absolution here on earth, so that I ought not doubt at all that it is valid in heaven also. And the Holy Spirit wants to be present in that very act (Jn 20:22-23) and strengthen and preserve faith through the Word. And for these reasons private absolution is justly to be both exalted and often and freely used.

286 *Are, then, all to be equally absolved regardless, be they penitent or impenitent? or is it in the discretion and power of the minister to bind and loose howsoever and whomever he will?*

By no means. But Christ says, Jn 20:21: As the Father has sent Me, so also send I you—namely that you administer the keys of the kingdom of heaven not according to your will or as it seems good to the world (Jn 6:38; 7:16), but according to the command and will of God (Jn 8:28; 12:49). Therefore, whom God binds in His Word, him the minister of the Word also should bind. On the other hand, whom God absolves, him the minister of the Word also should pronounce forgiven. But where God Himself does not bind or does not loose, there the minister also should not assume that power for Himself. But God does not absolve the impenitent and unbelieving but binds them in His just judgment (Jer 5:6-7; Lk 13:3; Jn 3:36). It therefore remains also for the minister to use, not the loosing, but the binding key against such people. On the other hand, God does not bind, but dismisses with forgiveness the sinner who heartily repents and in true confidence seeks the grace of God in Christ (Eze 33:14-16; Lk 15:10; cf. the story of the prodigal son, etc.). The minister of the Word should therefore do the same, not binding, but remitting sins to him (Mt 18:21-22; Lk 17:3-4).

287 *But how will a minister of the Word become clear regarding the true repentance and faith of a sinner?*

For that reason and for that purpose examination and exploration in private confession is observed in our churches with those who seek absolution and are about to approach the Table of the Lord.

288 *But the auricular confession of the papists is, at least in my opinion, null and void as a miserable torture of consciences and all out of harmony with the Word of God.*

The teaching of the papists regarding confession has chiefly three errors that conflict with the Word of God.

First, that in it there is required a full and express enumeration of each and every sin in the presence of a priest, with this notion added, that the sins that are not recounted to the priest cannot be forgiven.[45]

Second, that it is taught that by this work of confession, or by this recounting of sins, the one who confesses merits forgiveness of sins.

Third, that this recounting of sins is demanded of them for this purpose, that those who hear confession might, as spiritual judges, impose on those who make confession fitting and sufficient satisfaction by which they might atone for and expiate their sins, according to the measure of their offenses. Since all these things rest on no Scripture foundation, but diametrically conflict with it, therefore that auricular confession of the papist is justly rejected and abrogated in our churches.

289 *Yet is some kind of confession to be retained in the church?*

Holy Scriptures speak of threefold confession:

The first is that which is made to God, namely when the whole church, and everyone it in, confesses his sins individually to God with a humble and contrite heart and asks forgiveness (Ps 32:5; 1 Jn 1:9; Ps 106:6; Dn 9:4-7; Ez 9:6, 15; 10:1-3, 10-12).

The second [is] that which is made in brotherly reconciliation with [one's] neighbor, namely when he who has injured or offended [his] neighbor acknowledges and confesses his sin and asks forgiveness of the sin and reconciliation (Mt 5:23-25; 18:15; Lk 17:4; Ja 5:16).

Third, Scripture also testifies that, in the early church, before they that were to be baptized were admitted to Baptism they made a confession publicly or privately; one can gather from this that they were moved by serious repentance and sought Baptism in true faith (Mt 3:5-6; Lk 3:12; Acts 2:37-38; 8:36-38; 19:18). Thus David confessed his sins before absolution (2 Sm 12:13). So also the woman who was a sinner (Lk 7:38, 48). And Zacchaeus (Lk 19:8-9).

And hence there was introduced and received into practice both public and private exploration in the ancient church. And our churches also retain that kind of confession. For none are received to the Lord's Supper, unless they first, by general confession, attest their repentance and faith to the pastor of the church, who on that occasion also enters into private discussion with individuals. And this very thing, moreover, is observed in our churches for this purpose and for these reasons:

I. That from this kind of confession and private discussion pastors might note whether the hearers rightly hold and sufficiently understand the necessary parts of doctrine, and if they perceive that they still lack something in this matter, that they might thus have occasion to inform them more earnestly and better from the Word of God.

II. That in this way they might explore whether they that desire to be admitted to the Lord's Supper are moved by true repentance and at the same time teach them more precisely what sin is and what its reward [is]; likewise what things are required for true repentance and how they are to be rightly engaged in.

III. That in this way they might inquire and learn who believes what, [and] how, how seriously [and] with and through whom they seek remission of sins; where there is opportunity at the same time, to instruct and teach the unlearned more precisely what the nature and character of faith is, and likewise to remind them to learn to examine themselves whether they be in the faith (2 Co 13:5).

IV. That by that private exploration they might be able to determine what kind of intent to improve they have individually, and on that occasion diligently impress on them for what reasons new obedience is necessary and in what it consists.

V. That by that service they might, with salutary counsel and comfort from the Word of God, help pious consciences that are either pressed by temptation or troubled by some scruple; and that can be done best in that kind of private conversation.

Finally, the rite of private confession is retained and used in our churches chiefly for the sake of absolution, namely so that it might be rightly and salutarily sought, received, and used in earnest repentance and true faith.

Since these individual benefits, now enumerated, are of greatest importance and lack neither divine Word nor command, it is therefore clear and plain that this rite, namely as it is observed in our churches, rests on their foundations and [that] they are firm and drawn from Scripture. If these are rightly explained to the pious, they will of their own accord and by themselves present themselves for that confession, and there will be no need of any constraint. For that very benefit in itself will invite and attract them. Indeed the pastors themselves will also be reminded thereby how and why that private discussion is to be undertaken. As for the rest, the time of private confession is in our churches mostly connected with the Lord's Supper, so that no one might knowingly be admitted to it unworthily without true self-examination and bring judgment and damnation on himself. People are individually exhorted by pastors in private confession to examine and search themselves diligently and at the same time instructed why that should be done. All who are pious will understand that this is very important.

Prayer

290   *Is a Christian free to pray or not to pray?*

No. It is God's will and command that children of God call on God their Father, and that not only once or twice, but without ceasing (1 Th

5:17-18; Lk 18:1; 1 Ti 2:1; Dt 6:13 [and] Mt 4:10; Ps 50:15; Mt 7:7). In fact, they that do not call on the name of the Lord are regarded as Gentiles (who are an abomination in God's sight and on whom He has determined to pour out His wrath), Ps 14:3-4; Ps 79:6 and Jer 10:25. On the other hand, calling upon God's name is ascribed to the true church and to the saints of God as a kind of mark, 1 Co 1:2.

291   *What do you call prayer or invocation of God's name?*

Not this, when people only mutter many good words with the lips [but] without thought, meditation, and devotion (Mt 6:7; 1 Co 14:19; Is 29:13; Mt 15:8).

But that indeed is true prayer, when we pour out our heart before God (Ps 62:8; 25:1-2; 86:4; 143:8) and, coming thus to the throne of grace (Heb 4:16), address, with filial submission and true devotion of heart, God our Father, who is present and hears (Gl 4:6) and, both stirred up by His command and relying on [His] promise, set before Him our troubles and desires, in true faith, through and for the sake of Christ seeking mercy, grace, and help in the things that belong to His glory and are necessary, useful, and salutary for us (Heb 4:16; Jn 16:23-24) or give Him thanks for blessings received, and praise and glorify His name (1 Ti 2:1; 1 Co 14:16).

292   *What kinds of prayer are there?*

St. Paul classifies and enumerates them very simply in the following passages: Ph 4:6; 1 Ti 2:1; 1 Co 14:15-16; Eph 5:18-20. For we ask either that God would grant and give us good things [and] preserve, strengthen, and increase those that have been given, or we pray to be protected from imminent evil things, that He might turn them from us, guard us and free [us] from them, and sustain us under the cross itself, temper [our] troubles, give patience, and supply comfort; or we give thanks to God for good things received; or we extol and glorify with praises His name, that is, omnipotence, glory, righteousness, grace, and goodness; or we acknowledge and confess our sins in open confession and at the same time lament our miseries (Dn 9:5, 11).

And this kind of petitions, supplications, prayers, giving of thanks, praises, and confessions are made either in general for all needs, or in particular, when something is expressly mentioned in prayer. And likewise either for ourselves or for others. And we pray either alone or ask for something by common prayer in the united petitions of two or three or of the whole church (Mt 18:19). Moreover, those prayers or thanksgivings are sometimes made only with the inward affection, desire, or sighing of the mind, sometimes outward or spoken prayer is added at the same time, so that prayer is made with the heart and mouth. And that vocal prayer is made either by simple speaking of the words or rhythmically or with chants (1 Co 14:16; Eph 5:19).

Finally, even outward motions are used with prayers, e.g., kneeling (Eph 3:14), elevation of the hands (1 Ti 2:8; Ps 141:2), lifting up of the eyes to heaven (Ps 123:1), striking the breast (Lk 18:13). Or true prayers can be made in spirit and in truth without such outward motions (Jn 4:23). But they are used as being signs of or spurs to inward devotion.

293 *Does it make no difference how one makes his prayers?*

Yes it does, very much, for both the heathen and Pharisees pray, but Christ Himself testifies that their prayers are not acceptable to God (Mt 6:5, 7; Jas 4:3; Ps 109:7). Therefore let him who would pray rightly especially give himself to pay attention to this, with all care and thought: in what way he might so make His prayers, that they be acceptable to God and be heard by Him. But that way does not consist in wordiness or in elegance and a rhetorical display of words, but in this, that the prayers are formed according to the will of God revealed to us in His Word. For the sake of the common people this very thing can be very briefly summarized in these chief parts:

I. That each one who is about to pray consider above all whom he is about to address in prayer, so that [his] heart, mind, spirit, and all thoughts might be stirred, lifted up, and directed to that one true and eternal God, the Father, Son, and Holy Spirit, as He Himself has revealed His essence and will to us in the Word.

II. Since we address God in this way: "Abba, Father," as one who is not far absent (1 K 18:15; Acts 17:27), but is present and hears our prayers (Dt 4:7; Ps 145:18). Therefore we should carefully gather the thoughts of our mind and set forth our petitions with pious devotion and filial reverence and humility as in [His] presence and before His face (Ps 119:58; 142:2; Heb 4:16).

III. Since sincere repentance and true saving faith are required for devout prayer (for God does not hear impenitent sinners, Jn 9:31; Is 1:15), therefore he who would pray properly should consider most of all whether God, whom he is about to call upon, is so minded toward him, that he can truly and confidently call Him Father, since this is to be considered above all in prayer, that we might have forgiveness of sins and a merciful God, who as a most kind Father is willing to aid and assist us.

IV. That prayer be not only vain babbling of words, but ask, seek, and desire something definite from God (Mt 7:7), and that according to His will (1 Jn 5:14), and that we remember that we are spurred and constrained by divine command to ask and desire that very thing, whatever it is.

V. That we do not rely on any worthiness in us, either of person or of works, but rather on the other hand properly acknowledge and consider our extreme unworthiness. And therefore, trusting only in the boundless mercy of God and relying alone on the merit of our only mediator, intercessor, and advocate, Jesus Christ, lay our prayers in His name before our heavenly Father humbly and on bended knee (Dn 9:18-19; Jn 16:23).

V. Finally, it is necessary that in prayer faith, with firm assent, embrace that promise by which God gave solemn assurance that He would hear us without, in fact despite, all our merit, freely for the sake of Christ, and in confidence therein surely hold the more certainly that God will indeed hear also our prayers, and embrace us with fatherly favor and care, [and] likewise can and will relieve and ease our miseries and calamities, namely so far as the glory of His name and the salvation of our soul permits (Mt 21:22; Ja 1:6-7).

Hence it is clear and manifest how hard and very difficult true prayer is and that often many, in fact very many, worship not in spirit and truth but speak and babble their prayers only with the mouth and outward[46] lips. That is also clear from this, that to pray aright is not a work dependent on and springing from our natural powers, but is to be entirely ascribed to the power and work of the Holy Spirit (Gl 4:6; Zch 12:10).

Though that attitude of the mind and fervor of spirit, which is required for proper prayer, is very weak in us, and does not burn like a flame, but barely smokes like flax,[47] yet the practice of prayer is not therefore to be abandoned, but rather the more zealously pursued, and the divine promise insisted on, that God will give His Holy Spirit to them that ask Him (Lk 11:13). But zeal in prayer and piety in prayer are kindled and increased by both meditation of the Word and exercise of true faith.

For this reason also Christ commands us to speak, or pronounce words, when we pray (Lk 11:2; cf. Ro 8:26).

294 *What things, then, are to be asked of God?*

Cf. Mt 18:19; 21:22; Mk 11:24; Jn 16:23; 1 Jn 5:14. For we neither can nor ought to ask the things that are forbidden by God and are against His will. Moreover, Christ Himself, in the formula of prayer prescribed for the apostles, has set forth what that will of God is, or what He wants us to ask (Mt 6:9; Lk 11:2). Those things are in the main summarized in these chief parts. They look either to the glory of God, or to our need, benefit, and salvation. The things that pertain to us are either spiritual or bodily good things, namely of the soul, body, fortune, fame, etc., serving either the present or the future life, and are asked either for others or for ourselves, sometimes in general, sometimes in particular, as all these things are contained in order in the Lord's Prayer.

295 *But may one use another form of prayer, other words?*

The prophets, Christ Himself, and the apostles often used also other words in their prayers. We are therefore by no means bound only to the words of the Lord's Prayer; but we are surely bound to their sense: we should formulate our prayers according to those chief parts, in that way [and] order, and to [that] end.

It is therefore helpful if we become accustomed to include whatever we ask in some petition of the Lord's Prayer. It is also helpful, in all Psalms and other devout prayers, to consider to which petition of that prayer they are related and are to be connected. For that formula, prescribed for us by Christ Himself, ought properly be the standard and rule of any and all other prayers, surely the best and most perfect of all. For Christ does not say in vain: When ye pray, say, Our Father, etc.

296   *In what order, with what difference, and under what conditions are spiritual and bodily good things to be asked for?*

The formula of Christ teaches us to ask not only temporal and bodily good things, or these chiefly and in the first place, but both spiritual and bodily [good things]: first the kingdom of God and His righteousness, then the good things of life, not, when received, to be credited only to our effort and work, or to be expected from anyone else, but we are to regard these things also as to be sought and looked for nowhere else than from God, [and] only that they work for the glory of His name and our benefit and that of [our] neighbor. We should ask spiritual [gifts] indeed without any condition, in the firm confidence of prayer, but bodily [gifts] under qualification. For since God wants to exercise His own in this life with cross and calamities, and we do not know what is good for us or how God wants to promote our salvation, Christ has prescribed certain conditions under which we should ask for daily bread: First, if it is God's will; therefore we say, Thy will be done. Then, if that which we ask is connected with our benefit and salvation; therefore we pray, Lord, deliver us from all evil. Finally, if it works for the glory of God; hence we conclude our prayer with these words: Thine, O Lord, is the kingdom, the power, and the glory. Therefore we ought by no means prescribe to God either a certain way, or time, or limit in matters of this life and body, but submit ourselves to His will and yield in filial obedience, if another way seems better to Him than [what] we ask, according to the example of Christ (Mt 26:42), of David (2 Sm 15:25-26), of the Three Children (Dn 3:17-18), and of the leper (Mt 8:2). And yet both the promise and the confidence of being heard remain valid and firm, notwithstanding, in such prayers, namely that God wants to take care of us also in bodily matters and embrace us with fatherly affection and promote the things that He Himself knows will be profitable for us to salvation. And hence the ancients, in such needs and troubles, summarized their prayers no less briefly than fittingly in these words: that He would either deliver, or temper, or save by giving patience and comfort. And Augustine says: God always hears also in bodily matters, if not according to our will, yet certainly according to His will, for our benefit. Likewise: In such petitions God acts mercifully when He hears, and He acts mercifully when He does not hear.[48]

297   *Mention some reasons that should stir and move us to pray when we are otherwise slow and lax.*

Since nearly all of us are by nature cold and slow to pray, it is very helpful and necessary to know such reasons and have them ready at hand;

when we consider and meditate on them, the Holy Spirit stirs up and kindles zeal for prayer in us.

I. Since it is the will and command of God that we pray, as we have shown above from Scripture. Neglecting and ceasing to pray devoutly is therefore no light sin.

II. The great and manifold need by which we are burdened in this penitentiary of the world, and which we cannot sufficiently understand or comprehend by thinking, must less guard against or avert by our effort, should properly move us to pray even all by itself.

III. Also the boundless benefit and very abundant fruit of devout prayers should invite us. For spiritual good things are not obtained from God except by prayers (Lk 11:13). And temporal things are not good for us, unless they are sanctified by prayer (1 Ti 4:4-5). So also St. James describes at length the effect of devout prayer (Ja 5:15-18).

IV. Very sweet divine promises draw and incite us, namely that God the Father embraces us with such great love in Christ His Son, that He regards it as pleasing and acceptable if we approach and address Him with our prayers, and He has promised to incline His ears and hear us.

V. Likewise, that our mediator, Christ, has bound Himself with the firm promise that He would be present when we pray (Mt 18:20) and as our advocate and High Priest Himself bring our supplications to the Father, and intercede for us, and ask the Father together with us.

VI. Also that the Holy Spirit of God, as the Spirit of prayer, would kindle zeal for prayer, and devotion, in us, so that we cry in Him: Abba, Father (Gl 4:6). Indeed, He intercedes for us with unutterable sighs (Ro 8:26). They therefore sorely grieve that Spirit of prayer for whom prayers are not [a matter] for concern or for the heart.

VII. Since prayer is common to all members of Christ, who call upon one Father in heaven, whom we therefore call "our" [Father]. Therefore he that does not pray thereby severs and separates himself from Christ the head and from the members of His body, which is the church, or communion of saints. And God Himself regards and holds those as Gentiles, who do not call upon His name (Ps 79:6; Jer 10:25).

VIII. Since the practice of prayer is truly a training for all piety and a most useful exercise of all of Christianity, e.g., of repentance, faith, patience, comfort, hope, etc. For the Holy Spirit nourishes, preserves, and increases these gifts in us through persistence in prayer, just as, on the other hand, by ceasing them [i.e., prayers] those gifts are gradually diminished and finally disappear altogether.

IX. Where the exercise of prayer grows cold and is neglected, there the door and windows are open to the devil for all kinds of temptations (Mt 26:41; Lk 22:40).

298   *Does a place or time make prayer holier and more acceptable to God?*
In the New Testament the prayers of the pious are bound neither to a

certain place nor [a certain] time, as Christ expressly teaches (Jn 4:21). And Paul says that prayers can be made anywhere (1 Ti 2:8). In fact, everyone can pray in his private room (Mt 6:6) [and] in bed (Ps 63:6). And since we are to pray without ceasing (Lk 18:1), therefore any time is sacred and holy for prayer. But when, in Christian liberty, for the sake of training and good order, without superstition, a certain time is designated for prayer, and likewise a suitable place is chosen that is comparatively free of outside interference and interruptions, that neither can nor ought by right be censured. Thus, when in the assembled congregation, where the Word of God is taught, and the Sacraments are administered, the office of prayer is performed, this is done according to the example of the apostolic church (Acts 2:42, 46; 1 Co 14:26). But if one would do that in the opinion that prayer is holier and more acceptable to God by reason of a time or place consecrated by certain rites, that would indeed be rightly censured as a vain and pernicious superstition.

299 *Is there any difference between Christian and heathen and [between] papistic and evangelical prayers?*

True worshipers, who want to call upon God in spirit and in truth, should consider above all how to differentiate and dissociate their invocation from idolatrous and superstitious prayers of others (Mt 6:7-8). It is therefore helpful to know in what that difference consists.

Heathen and all other infidels call upon either their fabricated idols or the God whom they do not know (Jn 4:22). But they do not call upon the true God, who is the Father, Son, and Holy Spirit, since they do not know Him. They also do not call upon God in the name of, and [in] faith in, Christ, the Mediator, without whom no one comes to the Father (Jn 14:6). They base [their] confidence of being heard not on Christ but on their sacrifices and self-appointed acts of worship. In fact, they believe that they are heard if they use many words (Mt 6:7), yet are always unsure, uncertain about being heard and helped. If their wishes are not at all granted, they censure their idols and gods with abuses and blasphemies. Besides, they know nothing at all about asking for truly spiritual good things.

But the papists call not only on God, but with [Him] also [on] the dead saints as special patrons and helpers. They worship not only in the name of Christ, but choose and take for themselves many mediators and intercessors from among dead saints. But they base assurance of being heard either on their own merits or on those of other saints. Hence they also teach that one must always be in doubt regarding the grace and mercy of God. Likewise, they hold that if one prays before certain likenesses and images and in special places and temples, it is more likely that one will be heard. They also often pray in an unknown tongue and say that the longer the prayers are, and the more frequently repeated, the more pleasing they will be to God; accordingly, they count out Lord's

Prayers and Hail Marys to God as with certain counting stones[49]; and they hold that no matter how much prayers may lack all pious devotion, if only they are brought with a certain sounding out of words, they obtain from God, by performance of the act,[50] greater grace and salvation itself, despite the fact that in prayer we give nothing to God but wish to obtain and receive something freely from Him for Christ's sake. As for the rest, it is clear enough from the preceding how true prayer is to be made. And in order to be sincere it must be purged clean of all leaven, both heathen and papistic.

Invocation of Saints

300   *Should one pray to saints who have died?*

No! To worship someone else besides the only God is a sin against the First Commandment of the Decalog (Mt 4:10). And lest someone try to find a loophole in that fictitious difference between adoration and invocation, Scripture ascribes also the honor of invocation to God alone and shows that adoration at the same time includes calling upon the divine name in all needs (Ps 50:15). God does not give His glory to someone else, who is not God (Is 42:8). Therefore Christ, in the pattern for prayer, commands us to direct invocation to Him who is, and is called, our Father in heaven, with this kind of conclusion: For Thine is the glory, etc.

301   *But we are miserable sinners and not worthy to be heard. Do we therefore need some intercession that might have some influence with God? And does it behoove us to acknowledge this our unworthiness?*

This can indeed not be denied. And idolators of practically all nations trace the origin of [their] worship to that kind of speculations, as Ambrose also notes on Ro 1. But Holy Scripture shows us the royal and completely sure way; for we namely are unworthy to obtain anything from God, and therefore we have need of an advocate or intercessor who handles our cases—not anyone to be chosen for this by us in our fancy—but Him, whom God Himself has ordained and of whose intercession we are sure that it avails and is valid before God. It therefore teaches that only one Mediator and intercessor between God and us men has been appointed by God Himself, namely Jesus Christ (1 Ti 2:5). He is not only our Mediator with regard to redemption, but likewise also our advocate with the Father (1 Jn 2:1-2). He intercedes for us (Ro 8:34). He appears before the face of God for us (Heb 9:24). He intercedes for us, that we might come to God through Him (Heb 7:25). For in Christ we have free access to God with all confidence (Eph 3:12). And therefore He commanded us to pray to the Father in His name (Jn 14:14; 15:7; 16:24). And since both His merit is abundant and sufficient and [His] intercession pleasing to God and sufficiently efficacious, we therefore have, besides the command to pray in His name alone, in addition the sure and firm promise of being heard (Jn 16:23). For He is able also to save forever those who come to God through Him (Heb 7:25). Considering these basic facts, a pious mind will easily understand and judge what a fearful abomination and idolatry it is to make the merits and intercessions of the saints more than or equal to Christ.

302 *But Christ, established in heavenly majesty, is exalted above all angels; would He therefore either be moved by our ills, or should we miserable [people] dare to implore His intercession? And it is very likely that the saints, who have experienced the same misfortune as we, would be more concerned about our miseries, and have them commended to them, and therefore be more ready to help us.*

Heb 2:17-18 and 4:15-16 thoroughly remove this objection. And lest the excellence of His majesty seem to frighten us away, Christ Himself calls us miserable and unworthy [people] to Himself and commands us to come (Mt 11:28). And He does not reject those who come to Him (Jn 6:37). In fact, having entered His kingdom, He remembers the miserable robber (Lk 23:42-43). So also we are urged and compelled by both command and divine promise to pray in the name of Christ (Jn 16:24). But none of these things is found anywhere in the Scriptures about the saints.

303 *Yet there is no doubt that the saints who live with God, like also the holy angels of God, wish and desire the best for us, who still live on earth. Why, then, is it not permitted to call upon them?*

Some Scripture passages indeed seem to refer to this, that the saints, enjoying heavenly glory with God, even as also the blessed angels, in general desire and wish all of the best things for the church of God still militant on earth under the banner of the cross and struggling with various afflictions. But it by no means follows from this that they are to be called upon in times of need, especially since we are altogether without both command and promise regarding that matter. And Scripture expressly says that God alone is to be called upon, and not the saints for this reason, that since they live in another world they are unaware and ignorant of our matters (Is 63:16). And since they are no longer in this world, they can neither understand our thoughts, sighs, and desires nor look into and search [our] hearts. For only God and the man Christ are capable of this (Jer 17:10; Ro 8:27; Rv 2:23; Jn 2:24-25; Lk 24:38).

304 *But could God reveal our dangers, prayers, and sighs to the saints, and perhaps, when He is about to help us, use their ministry and work for this, even as also the angels are servants of the Spirit?*

Prayer and invocation must rest not on opinions that are uncertain and humanly preconceived, but on the express command and sure promise taught in the Word of God. For it should be made in faith (Ja

1:6). And faith must rest on the divine Word (Ps 119:105). But the things that they come out with here regarding saints are only figments of human opinions, devoid of any plain Word of God, command, and promise, in fact contrary to the clear text of Scripture (Is 63:16; Acts 13:36). And even if the condition of the saints and angels were the same regarding services and ministries to be rendered for us, it would nevertheless not follow from that, that they are to be adored and invoked. For though the blessed angels themselves sometimes declare that the prayers of the pious are heard, yet they do not want to be adored (Dn 9:22-23; 10:12; Lk 1:13; Acts 10:4; Rv 19:10; 22:8-9).

305   *Yet that formula of prayer was frequent and common among the people of Israel in the Old Testament: Lord God, remember Thy servants Abraham, Isaac, and Jacob, etc.*

With this form of prayer the Israelites remind God of [His] most gracious promises regarding the blessed seed and regarding the adoption, made to the patriarch, and they support their prayers with them. But nowhere do we read that they called upon the departed patriarchs or asked that they be heard by God because of their merits and intercessions. Indeed, they plainly confess on the contrary, Is 63:16: Thou art our Father; for Abraham does not know us, and Israel is ignorant of us, etc. Here they indeed mention the patriarchs, but they call not upon them, but upon God alone.

Also Gn 48:16, which is raised in objection, means nothing else than that Jacob prays, and by testament commands, that the sons of Joseph (Ephraim and Manasseh) be included and counted with his family and called by his name, just as if they had been begotten by Jacob himself, even as this explanation of that phrase is clear from Is 4:1: And in that day seven women will take hold of one man, saying, We will eat our own bread and be covered with our own garments, only let thy name be called upon us (that is, let us be thy wives and called by thy name). Likewise Jer 15:1 in no way whatsoever establishes the intercession of the dead, but means this: If there were some among them who could pray with such zeal and fervor of spirit as that with which Moses and Samuel once interceded for their people when they were still among the living, yet I would not spare that very wicked people. This explanation is not invented by us but is expressly taught Eze 14:14, 16, 18.

306   *Are then the saints of God not to be honored at all?*

They are indeed to be honored, but both in the way in which God has prescribed and they themselves want to be honored—just as the blessed Virgin Mary says in her song: From henceforth they shall now call me blessed, not because I can do great things and as though my name were holy, but because the Lord has done great things for me; He is mighty and only His name is holy [Lk 1:48-49]. On the basis of the Apology of the Augsburg Confession the position of Scripture on honoring the saints

146

comes down to these three chief parts:

First, that we praise God by true thanksgiving with regard to the saints; He has adorned them with such various and excellent gifts (Gl 1:24; Mt 5:14, 16). And at the same time let us magnify those gifts and praise the saints themselves, who used those gifts faithfully, just as Christ commended the faithful servant (Mt 25:21; 11:11).

Second, that we might strengthen our faith and draw patience, comfort, and hope from their doctrine, confession, cross, affliction, constancy, relief from the cross, and deliverance. (Ro 15:4).

Third, that, everyone according to his calling, we might imitate their faith, hope, love, and the other Christian virtues (Heb 13:7; 1 Co 11:1). And this is the true honor, this the true veneration of the saints. For the acts of worship, which are due to God alone, e.g., invocation and adoration, ought not be directed either to angels or saints. And the saints themselves doubtlessly neither desire such honors or acts of worship nor regard them as pleasing and acceptable; in fact, they reject them, e.g., Peter (Acts 10:25-26) and Paul (Acts 14:15).

Matrimony and the Marriage of Priests

307   *What is matrimony?*

It is a holy and honorable order or state first instituted by God Himself in paradise, and thereupon after the Fall, and likewise after the Flood, and finally also confirmed and approved in the New Testament, consisting in the lawful and indissoluble union of one man and one woman, so that mankind might be propagated according to a specific order (Gn 1:28), that promiscuous lusts might be avoided (1 Co 7:2), and that the spouses themselves might be mutually bound to each other by the mutual functions and helps of love and benevolence, according as those functions of pious spouses are set forth in the table of domestic matters (Eph 5:22, 25; Cl 3:18-19; 1 Ptr 3:1-2, 7).

308   *Is this state to be regarded pure, holy, and chaste before God?*

God solemnly forbids all other unions of male and female outside of matrimony and has determined to punish them in this life and in that which is to come (Gl 5:19-21; Heb 13:4). But He has permitted that conjugal intercourse and cohabitation only in lawfully contracted matrimony. Therefore this state is by no means to be regarded as an impure kind of life, but it is adorned with that blessing by God, that among believers it might be, and be regarded before God as, honorable, pure, holy, chaste, and respectable (for Scripture deems marriage and pious spouses worthy of these designations [Heb 13:4; 1 Th 4:3-4; 1 Ti 2:15; Tts 2:4-5]). In this [state] Christians can in good conscience live and cohabit and at the same time call upon God and be saved (1 Ti 2:15; 1 Co 7:5; 1 Ptr 3:7).

309 *Are all people bound to enter matrimony under threat of damnation?*

No. For Christ makes some exceptions: (1) Those who either by nature or for some other reason are not suitable and fit for matrimony; (2) Those to whom the gift of continence has been divinely given, so that they can live chastely and modestly outside of marriage, either in virginity or in the state of widowhood (Mt 19:11-12). And Paul indeed counsels those who have been endowed with the gift of continence, to remain so, since in that celibate life they would both have fewer afflictions and be able to have opportunity for divine worship more freely and easily, without outward hindrances, so that they might be holy in body and spirit (1 Co 7:8, 26, 34-35). But, says Paul, if these also want to enter matrimony, they can do so without sin (1 Co 7:26, 28). But Paul likewise says to the rest, who cannot contain themselves, that marriage was ordained and commanded to avoid debauchery, and that it is better to marry than to burn (1 Co 7:1-2, 9).

310 *Do they do right, who, though they do not have the gift of continence, yet, abjuring marriage, vow perpetual celibacy?*

Scripture says: Thou shalt not tempt the Lord thy God (Dt 6:16; Mt 4:7). But they tempt God, who, to avoid fornication, do not want to use the means, e.g., marriage, ordained and given by Him, lest something worse result. And Christ declares that it is not given to all to live chastely outside of matrimony and that no one is capable of this, except he to whom it has been given (Mt 19:11). Paul likewise says that the prohibition to marry, which occurs in the papistic vows under the guise of holiness, is a doctrine of the devil (1 Ti 4:1-3).

311 *Can the dignity and holiness of the ministry bear it that a priest have a lawful spouse?*

By all means. For not only did priests in the Old Testament have their lawful wives, but Paul also writes, in the New Testament, that such a bishop and elder is to be chosen as is both of blameless life and the husband of one wife (1 Ti 3:2; Tts 1:5-6).

312 *But some say: Paul is to be understood allegorically, namely that a bishop is to be appointed over only one church, or that he indeed can be chosen bishop who formerly was the husband of one wife, but not he who still is, or he who still has his own wife.*

Paul himself is his own clear interpreter, namely that by husband of one wife he means him who has children, and not only of the church, but also of a family, that is, he rules well a wife, children, and servants (1 Ti 3:4; Tts 1:6). So also some of the apostles had their own wives, not only before they became apostles, but they also lived in marriage with them at the very time when they were apostles (1 Co 9:5). So also Ignatius and Clemens explain that passage of Paul. Moreover, Paul does not say, He who was the husband of one wife, but: He who is. And if these words were to be wrested to the past tense, it would necessarily also follow therefrom that a bishop is to be chosen who was at one time sober and able to teach, but is no longer so.

313 *But the office of the ministry is very holy, and is marriage not a carnal state?*

It is plainly diabolic blasphemy that some Roman popes have not hesitated to misapply to marriage those statements of Paul: They that are in the flesh cannot please God, and if ye live according to the flesh ye shall die (Ro 8:8, 13). For marriage is a divine ordinance, sanctified with the Word and blessing of God (Gn 1:27-28; 9:1). Hence Christ declares that God Himself joins spouses (Mt 19:6). And Paul says expressly: He that marries does not sin (1 Co 7:28). For he declares likewise that in conjugal intercourse there is holiness, honor, and chastity (1 Ti 2:15; 1 Th 4:4; Tts 2:4-5). Peter also calls the wives who are obedient to their husbands holy (1 Ptr 3:5). And Heb 13:4 calls matrimony and the undefiled bed honorable. In fact, also the cohabitation of believing wives with unbelieving husbands is holy (1 Co 7:14).

Paul therefore declares that the prohibition of matrimony is a doctrine of demons (1 Ti 4:1, 3), especially since Christians also can be saved in the marriage relationship (1 Ti 2:15). Hence canon 4 of the Council of Gangra piously decrees regarding ministers of the Word and of the Sacraments: If one holds that one should not worship under leadership of married priests, as though it is not necessary to take part in a service under such ministration, let him be anathema.

314 *But doesn't Paul say, 1 Co 7:1: It is good not to touch a woman; likewise, v. 32: He that is unmarried cares for the things of the Lord, etc.; [and] therefore concludes, v. 38: It is better not to marry?*

In that very same place Paul immediately adds a clear explanation of his words. For he does not say that it is sin, or a wicked thing, to enter marriage. But he says, v. 26: I hold that this (namely to remain celibate) is good for a man, that is, it is advantageous or expedient because of the present necessity. For since in matrimony many adversities, annoyances, and difficulties are encountered, by which spouses are often hindered from giving more proper and diligent attention to the things of the Lord, it would therefore be better and more expedient for carrying out the functions of the ministry, if they that function in the ministry could remain celibate. But Paul adds, vv. 35 and 7: I say this, not by way of precept, but for your own good, not to cast a snare on you, for everyone has his own gift from God, one indeed this, but another that. And let each one choose what is good and suitable for him, namely marriage or celibacy, according to the gift that is given to him by God; and he that marries does not sin (1 Co 7:28). He can even function in the office of bishop (1 Ti 3:2). And conjugal cohabitation and domestic concern in themselves do not hinder the things that belong to the church ministry, especially in those that apply piety and faithfulness in the office, as witness many outstanding examples of the patriarchs, prophets, the priest Zacharias, the apostles, the ancient bishops, and the holy martyrs. In fact, Paul wants a bishop to rule his own house well (1 Ti 3:4-5). But 1 Co 7 he speaks mainly of the things that commonly happen in unequal marriages, when the spouses are either not of the same religion, or are not equally given to piety and faithfulness, and he does not want to cast a snare on anyone even in that case.

315   *Can no one, then, be a priest or minister of the church unless he has a wife?*

He that has the gift of continence does well if he remains celibate. For he can administer his office with less hindrance and difficulty, especially in time of persecution (1 Co 7:35). Let each one therefore examine himself, and at the same time take pains in solemn prayer, whether he can remain in the celibate state. For Christ praises the self-appointed celibacy of those who castrate themselves for the sake of the kingdom of God (Mt 19:12). But he adds that this gift is not obtained either by prayers alone or by diligence alone, and deliberate choice; for He says, Not all are able to receive this saying, but those to whom it has been given; wherefore let him who can receive it, receive it. Therefore let him who has been adorned by God with this gift use it to promote the kingdom of heaven; but to him who lacks it Paul says, 1 Co 7:2: In order to avoid fornication, let every man have his own wife; likewise, v. 9: Let those marry who cannot contain themselves, for this is better than to burn; and he that marries not only does not sin (1 Co 7:28), but he can also function in the office of bishop (Tts 1:5-6).

The Last Judgment and Purgatory

316   *What is the end of faith, and what [is the end] of unbelief?*

The end of our faith is the salvation of our souls (1 Ptr 1:8-9) and life eternal (Jn 3:36). But the end of unbelief is damnation (Mk 16:16) and eternal perdition (2 Th 1:8-9). And we are also saved even in this life, but by hope ([Ro 8:24]; 2 Co 5:7). But finally at the end of time, when Christ will come as judge of the living and the dead, the end of both faith and unbelief will be plainly and perfectly revealed (1 Ptr 1:5; 2 Th 1:6-7). Then the righteous shall go into life eternal, but the wicked into the punishment of eternal fire (Mt 25:46; Jn 5:29).

317   *What does Scripture teach regarding the last judgment?*

It teaches that the world and the things that are in the world will not last forever but will have an end (Mt 24:35; 1 Co 7:31) and that the heavens, on fire, shall be destroyed, the elements, burning, will melt, and the earth and the works that are in it will be burned up (2 Ptr 3:10); and that [will take place] when the Son of man comes from heaven in manifest power and majesty (Mt 24:30), in such a way that flames of fire shall precede Him (2 Th 1:7-8). And then it will come to pass that all the dead will rise with their bodies (1 Co 15:44). Immediately the judgment shall be made, in which the elect will be placed to the right of Christ the judge, but the accursed to the left. And they shall come forth, they that have done good, to the resurrection of life, but they that have done evil, to the resurrection of judgment (Jn 5:29). Thus this form of judgment is described Mt 25:31-46. But no one knows about the day and hour of that judgment, except the Father only. We should therefore watch and pray, since we do not know the hour and the time of the Lord's coming (Mt 24:36, 42).

318   *But what is the state of both bodies and souls between the time of death and the last day?*

With regard to the souls of the dead, Scripture declares that when the souls of the righteous are separated from the bodies by death, they are gathered to their people (Gn 25:8; 35:29), bound in the bundle of the living (1 Sm 25:29), to be in the hand of God (Wis 3:1), in the bosom of Abraham (Lk 16:22). Thus they depart to the Lord and are with Christ in paradise (Ec 12:7; 2 Co 5:8; Ph 1:23; Lk 23:43). There they enjoy rest (Lk 16:25); they rest from their labors (Rv 14:13). They await that last day with joy, when they will finally be fully perfected (Rv 6:11; Heb 11:39-40). But Holy Scriptures testify regarding the souls of the wicked set free from [their] bodies by the intervention of death, that they come to the place of torments, where they are in anguish (Lk 16:24, 28). They await with terror the fearful judgment of God and the punishment of eternal fire (Heb 9:27; 2 Ptr 2:4).

Moreover, the Word of God teaches regarding the bodies of the dead that the bodies of both righteous and wicked sleep and rest in graves till the last day, when they will rise again, quickened by the voice of the Son of God, and they will be united again with their souls (Jn 5:28); and finally, when the last judgment has been pronounced, the righteous shall go into life eternal, but the wicked shall be cast into eternal fire (Mt 25:46).

319   *What, then, do the papists teach regarding purgatory?*

The papists make a threefold distinction regarding the dead:

I. They say that some are so pure, holy, and perfect in this life, that when they die [their] souls fly away directly to heaven.

II. They say that some live so sinfully and wickedly in the world, that [their] souls are cast down to hell immediately after death.

III. They put some in between, namely those, who, though they were not unbelievers nor altogether wicked, yet they left this life with the stains of sin not yet fully blotted out and satisfaction for sins not yet fully accomplished.

They therefore imagine that these are cast together into the fire of purgatory, so that by that fire the remaining blots of sin might be burned out and purged away, and that with the exceeding torment of purgatory they might fully and completely supply that which was lacking in this life for accomplishing satisfaction for [their] sins. When that purging out and satisfaction is complete, they will finally be delivered from that fire and transferred to the place of the blessed.

But this modification of the fire of purgatory is added by the papists, that its flame can be somewhat cooled by holy or blessed water and that souls in purgatory can be helped by vigils, obsequies, memorials, anniversary memorials, masses for the dead, alms, and other works of the living for the dead, so that they might be delivered from it more quickly and easily.

320 *Is this invention of the papists based on the Word of God?*

No; it is diametrically opposed to it. For the Word of God teaches first, that there are only two ways in this life and out of this life; one of them leads to life eternal, the other to eternal condemnation (Mt 7:13-14; Mk 16:16; Jn 3:18, 36).

Second, there is a twofold difference in bodily death: whether it be either the death of the righteous (Nm 23:10; Ps 116:15), who die and sleep in Christ (1 Th 4:14, 16; Rv 14:13), or the death of sinners (Ps 34:21), who die in sins without faith (Jn 8:24).

Third, after death, before the last day, there are only two different places in which the souls of the dead go, namely, the place of comfort of the blessed and the place of torment of the damned (Lk 16:25). But Scripture knows no third place as intermediate, as Augustine also testifies (*Hypognosticon,* Book 5).

Fourth, they that die in faith in the Lord are immediately, from that time on, blessed, and at rest (Rv 14:13), in such a way that they shall be touched by no torment (Wis 3:1). For they shall not come into judgment, but shall pass through death into life (Jn 5:24). But they that do not believe are also judged, and they shall not see life, for the wrath of God remains on them (Jn 3:18, 36).

Fifth, immediately after death that great gulf is fixed, so that no one can pass over from the place of torment to the place of comfort (Lk 16:26).

Sixth, the time of this life is the acceptable time and day of salvation (2 Co 6:1-2), and to the end of life the day is called Today (Heb 3:13), after which there is no more room for repentance (Lk 16:26). For that which should be loosed in heaven must be loosed on earth (Mt 16:19; 18:18). But Scripture knows nothing whatever of that doctrine of the papists, that after this life there remains some time for repentance and reconciliation with God, even as it knows nothing of this, that the prayers of the living for the dead are profitable unto salvation. For everyone will there receive according to that which he did here in the body (2 Co 5:10). Hence Cyprian (Tract 1. *Contra Demetrianum*): When one has gone there, there is no more room for repentance; life is lost or retained here. Ambrose *(De bono mortis):* He that does not receive remission of sins here will not be there; but he will not be there for this reason, that he will not attain to life eternal; for life eternal is remission of sins. And he quotes this [passage] of David [Ps 39:13]: That I may be refreshed before I go hence and be no more.

321   *But in fact Scripture says, Rv 21:27: Nothing defiled shall enter heaven. And God is not only merciful, but also just; He wants sin to be atoned for with full satisfaction.*

These things are indeed true. But if this purging, expiation, and satisfaction for sins depends on us and on our works, no man would ever be saved. Therefore God sent His Son as Mediator and Redeemer, who alone is the satisfaction or propitiation for our sins (Ro 3:25; 1 Jn 2:2). He also purged our sins (Heb 1:3). For his blood cleanses us from all sin (1 Jn 1:7). He cleansed us with the washing of water (Eph 5:25-26). And hearts are washed in the blood of the Lamb (Rv 7:14), having our conscience sprinkled and cleansed (Ps 51:7; Heb 9:14; 10:22; 1 Ptr 1:22), so that through Him and in Him we might be holy, unblameable, and spotless (Cl 1:22). But these very great benefits of the Son of God are wickedly obscured and minimized by the papistic doctrine of purgatory.

322   *But those words of Paul seem to stand in the way, 1 Co 3:15: He shall be saved, yet so as by fire.*

None of the fathers explained this statement of Paul simply, properly, and surely of purgatory. In fact, neither Augustine nor Gregory, though they refer to this passage, dared to construct purgatory surely and firmly on the basis of those words. For they say that this passage can be understood of the fire of affliction in this life. And since Paul says that everyone's work is tried by fire, it would surely follow that all the saints would have to be subjected to the flaming fire of purgatory; and the papists themselves do not grant this. But the true meaning of Paul is clear from the context. For he speaks of teachers in the church, and hearers, who retain the foundation intact, and says: Whatever they build, either of doctrine or of opinions, on this foundation, all this is tried by the fire of temptation, tribulation, and persecution; in this fire some things stand, [but] some are burned up as unfit and useless, yet in such a way, that if the foundation is retained intact and entire, it does not hinder salvation. For since all the words of the text, e.g., gold, silver, wood, hay, etc. are meant allegorically, surely the word fire should also not be taken in a material sense as the kind of fire the papist imagine and invent in their purgatory.

323   *Yet Christ declares Mt 12:31-32 that there are some sins that are forgiven neither in this world nor in that which is to come.*

Christ explains this His statement Mk 3:29, that is, the sin against the

Holy Spirit will be punished both in this life and in the life to come, even though many other sins remain unpunished in this life.

324 *But Maccabeus offered sacrifices for the sins of the dead (2 Mac 12:43-46).*

The Books of the Maccabees are not in the canon of the sacred books, by which articles of faith can be established and proved or confirmed. And nowhere else in all sacred Scripture is there either a command or an example regarding any sacrifice for the dead, though it teaches many things about sacrifices. Maccabeus therefore did this not on the basis of divine command, but by his own design. But God has prohibited this in so many words (Dt 12:8, 32).

And Maccabeus mentions neither any fire nor torment of the dead from which they are to be redeemed by works of the living.

325 *Even so, the holy fathers taught and defended purgatory as an article of faith.*

The fathers cannot establish articles of faith without the express Word of God. In fact, this is falsely attributed to the fathers. For the Greeks never were and are not even now willing to acknowledge purgatory. Augustine indeed discusses purgatory but does not defend it as an article of faith; but he leaves it in doubt whether or not it exists (*Enchiridion,* ch. 69; *Ad dulc.,* quaest. 1; *De civitat.,* Book 21, ch 26).

The Universal Church

326 *What are the marks that point out the true church of God on earth?*

The true church of God on earth is not determined by the multitude of people (Mt 7:13-14), even as it is not to be determined by power, nobility, and wisdom according to the flesh (1 Co 1:26-28). Nor does this assembly always represent the true church, which carries and bears before itself the name "church," even as the universal or Christian church is truly not definitely recognized by the ordinary succession; the accounts of the prophets, Christ, and the apostles point this out. Nor is it enough, to identify it, to put forward what was written many years ago and the authority of the ancients (Mt 5:21-48; 15:1-3). But these are the genuine marks that distinctly identify the true church of God on earth:

I. Where the Word of God is taught purely and in truth, without corruptions (Jn 10:5, 27; Eph 2:19-21; 4:11-12; 2 Co 2:17; 1 Ti 3:15).

II. Where sins are bound and loosed through the Word and according to the Word of God (Mt 16:18-19; Jn 20:22-23).

III. Where the Sacraments are administered according to the divine injunction and institution (Mt 28:19-20).

IV. Where there are people who use the Sacraments (Mk 16:16; 1 Co 10:17; 11:33), hear the Word of God (Jn 10:27, receive [it] (1 Th 1:6; 1 Co

15:1, confess [Christ] (Mt 10:32), follow [Him] (Jn 10:27), and call upon God, as He has commanded in the Word (Lk 19:46; 1 Co 1:2; Ps 79:6). And these signs are sometimes more in evidence, sometimes less evident. For on this foundation some build gold, some stubble (1 Co 3:12-13). And yet if the foundation remains intact, God has His church there (1 K 19:18).

327 *Are all those holy and saved who join themselves to and associate with this assembly by outward profession?*

Not all, for not all are doers of the Word, and not all that hear the Word keep it (Lk 8:15; 11:28; Mt 7:26). The parables of the gospels also show this clearly (Mt 13:24-30, 47-48; 22:1-14).

328 *Why, then, is it called holy universal church in the creed?*

Because the Holy Spirit is efficacious and works in that assembly through the Word and the Sacraments in such a way that He calls, enlightens, converts, sanctifies, and preserves those who are saved, namely so that they repent, believe in Christ, and bear fruits worthy of repentance (Acts 26:20).

329 *Can anyone be saved outside of this church of Christ, or if he is not a part and member of the true church?*

Scripture uses this comparison, that the church is like a body consisting of many members, the Head of which body is Christ, who is the Savior of His body, so that the things that the members need for salvation flow out to them from the Head (Eph 1:22-23; 4:15-16; 5:23, 30; Cl 1:18; 1 Co 12:12, 27). For this reason he that is not a member of this body, whose Head is Christ, cannot be saved. For salvation, accomplished through Christ, is distributed and applied to believers through the ministry of the Gospel, which is in the only true church (2 Co 5:18-20). Thus Paul very aptly describes and summarizes[51] the order that God observed in saving men, Ro 8:30. But the call takes place through the Word in the true church. Therefore also those two points in the creed are connected: I believe in the holy universal church, the communion of saints. People are therefore repeatedly and diligently to be admonished to withdraw [from] and leave a false church (Ps 1:1; 26:5; 2 Co 6:14, 17; Rv 18:4; Mt 7:15; 16:6; Acts 20:28-29; Gl 1:9; 1 Jn 4:1). Let them attach and join themselves to the assembly that has the signs and marks of the true church of Christ (Heb 10:25; Ps 27:4; 42:4; 119:63; Mt 12:30).

330 *Who is the head of the universal church?*

The true universal church acknowledges only a single Head, who is Christ (Eph 1:22; 4:15; Cl 1:18). For though there is a certain order and difference of gifts among the members of the church (Ro 12:4-6; Eph 4:16), yet all are members of one body, and to none of these belong the things that are characteristic of the Head of the church (Eph 1:22-23), who fully fills all in all (Eph 5:23).

331 *Is it in the power of the church to change anything in the Word of God* *or to establish new articles of faith?*

By no means. For the church is built on the Word of God (Eph 2:20). And it is bound to that Word (Mt 28:20). If it rejects this Word, it is not the church (Jn 10:26; Gl 1:9). For the church ought not rule Christ but be subject to Him (Eph 5:24).

332 *Why is the church called universal?*

I. Because it is not restricted to a certain place, but [is] scattered here and there through the whole world.

II. Because God at all times, to the end of the world, gathers for Himself a church out of mankind on earth.

III. Because it is not bound to the persons of certain people, but only to its single Head, Christ, and to His Head (1 Co 11:3), so that, though by way of time, place, and persons, its members are separated, yet they are and constitute one body under one Head, Christ; hence it is also called communion of saints.

IV. But it is not necessarily required for the true unity of the church that there always and everywhere be conformity in outward ceremonies or rites instituted by men, but only this, that there be one foundation (1 Co 3:11), one faith, one baptism (Eph 4:5). And briefly, the Nicene Creed well explains what the "universal" is in these words: I believe one holy universal and apostolic church.

333 *Why is the matter of the church reckoned among the articles of faith?*

Not for this reason, that as we believe in God, so we also believe in the church, or that we make the church equal to or more than God and His Word, but because we firmly know and believe, on the basis of the divine promise, that though the church in this life labors under great and varied infirmities and is completely devoid of human resources, and in addition the devil, with the world and the flesh, tries with both power and guile utterly to destroy and uproot that small and forsaken flock—yet God would defend and protect His church against all the gates of hell (Mt 16:18), so that He will preserve the purity of His Word and Sacraments and also His elect to the end of the world (Mt 28:20; 1 Co 11:26; Mt 24:31; 1 Th 4:17). As for the rest, the reasons why the church is under the cross and with what comfort it should sustain itself under the cross, and what things will appear to be necessary matters of discussion regarding some other articles of faith in the examination, should be drawn from other booklets on this subject.

For these things [in this booklet] have not been written with this in mind, that they replace helpful booklets of others in the hands of students, but only that they might be a directive and guide how the unlearned can and should, on the basis of true foundations, understand the things that they read in other booklets, and apply them to popular use, so that purity of doctrine might be preserved, and they be applied in simple, common terms for the edification of the church.[52]

Part 3

With regard to the doctrine concerning ecclesiastical ceremonies (which we first said would be the third chief part of this examination), it is contained and set forth in the church order. Pastors should also be examined with regard to that very doctrine, so that they might both have the right understanding of it and be able rightly to explain it to their hearers. Likewise, one should inquire whether and how they observe those ceremonies. Superintendents should also confer with pastors regarding marriage orders, incorporated in the church order, that they might have the necessary understanding also of them.

Part 4

Finally (this will be the last chief part of the examination), pastors should, by solemn exhortation be spurred to render due faithfulness in [their] office and to lead a pious, honorable, and blameless life, and to be earnestly reminded on basis of Scripture, how very important this is.

The End

Notes

Unsigned preface in the (Latin) 1603 edition

1. This unsigned preface is in the (Latin) 1603 edition, where it has the running heads *Praefatio*.
2. Latin *pio*. This word is used repeatedly in the Latin preface of the 1574 edition, where Chemnitz uses the German *Christlich*.
3. *candido*.
4. *S*. Abbreviation of *salve*.
5. *candide*.
6. *minus exercitatorum*.
7. *Dn*. The word *Dominus* is often abbreviated *D*. or *Dn*. In the Middle Ages, *Domine* (vocative of *Dominus*) was the usual title by which learned men were addressed. Sometimes omitted in translation.
8. 1517—April 5, 1571; born in Weinbrueck, Hungary; pastor in Brunswick 1553. Translated many works of Chemnitz into German.
9. *D*.
10. *pie*.
11. *candide*.

Preface by Martin Chemnitz

1. This preface by Chemnitz is in German in the 1593 edition, in Latin by Zanger in the 1603 edition. It has the running heads *Vorrede* and *Praefatio* respectively. The present English translation reproduces both. The notes draw attention to the main differences between the two.
2. German: *Ebten*. Latin: *Dominis Abbatibus*.
3. Ger.: *in Gott*. Lat.: *in Christo*.
4. Ger.: *Andächtige*. No counterpart in the Latin.
5. Ger.: *in Christo*. Lat.: *in Domino*.
6. In this preface the verses are not in the German text and are for the most part not in the Latin text. Where they are lacking they are added by the present translator.

7. The Latin text does not have these references to Ps 19 and 119.
8. Ger.: *Christliche.* Lat.: *Catholicam.*
9. Ger.: *nach diesem Leben.* Lat.: *in futura.*
10. Ger.: *der liebe Gott.* Lat.: *benignissimus Deus.*
11. Ger.: *losen, faulen, falschen und gifftigen.* Lat.: *putidis, pravis & venenatis.*
12. Ger.: *Christliche.* Lat.: *piam.*
13. Ger.: *frommen trewen Gott.* Lat.: *Deo opt. max.*
14. Ger.: *gleichwol.* Lat.: *omnino.*
15. Ger.: *erkennen, behertzigen und bedencken.* Lat.: *agnoscamus & consideramus.*
16. Ger.: *beweisen und erzeigen.* Lat.: *testandam.*
17. Ger.: *unser Christliches danckbares Hertz und Gemüth.* Lat.: *piam nostram gratitudinem.*
18. Ger.: *zu seinen Ehren.* Lat.: *ad nominis ipsius gloriam.*
19. Ger.: *Heil und Seligkeit.* Lat.: *salutem.*
20. Ger.: *unserer armen Seel.* Lat.: *animarumque nostrarum.*
21. Here and in the next four references the verses are in the Latin text.—And beginning here the notes are less detailed.
22. Ger.: *in die Hölle.* Lat.: *usque ad infernum.*
23. Ger.: *angehenden.* Lat.: *nascentis.*
24. Ger.: *der liebe Gott.* Lat.: *Deus.*
25. Ger.: *Gemein.* Lat.: *Ecclesia.*
26. From here to the end of this preface the verses are neither in the German text nor in the Latin text.
27. Ger.: *Unkraut.* Lat.: *fermentum.*
28. The Latin text does not have these last five words.
29. These two references are not in the Latin text.
30. Ger.: *alle Jar Zweymal.* Lat.: *bis quotannis.*
31. Ger.: *einfältige Pastores.* Lat.: *rudiores.*
32. This word is not in the Latin text.
33. Philipp Melanchthon.
34. Ger.: *eytel Teutsche Baccularij solten seyn.*
35. Literally "Sleep without a care!" Chemnitz warns against the thought: "This book is all I need."—This longer part of the sentence reads in the Latin: "not that it might be a kind of cover [*subsidium*] for the ignorance and indolence of the less-learned, as though, content with only the vernacular tongue, there is no need for them to be concerned about others."
36. *more Psittaci.*
37. *populariter.*
38. Ger.: *oder ob sie eine frembde Stimme führen.* Lat.: *an vero alienam sonent.*
39. Ger.: *nach dem es zum Druck verfertigt, hab ichs anfänglich.* Lat.: *cum in lucem libellus hic primum emittendus esset.*
40. Ger.: *Christlicher.* Lat.: *pium.*
41. This word is not in the Latin text.
42. Ger.: *der liebe Gott.* Lat.: *quadam benedictione divina.*
43. Ger.: *fromme treuwe.* Lat.: *fidelis ac benignissimus.*
44. Ger.: *segne.* Lat.: *confirmet.*

Preface by Polycarp Leyser in the (German) 1593 edition

1. This preface by Leyser is in the (German) 1593 edition, where it has the running heads *Vorrede*.
2. *Christmilder*.
3. *wolermelte*.
4. *jener*.
5. The 1593 edition. In *Wie man fürsichtiglich* . . . . See the present translator's Foreword.
6. *Herrn Martinum Lutherum*.
7. *Christmilder*.
8. In the 1593 edition.
9. *Theologis, Pastoribus und Seelsorgern*.
10. *dieselben werden ihnen solches nit missfallen lassen*.
11. That part is Chemnitz's *Enchiridion*.

Introduction

1. Ger.: *wie die Weyh-Bischöff thun*. Lat.: *sicut apud Pontificios suffraganeos plerunque fit*.
2. Canon IX; cf. *Corpus iuris canonici*, c. 4, Dist. 81.
3. This book concerns itself in the main only with the first two.

Part 1

1. The questions regarding pious rulers (22—26) and patronage (27) reflect the practice of those times.
2. See note 1.
3. Ger.: *die alten* Canones. Lat.: *vetus Ecclesia*.

Part 2

1. Ger.: *der Layen Bibel*.
2. Questions 46—first part of 50 are not in the German edition.
3. See note 4.
4. We would say *"antilegomena"* (Greek "disputed"; they were in the canon and in that sense not apocryphal). Cf. J. T. Mueller, *Christian Dogmatics* (St. Louis: Concordia Publishing House, 1934), pp. 117, 130—131; Eusebius, *Church History*, Book III.
5. Questions 46—50 up to this point are not in the German edition of 1593.
6. Gregory of Nazianzus.
7. Abbreviation for either *Domini* (title given learned men) or *Divi* ("Blessed"). Sometimes omitted in translation.

161

8. Lat.: *substantia*. Ger.: *Wesen*.
9. E.g., *The Lutheran Hymnal*, No. 369: "All Mankind Fell in Adam's Fall."
10. Lat.: *nobis*. Ger. *seinen*. Heb 2:17 has no pronoun in the Greek. King James Version: *his*.
11. Lat.: *substantia*.
12. Lat.: *substantia*.
13. Lat.: *genuinas*.
14. Commentators disagree as to whether this refers to the Holy Spirit (capitalized) or should be "spirit" in reference to man's spirit.
15. Lat.: *gestibus*. Ger.: *Geberden*.—Postures.
16. Lat.: *usum*.
17. Lat.: *ad inferos*. Douai: to hell.
18. IV, 257.
19. IV, 62; XII, 29—30.
20. IV, 5.
21. Lat.: *desiderando*.
22. Lat.: *ministerium*.
23. Lat.: *rei*.
24. Lat.: *una* (adv.).
25. Lat. *formata;* cf. *Cath. Enc.*, V, 757, cited in Th. Engelder, W. Arndt, Th. Graebner, and F. E. Mayer, *Popular Symbolics* (St. Louis: Concordia Publishing House, 1934), p. 173.
26. Lat.: *amen*.
27. Lat.: *silentio et sicco pede*.
28. This reflects the context in the Vulgate.
29. Lat.: *substantia*.
30. 1941 Roman Catholic translation *(The New Testament of Our Lord and Savior Jesus Christ* [Paterson, N.J.: St. Anthony Guild Press], p. 616): "hold fast our first confidence in him."
31. Or: because; in order that; so that.
32. Pride, covetousness, lust, anger, gluttony, envy, sloth.
33. Compare *A Select Library of the Nicene and Post-Nicene Fathers of the Christian Church,* First Series, ed. P. Schaff, VI (preface dated New York, 1887; photolithoprinted Grand Rapids, Mich.: Wm. B. Eerdmans Publishing Company, 1956), 325—326, 330—331.
34. Lat.: *de impunitate peccati*.
35. Lat.: *mersio*. The manner of baptism was not a confessional issue in this connection. Here *mersio in aquam* is simply another term for "baptism." We also recognize immersion as one form of baptism.
36. Lat.: *Catholica*. Ger.: *christlich*.
37. Cf. Is 49:22.
38. Lat.: *Catholica*. Ger.: *christlich*.
39. Lat.: *iudicium*. Ger.: *Gericht*. The context ("unworthily") indicates that it is an adverse judgment, hence "damnation" (King James Version).
40. Nicene Creed. The congregation joined in its recitation beginning with the word *Patrem*.
41. Cf. *ex opere operato,* note 50.
42. See note 39.

43. See note 39.
44. See note 39.
45. According to Roman Catholic doctrine, *mortal* sins are not forgiven unless they are so confessed.
46. The thought of Mt 15:8 and Mk 7:6 is reflected here.
47. Cf. Is 42.3; Mt 12:20.
48. That is, does not answer as we hope.
49. A reference to the rosary.
50. Lat.: *ex opere operato;* cf. note 41.
51. Ger.: *zusammenfasset.* Lat.: *quadam quasi catena connectit,* "makes a kind of chain of it, as it were."
52. In the (German) 1593 edition the questions on the church (326—333) immediately precede the questions on the Last Judgment and purgatory (316—325).

Index

LUTHER POELLOT

The ministry (and ministers), the Word (Bible, Holy Scripture, Word of God), and the Sacraments (Baptism and the Lord's Supper) are mentioned also elsewhere, here and there throughout the book, besides on the pages listed in the index. Other entries also are selective, not exhaustive. In order to avoid clutter, *passim* is not used.

rejected or changed because of
abuse 79-80, 85
Formal of original sin 62-63
Free will
of God 31
of man 57, 66-68, 76-77, 93, 101
Freedom from the law of God 50, 100

Gangra, council of, on the ministry of
married priests 149
General call to proclaim the Gospel 29
Gentiles 42, 52, 138, 142
Gerson describes justification by the
simile of forensic appeal 73
Glorification 89
God 48
calls into the ministry 29-32, 36-37
dismisses or removes from office 37
natural knowledge of 39-40
speaks, exhorts, absolves, baptizes,
etc. in and through the ministry
and the Sacraments 29-30, 37,
113-114
Good works (new obedience) 66, 73-74,
78-84, 88, 96-102, 108, 132
necessary 78-79, 81, 96-98
do not merit justification 79
not necessary to justification or salvation 81, 97
pleasing to God 101-102
as a second plank 115
what good works are to be taught and
done 99-101
why to be done 98-99
see also Renewal, spiritual
Gospel 48, 54-55, 68-73, 75, 82, 84, 89-
90, 103-106, 109-111, 118, 129,
131, 134
comfort 133-135
difference between Law and Gospel
55, 69-72, 79
and Law involved in conversion 49
a mystery to human reason 40
in the sense of the whole doctrine of
the divine Word 54, 68-69
use of 54-55, 68-70
Grace (mercy) 69-70, 72-95, 98-99, 101,
103-104, 107-120, 127, 129-130,

133-135, 138
Catholic doubt regarding God's grace
143-144
means of see Means of grace
Gregory of Nazianzus on giving offense
47

Hail Marys 144
Hardening of the heart 88-89, 92, 94-95,
107-108
Heaven (eternal life) 61, 73-74, 81, 84-
85, 88-89, 91-92, 103-104, 106,
112-114, 116, 118, 125, 133-135,
150-153
Heaven, kingdom of 133, 150
see also Keys of the kingdom of
heaven
Hell (eternal death) 73-74, 88, 103-104,
108, 150-154
Hilary on justification by faith alone 78
Holy Baptism see Baptism
Holy Communion see Lord's Supper
Holy Scripture 40-48
interprets itself 42, 123-124
purpose of 86, 93
sufficient 41-42
see also Word of God
Holy water 152
Human nature 40
not the same as original sin 59-62
Human powers see Natural powers
Human reason see Reason
Hypocrisy 88

Idolatry 40, 42, 144
Image of God 57-58
Immediate (or direct) call 30-32
Immersion 112
Impenitence 85-86, 89, 103, 131, 133
final 91, 107-108
Indifferent things see Adiaphora
Indirect (or mediate) call 30-37
Infant baptism 116-120
Inspirations, new, not to be expected
40-41
Invocation of saints 51, 126, 143-147
fictitious difference between adora-
tion and 144

168

169

170

Opus operatum; ex opere operato 126, 144, 162, 163
Orders of the church, chief (clergy, pious ruler, faithful people) 35
Ordinary or regular call into the ministry 28-38
Ordination 26-27, 36-37, 111
 not a Sacrament 111
Origen on the work of a priest 38
Original sin 57-64, 103-104
 and Baptism 62-63
 chief sin 59
 not the same as human nature 59-62

Particular or special call 28-29
Pastors *see* Ministers
Patronage 35
Paul 28, 31-32
Pelagians on Baptism 119
Perdition or hell 150-154
Personal sin 59
Personal union 120, 125
Pharaoh 108
Pharisaism 42, 54, 69, 83, 94, 103, 107, 132, 139
Philosophy 62
Political authority 26, 30, 33
Political functions of government, Christians can perform 53
Political laws 50-53
Pope 33, 42
 not a source of new revelations 41
Prayer 47, 79, 120, 137-147
 comfort of 120
 for the dead 127, 152
 for what to ask 140
 form of 140-141
 how to pray 139-141
 invocation of saints 51, 126, 143-147
 kinds of 138-139
 in the name of Jesus Christ 139, 144-145
 Lord's Prayer 140-141, 143-144
 to our Father 139, 142
 outward motions used with 138-139
 place of 142-143
 should be made in faith 145-146
 time of 142-143

training for all piety 142
why to pray 141-142
not a vain and useless babbling 132-133
of repentance 105
Prebirth infants 119-120
Predestination 85-96
 to be approached a posteriori, not a priori 87
 comfort of 93-96
 distinguished from foreknowledge or foresight 86-87
 not in view of faith or good works 89-90
 precedes faith 90
 use and usefulness of the doctrine of 92-94
 why are some predestinated, others not? 94-96
Preordination *see* Predestination
Presbytery 31-33, 35
Presumption regarding God's mercy 107
Priests
 have no corner on both kinds in Communion 122
 marriage of 147-150
Priests, spiritual 29
Private absolution 133-135
Private confession 135-137
 auricular confession 135-136
Public ministry 29
Purgatory 150-154

Quality or accident (dialectic term) 61-62

Reason 39-40, 52, 76-77, 90, 94-96, 124
Reconciliation 79-80, 82, 84, 97, 101, 127, 130, 136
Redemption 61
Regalia 33
Regeneration 63, 96, 112, 115-117, 119
Regular or ordinary call into the ministry 28-38
Remission of sin *see* Forgiveness of sin
Removal from office 37
Renewal, spiritual, or sanctification 61,

171

63, 73, 79-83, 88, 91, 96, 101,
108, 133, 137
in Baptism 115-116
justification precedes 79
see also Good works
Renunciation in Baptism 116
Repentance 43, 48-49, 54, 64-69, 76, 79,
84-86, 88-89, 91-92, 103-108,
114-115, 128-130, 132-137, 139,
142, 152
see also Contrition
Resurrection of the flesh or of the body
61, 151
Revelations, new, not to be expected
40-41, 77
Rhegius, Urbanus, on the necessity of
good works 98
Right hand of God 125-126
Righteousness 69-74, 77-84, 90-91, 96-
99, 104, 113, 116, 130, 138
of the Law and of the Gospel 84
Rites 36-37, 50-52, 111, 132, 156-157
Rosary 144, 163
Rulers, pious, are nursing fathers of the
church 33-34

Sabbath 49
Sacrament of Holy Baptism *see* Baptism
Sacrament of the Altar *see* Lord's
Supper
Sacramental eating and drinking
127-128
Sacramental union 120-121
Sacramentarians 109, 114, 119, 126
Sacraments 26-30, 33, 37-39, 43, 75,
109-132
deal with everyone personally and
specifically 112
definition of 109
and faith 109-110, 130-131
God deals through 37, 113-114
number of 110
Sacrifice of the mass 126-127
Sacrifices, spiritual 29, 126-127
Saints
Apology of the Augsburg Confession
on honoring 146-147
invocation of 51, 144-147

true veneration of 147
Salvation 71-100, 104, 108, 110-111,
115, 128, 130-132, 140, 150
also for infants 118
assurance of 90-95
difference between Catholic and
evangelical doctrine 81, 144
distributed, applied, and sealed in
and through Baptism 114
why some are lost 74, 92, 95-96
Sanctification *see* Renewal, spiritual
Scholasticism 62
Scripture *see* Holy Scripture
Seal of the covenant of grace
Baptism 119
Lord's Supper 128
Seal of the righteousness of faith (circumcision) 118-119
Second plank (i.e., of repentance and
works) 115
Security, carnal 54, 85-86, 103, 129, 131
Self-examination for Communion 131-
132, 137
Sergius 53
Seven deadly sins 103, 162
Silvanus (Silas) 31-32, 34
Simon Magus, binding key used against
134
Sin 56-64, 96-97, 101-108, 130-139
actual 57, 59, 63-64
chief 59
against the Holy Spirit 105-108,
153-154
sins of commission 64
enumeration 136
forgiveness of 54, 63, 69-70, 72-76,
79-80, 84, 88, 92, 97, 99, 103-108,
111-112, 115-117, 120, 127-128,
130, 132-137, 139, 153
mortal 57, 64, 102-104
natural 59
sins of omission 64
original 57-64, 103-104
personal 59
seven deadly sins 103, 162
venial 57, 64, 102-104
see also Absolution
Smalcald Articles on original sin 59

172